MIRROR OF THE
ARAB WORLD

LEBANON IN CONFLICT

MIRROR OF THE ARAB WORLD

LEBANON IN CONFLICT

SANDRA MACKEY

W. W. NORTON & COMPANY

NEW YORK · LONDON

For information about permission to reproduce selections from this book, write to Permissions, W. W. Norton & Company, Inc., 500 Fifth Avenue, New York, NY 10110

For information about special discounts for bulk purchases, please contact W. W. Norton Special Sales at specialsales@wwnorton.com or 800-233-4830

Manufacturing by RR Donnelley, Harrisonburg, VA
Book design by Chris Welch
Production manager: Anna Oler

Library of Congress Cataloging-in-Publication Data

Mackey, Sandra, 1937–
Mirror of the Arab world : Lebanon in conflict / Sandra Mackey.
p. cm.
Includes bibliographical references and index.
ISBN 978-0-393-06218-2 (hardcover)
1. Lebanon—politics and government—20th century. 2. Palestinian Arabs—Lebanon. 3. Shi'ah—Lebanon. 4. Religion and state—Lebanon. I. Title.
DS87.M282 2008
956.9204—dc22   2007051960

W. W. Norton & Company, Inc.
500 Fifth Avenue, New York, N.Y. 10110
www.wwnorton.com

W. W. Norton & Company Ltd.
Castle House, 75/76 Wells Street, London W1T 3QT

1 2 3 4 5 6 7 8 9 0

To Adrian

The next generation

CONTENTS

MIRROR OF THE

ARAB WORLD

LEBANON IN CONFLICT

AUTHOR'S NOTE

When one is writing about as vast a subject as the Arab world in a slim volume, it is necessary to explain the scope and focus. The Arab world can be defined in different ways. In its broadest sense, it reaches from Iraq on the Persian Gulf to Morocco on the Atlantic Ocean and splits between the *maghrib,* the Arab west, and the *mashriq,* the Arab east. The *mashriq,* composed of the states of Egypt, Lebanon, Jordan, Syria, Iraq, Saudi Arabia, Yemen, Oman, the United Arab Emirates, Qatar, Bahrain, and Kuwait, constitutes the cultural and political core of the Arab world. These countries are joined by the fragile political entity known as the Palestinian Authority, which most Palestinians regard as the seed of their own independent state.

The primary purpose of this book is to help the nonspecialist reader learn how to think about the Arab world as it confronts the West with a range of challenges, from political and social instability in a region vital to the global economy, to the security of people living within the borders of Western nations. Ironically it is Lebanon, the most uncommon of Arab states, that provides a case study of the Arab world, for three reasons: Lebanon shares many of the characteristics found in all

Arab societies and states; the Lebanese have run the gamut of national experience, from the conflicts of family and group to civil war to near destruction at the hands of domestic and foreign forces, to the practice of politics through Islam in its Shia form; and Lebanon is the most transparent of all Arab states.

By examining the Lebanese experience, I intend to lead the reader into the Arab world to glimpse its complexities, frustrations, and virtues.

A note about language: The transliteration of Arabic to English is problematic at best. There is no standard system recognized for either academic or general audiences. Since no method of transliteration is without critics, I have chosen to use the simplified forms of Arabic words, names, and locations commonly used by newspapers and periodicals in the United States. The diacritical marks, glottal stops, and consonant sounds unique to Arabic, as well as marks for long vowels, have been omitted. However, transliterations in quotations from other writers have not been changed. This is a choice of style, not the dictate of either Arabic or English.

A final note, about references: The bibliography contains only significant articles and books. Common periodicals and newspapers from which quotes are drawn are not listed.

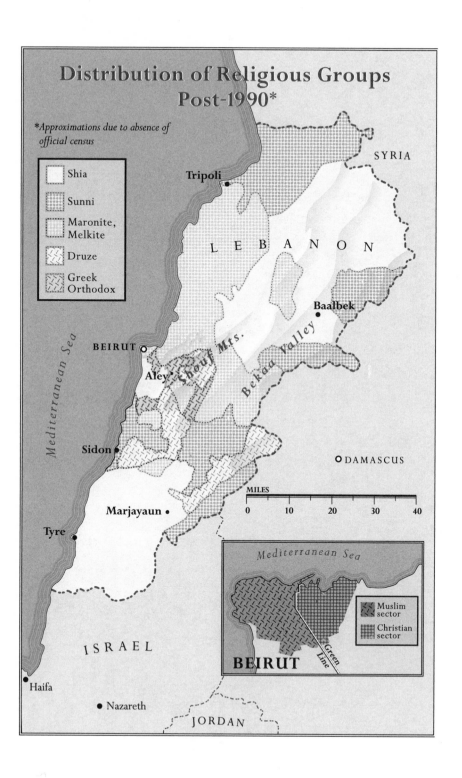

Distribution of Religious Groups Post-1990*

*Approximations due to absence of official census

Legend:
- Shia
- Sunni
- Maronite, Melkite
- Druze
- Greek Orthodox

SYRIA

Tripoli

L E B A N O N

Baalbek

BEIRUT

Aley

Shouf Mts.

Bekaa Valley

Sidon

DAMASCUS

Marjayaun

MILES

0   10   20   30   40

Tyre

Mediterranean Sea

Inset (BEIRUT):
Mediterranean Sea

Green Line

- Muslim sector
- Christian sector

BEIRUT

ISRAEL

Haifa

Nazareth

JORDAN

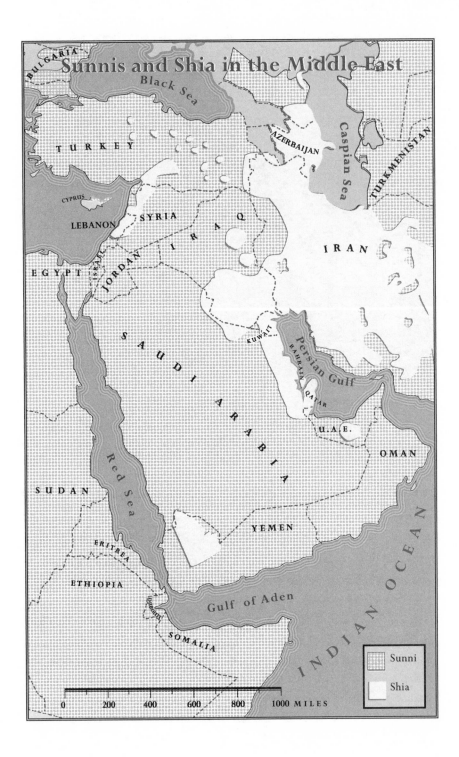

Sunnis and Shia in the Middle East

Legend:
- Sunni
- Shia

Introduction

The soft pinks and muted oranges of a perfect sunset washed over the ancient stones of Byblos, twenty-two miles up the Mediterranean coast from Beirut. The fishing boats had returned hours earlier with the day's catch. The nets had dried and now lay coiled on the low seawall that curved along the tight little harbor. Beyond the quay, on a promontory just to the west, two classical columns built by the Romans faced the sea, anchored in the same place where they had stood for centuries. To the east, the aged stone streets originally laid by the Phoenicians as early as 1200 BC surrounded the walls of a Crusader castle built in the twelfth century AD. At the instant the sun sank into the sea on this evening in early July 2006, one sensed a moment of perfect tranquility.

On July 12 the serenity ended. Hezbollah, a militant Islamic group that was born during the 1982 Israeli invasion of Lebanon, sent its commandoes into a sixteen-acre sliver of land at the junction of Lebanon, Syria, and Israel. Rejecting Israel's occupation of Lebanese-claimed land, Hezbollah militiamen killed three Israeli soldiers and whisked two more into captivity.* The

---

* Five more Israelis died when a tank hit a mine during a rescue attempt.

ransom for the two captured Israelis was the release of an undetermined
number of Lebanese prisoners held within Israel.

Refusing to negotiate and determined to destroy Hezbollah's weapons and infrastructure, the Israeli government of Ehud Olmert sent
high-performance aircraft equipped with state-of-the-art technology and
precision-guided missiles north over Lebanon. As destruction rained
down on its strongholds in the southern neighborhoods of Beirut and the
towns of south Lebanon, Hezbollah struck back by firing low-tech and
inaccurate Katyusha rockets and the far more advanced and destructive
Iranian-made Farj 3 and Farj 5 missiles into northern Israel. Although
Israel suffered its own casualties and physical destruction, Lebanon
took the brunt of the conflict. For thirty-four days, Israel ran thousands of sorties over Lebanon that ripped apart civilian life, destroyed
major bridges and roads, wiped out electrical grids and water stations,
reduced neighborhoods to ruin, displaced over a million people, and
threatened the very survival of the Lebanese state. As images of rubble
and despair flickered across millions of television screens throughout
the Arab world, angry demonstrators took to the streets of cities and
towns to denounce Israel and its American patron. For the United States
and the larger West, the crisis in Lebanon mushroomed into a crisis in
the Arab world. Combined with problems arising from Western depen-
dence on Arab oil; rising discontent among the lower classes within
countries ruled by pro-Western elites; alternative, non-Western power
brokers; the American debacle in Iraq; and the militancy within Islam,
the war in Lebanon in the summer of 2006 signaled the death of a long
era. Unlike in the nineteenth and twentieth centuries, the West can no
longer tame the Arab world to respond to Western needs and desires.

THE ARAB WORLD is a region woven together by language and culture.
It begins on the Nile River south of Cairo where a single-sail falucca dragging a frayed fishing net glides in near silence under a brilliant sun. It ends

nearly two thousand miles to the east in the wake of a high-backed dhow weighted with cargo that slips past the sixteenth-century stone battlements of Muscat to enter the Gulf of Oman en route to the Persian Gulf. Two boats constructed in centuries-old designs visually create the western and eastern boundaries of the Arab world. From north to south, that world extends from the southern boundary of Turkey to the unbroken sands of Saudi Arabia's Rub al-Khali. In all, the Arab world encompasses eleven countries and an estimated 171 million people united by the commonalities of language and culture.* Although linked to oil in the Western mind, the importance of the region exceeds the vast and vital petroleum reserves of the Arabian Peninsula and the Persian Gulf. It is the bridge of land that connects Europe, Asia, and Africa. It is warehouse to arsenals of weapons that in less than half a century have evolved from rifles to tanks to missiles to nuclear bombs. Over the same period, events in the area, like jagged pieces of glass in a kaleidoscope, have tumbled, paused, and reordered in dizzying sequence. Red, green, blue, and yellow translating into passions, interests, ambitions, and fears build ever-new designs. And with increasing rapidity and menace, they transfix a West looking at the complex, multifaceted patterns through the lens of its own, often disruptive, interests.

The forces that drive the Arab world layer one upon the other. They are cultural. They are religious. They are historical. They are economic. They are neatly reasoned and they are wildly illogical. Thus perceptions and realities fall over each other, making ever stronger the inescapable link that the age of globalization has forged between the Arabs and the West. It was not always so.

---

* What countries constitute the Arab world is open to interpretation. The string of states along the coast of North Africa as well as Yemen, curving around the tip of the Arabian Peninsula, are often included in the Arab world. For reasons of culture and politics, the author has limited discussion of the Arab world to Egypt, Jordan, Syria, Iraq, Saudi Arabia, Kuwait, Bahrain, Qatar, the United Arab Emirates, Oman, and Lebanon.

———

THE WEST BECAME isolated from the Arab world in the fifth century AD after the final dissolution of the western part of the Roman Empire. Tumbling into the isolation of the Dark Ages, Europe was absent in the seventh century when Islam delivered Arab culture to the Fertile Crescent, which arcs from the Tigris River to the Nile. While Charlemagne and his lords were learning to write their names, Arab scholars of the Islamic Empire studied Aristotle, algebra, and anatomy. After breaking out of isolation and ignorance during the Crusades, Europe retreated once again when the search for the Holy Grail and unholy territory failed. But the Europeans returned to Europe bearing the learning of the Arabs that laid the foundation of the Renaissance and the Industrial Revolution.

Yet in the early nineteenth century, God-fearing Christians, sitting in hard, straight-backed pews and clutching their well-worn Bibles, still defined the Arab world through the oft-told story of young David confronting the hulking Goliath. If the conscious mind of a Westerner ever engaged an Arab, the image was that of a fanatic, uncivilized "Mohammedan." It was this basic attitude that led most to concur with the judgment of the British scholar Sir William Muir that "the sword of Muhammad, and the Kor'an are the most stubborn enemies of Civilization, Liberty, and the Truth which the world has yet known."*

By the middle of the nineteenth century, a few widely scattered Christian groups began to dispatch emissaries to the Arab world for the purpose of revitalizing the gospel for the Christian churches of Europe. Before the century closed, small contingents of European tourists followed the archeologists and the Bible scholars into the Arab east. They were joined by a few Americans who crept out of the cocoon of North America to join their wealthy European cousins on the Grand Tour. They came home with brassware and fat leather ottomans but almost

* Quoted in Albert Hourani, *Europe and the Middle East* (Berkeley: University of California Press, 1980), p. 34.

no comprehension of Arab history and culture or Arab resentments and anxieties.

In what was an age of innocence, naiveté about the Arabs mattered little. But in the prelude to World War I, the relationship between the West and the world of the Arabs shifted as the new ships of war sliding out of the docks of Glasgow, Devonport, and Bremen required oil rather than coal. And horseless carriages propelled by gasoline revolutionized transportation. For Europe, the fuel for both lay under the sands and marshes surrounding the Persian Gulf. Thus, at the close of World War I, victorious Britain and France colonized much of the Arab world. It was not until the end of World War II that the United States replaced exhausted Britain and France as the major power in the Arab east.

Over the years since, America has been called to the Arab world to protect the Zionist dream; roused to halt the perceived march of communism into the heart of Islam and of the Soviet Union into the Middle East's oil fields; lured into Lebanon in the naive belief that order could be imposed on a multilayered civil war; coaxed to keep the oil flowing out of the Persian Gulf during the Iran-Iraq War; stirred to intervene against Saddam Hussein's ambition and naked aggression in Kuwait; challenged by deadly messengers of politicized Islam; and befooled by the belief that an Arab country would bow before overwhelming military power and the promise of democracy as defined by Western terms.

Gone is the time when the Arab world was so far away from everyday Western life that it existed only in old stereopticon photos and travel articles written by those who plied obscure back roads far removed from the realities that plagued Arab life. But the world of the Arabs is no longer a mysterious, romanticized region lying somewhere between Europe and Asia. It is here. It is now. And it is difficult.

FOR CENTURIES THE Arabs have sat on the invasion routes from west to east and east to west. Almost all of the countries in which they live are little more than contrived states whose borders were drawn at the end of World War I to meet the needs and desires of European powers. Universally their societies are segmented into family, tribe, ethnicity, religion, and sect. Wedded to group, the individual Arab is reluctant to invest his or her identity or security in the state. All are impacted by the creation of Israel in 1948, which left the bitter legacy of the displaced Palestinians. None of these countries have developed institutions of state strong enough to resolve the internal struggles that pit family against family, tribe against tribe, region against region, religion against religion, sect against sect, or ideology against ideology. Nor are they strong enough to confront threats from sparring foreign powers who often fight proxy wars on the territory of weak Arab states. All Arab societies face the demands of modernization and struggle with the power of tradition. And none has seriously addressed the inequitable distribution of political and economic power. As a result, those on the bottom rungs of the social ladder who once sought equality through various renditions of Western socialism now channel their demands through a politicized Islam that promises social justice to the disenfranchised and an idealized past to the alienated. In a few of these Arab countries, the demand for social justice feeds the centuries-old antagonisms between the orthodox Sunnis and the deviating Shia. Whether these Arab societies reside in Iraq, Saudi Arabia, Egypt, Jordan, Syria, the sheikhdoms of the Persian Gulf, or the Palestinian territories, they are all engaged in a process crucial to their very survival—the transformation of fragile states into authentic nations capable of achieving political stability and economic progress. Until Iraq took a share of the title in 2003, the most tormented of all Arab countries was Lebanon.

LEBANON WANDERS DOWN 125 miles of the scenic coastline of the eastern Mediterranean. Its undulating shoreline cradles cities and towns built around wide bays and nestled in narrow inlets framed by the Lebanon Mountains. To the east, the rugged topography flattens out in the fertile red and black fields of the Bekaa Valley before climbing again in the anti-Lebanon mountains that front the western border of Syria. A country comprising only four thousand square miles, Lebanon has for centuries served as the gateway between the European West and the Arab East.

Lebanon is unique to the Arab world for two reasons: its large Christian population and its cosmopolitanism. At one time, Christians comprised perhaps just over fifty percent of the country's population. Their presence was a critical factor in the construction of the Lebanese state. Their influence shaped its history and culture. And their fears of marginalization played a major role in charting the course that led to the civil war of 1975–1990. Although the numbers of Christians have been greatly reduced by war and emigration, the "Christian question" still eats at the foundation of a state that has declared itself Arab.

Within the Christian community, large blocks of Lebanese vehemently deny Lebanon's Arab culture. For generations, they have carefully devised histories that nurture the myth that Lebanon's Christians are descendants of the ancient Phoenicians. Others passionately claim they are Greeks by blood. Others simply describe themselves as "Lebanese Christian," a term that implies non-Arab bloodlines and the Arabic they speak as "Lebanese." Expanding on the same theme, most Christians, regardless of sect, assert that Lebanon is part of the Arab world only by geography. By history and culture, it belongs to the West.

But it is not only Christians who draw a distinction between Lebanon and the rest of the Arab Middle East. Almost all Lebanese, regardless of religion, possess a strong pride in Lebanon and feel a sense of superiority over the peoples of the rest of the Arab world. There is both a superficial and a deeper truth to this claim. The polished Beirut entrepreneur and the rough Saudi Bedouin, the intellectual of Tripoli and the illiterate peasant of Luxor, the Christian priest of northern Lebanon and the Shia cleric of southern Iraq are vastly different. And the states within which they live are different. There is a sophistication and worldliness among the Lebanese that distinguishes Lebanon from the countries of the Arab hinterland.

The aim of this book is not to argue whether Lebanon is or is not an Arab country. Nor is it to recount the history of Lebanon. Nor is it to picture Lebanon as a replication of the Arab world. Rather its purpose is to observe through the lens of Lebanon many of the dynamics at work in all Arab states. It is those dynamics that are feeding the turmoil from Iraq to Palestine that is undercutting the stability of a region vital to the West.

Despite its unique characteristics, Lebanon provides a case study for the Arab world because it is, and has always been, the most open Arab society. Although it carries a shadowy history played out in a closed political system, it is home to a democratic tradition, no matter how imperfect, which makes it the most transparent country in the Arab world. On a deeper level, the endemic problems of Lebanon are the same as those of other Arab countries. But only Lebanon has experienced the wide range of circumstances resulting from a fragmented society; externally imposed borders; a hollow state housing weak institutions; the origin and effects of the Palestinian question; civil war; the absence of a common identity that is essential to turning a fragile state into a viable nation; the recycling of old grievances into new patterns of conflict; resistance to societal and political change; the rise of Shia political power; meddling foreigners; militant Islam as a political ideology; and the escalating rivalry between Sunnis and Shia, currently adding a new dimension to the already fragmented Arab world.

Thus Lebanon, a small, tortured country at the gate of the Arab east, can help Westerners learn how to think about the Arab world. Part of the process involves an understanding of the challenges the Arabs pose to themselves. Equally important is a comprehension of Arab fears and hostilities that rise out of experience and threats the West poses to them. The reader is undertaking an exercise in learning and perception that is crucial because the stakes are enormous, for the Arab world and the West are standing at the very precipice of a tragic conflict that could prove catastrophic for both.

Chapter 1

A COLLECTION OF TRIBES

Whether . . . religion, class or culture—the more one
loved one's own, the more one was entitled to hate
the other.

—PETER GAY,
The Cultivation of Hatred

The Nejd is a waterless ocean. For centuries, this central core
of the Arabian Peninsula was nothing but a seemingly endless wasteland occasionally broken by a cluster of date palms
and a few mud-walled structures that huddled around a source of precious water. Beyond these oases, open-fronted tents woven of goat hair
floated randomly in isolation on the lunar landscape of the barren desert. Within each of them, father, sons and brothers, mother, daughters-
in-law, and cousins lived within tight boundaries of kinship drawn by
precise bloodlines. This was Bedouin society, rooted in a fierce pride
that comes from an extraordinary ability to survive on the hellish desert. Still a potent part of the culture and politics of Saudi Arabia, the
Bedouin lived by a deeply ingrained code of personal honor, the dictates of vengeance, the obligation of hospitality, and the near-sacred
dedication to family. It is the Bedouin who was the original Arab and it
is the Bedouin who remains the true Arab.

The Arab world began to take form in the seventh century AD when
the Prophet Muhammad, according to Islamic history, received the

word of God and revealed it to the people of Mecca, located in what is now western Saudi Arabia. Speaking to those left out of the merchant elite of Mecca, Islam incorporated Bedouin values.

After the Prophet's death in 632, Muslim warriors garbed in tattered clothes, mounted on camels, and armed with nothing but primitive weapons, took Islam beyond the Arabian Peninsula. In the Fertile Crescent they met a far more advanced people who over the centuries had absorbed pieces of the Sumerian culture of Mesopotamia and the skills of ancient Egypt; had incorporated aspects of Persian learning at the time of Cyrus the Great and embraced elements of Hellenism delivered by the great Alexander; and had lived under the Romans and accepted inclusion in Christian Byzantium. In a feat remarkable by any standard, the painfully poor, illiterate warriors of the desert had by 750 imposed their faith, their language, and many of the values and traditions of the Bedouin on these far more advanced and worldly people.

With most of the Fertile Crescent's older religions discredited, the Arab Muslim armies seldom converted by the sword. Riding behind the green banner of the Prophet, they thundered toward a town. Halting at the perimeter, they sounded a horn to summon the people to Islam. And then they waited. In the stillness, doors flew open and new converts flocked out to surrender to Allah.* Jews and Christians—as monotheists protected by Koranic injunction—kept their religion by paying tribute. Thus it was never religion—but language—that laid the foundation of the Arab world. By the eleventh century, Arabic as a cultural vehicle had completely supplanted such old and distinguished languages as Coptic, Aramaic, Greek, and Latin. Through language, peoples of different regions, different histories, and different ethnic roots became Arabs. As a result, "the Babylonians, the

---

* Many simply surrendered. Conversion to Islam of the vast majority of the population of the Fertile Crescent was a process covering several centuries.

Assyrians, the Phoenicians [who] were . . . are no more. The Arabs
were and remain."*

Whereas language has proved the great unifier of the Arabs, the concept of family, so central to Bedouin life, has proved the most divisive
force in the Arab world. The centrality and exclusivity of family that
developed out of multiple sources and cultural traditions were present in the Fertile Crescent before the Bedouins arrived. But it is the
Bedouin who most clearly exemplify the power that family holds over
individual Arabs.

Although wealth and urbanization have swept most of the nomads
of Saudi Arabia off the desert, Bedouin attitudes toward blood kin still
persist. The well-to-do descendants of the Bedouin who have settled in
Riyadh, Jeddah, and the other sprawling metropolises live as extended
families inside the stucco walls of a housing compound that re-creates
the sense of exclusiveness once provided by a knot of tents pitched on
the vastness of the desert. Those without significant resources live in
neighborhoods or apartment houses where units of the family reside in
close proximity to each other. Those forced by employment in a modern
economy to reside in a different town consume hours of cell phone time
connecting with parents, brothers, sisters, and cousins, and frequently
travel back to where the family lives, to remain tightly merged in the
kinship group where the individual finds his or her primary source of
identity and security.

The overwhelming need for security led the Bedouin of centuries
ago to gather in patrilineal families locked in steadfast fidelity and absolute obligation to one another. In the brutal, open desert where survival
depended on numbers and cohesion, each tent represented a family,
each encampment constituted a clan, and several clans linked together
through descent from a common ancestor became a tribe. Within

* Philip Hitti, *The Arabs: A Short History* (Princeton: Princeton University Press,
1949), p. 1.

these protective walls of kinship, father and son, brother and brother, cousin and cousin searched for pasture, camped together, married first cousins to first cousins, and defended each other and their collective honor. Within the group, cohesion held because overpowering cultural and social pressures instilled within each individual the supreme and unquestioned value of life—the commitment to family solidarity and the assumption of mutual responsibility. In these family units in which every person knew every other person, in which all were related by blood, or at least by a fiction of common descent, the imperative of the collective good of the family passed from generation to generation. Near-absolute necessity guaranteed enforcement.

Expulsion from the family descended on anyone who broke the near-sacred code of kinship. The disgraced individual not only became an outlaw against whom the hand of every family member was turned but also wandered as a lost soul in a society that required every person to be attached to his or her kinship group. In the dire reality of loss of support and protection of the family, each individual, in both emotional and practical terms, surrendered his or her identity to the family. And like the rest of the family, these individuals distrusted and largely disliked those outside the boundaries of kinship.

The definition of family in Arab culture is not nuclear or even extended. The concept of *ahl* (kin) means a first cousin is like a brother and a distant cousin is an integral part of the total family, regardless of gaps in wealth, education, and social status. This potent sense of family has cast societies into an amalgam of primordial allegiances governed by the most Arab of all utterances: "My brother and I against my cousin, my cousin and I against the alien."

ANYONE WHO HAS lived within Arab culture realizes that the tight cohesion of the family results from more than the dictates of conformity and the fear of exclusion. Arab families derive a deep contentment in

simply being in each other's company. Most often living in close proximity to each other, relatives come and go in each other's living space as
if doors do not exist. In this easy movement between households, cousins essentially grow up like brothers and sisters. Preferred marriages are
those arranged within the kinship group. And by common acceptance,
everyone's business is everyone else's business. Consequently hour
by hour, day by day, year by year, members of a family tend the dense
strands that hold them together in triumph and adversity. Nepotism in
business and the awarding of government jobs is a given. In times of
unemployment, business failure, personal crisis, or old age, the family
comes to the rescue of the individual. In starkly practical terms, the
most unenviable position for any Arab is to be the oldest son in the family. He becomes the patriarch when his father retires or dies. As such,
he inherits the responsibility for his unmarried, divorced, or widowed
sisters. He pays the tuition and school fees for his younger siblings. And
he is held responsible for solving the problems of anyone who falls into
the category of his family. The reward is that if he becomes disabled
physically or financially, his family takes care of him.

Thus, throughout the Arab world "the family is the alpha and omega
of the whole system; . . . the indissoluble atom of society which assigns
and assures to each of its members his place, his function, his very reason for existence and, to a certain degree, his existence itself."*

Although societies within the various countries of the Arab world
are not replications of each other in that group dynamics within each
differ in both particulars and intensity, all Arab societies are in some
degree tribal. Tribes are most commonly defined by ties of kinship that
can wrap thousands of people together in one bundle. Or tribe is created by the wedding of interests and the embracing of an identity that is
not necessarily determined by bloodlines. Or vast and not so vast fami-

---

* Pierre Bourdieu, quoted in David Pryce-Jones, *The Closed Circle: An Interpretation
of the Arabs* (New York: Harper Perennial, 1991), p. 27.

lies can coalesce into clans descended from different bloodlines. These clans coagulate into regional groupings or religious sects or sometimes pseudo-political parties that compete for power in the political process. These are not interest groups. Rather they are self-contained units in which the central function is to protect one's little world from outside encroachment. As such, they are the great deterrent to political stability and economic development in Arab countries in which few perceive themselves as first and foremost citizens of a nation-state, the organizational unit on which the international community currently operates.

In terms of the contemporary Arab world, the largest tribe in the metaphorical sense is housed in Islam. Within it there are subtribes composed of the orthodox and the dissenters. In the first decade of the twenty-first century, the sectarian split between the orthodox Sunnis and the dissenting Shia is the most poisonous divide among the Arabs from Iraq in the east to Lebanon in the west.[*] Knowledge of the origins of each of these sects, their differing theologies, their attitudes toward authority, their differing definitions of the nation-state, and their means of pursuing political power is essential to understanding the mounting tensions within Islam that are threatening to rip the world of the Arabs apart.

FOR ALMOST FIFTY years after the Prophet's death, Islam would be as much of a monolith as it would ever be. Both those who delivered Islam and those who accepted it would come to be Sunnis, followers of "the path" or "the way" of the Prophet. In general terms, this meant embracing Muhammad's original teachings unadorned by heavy cultural variations, intrusions of mysticism, or a hierarchical system of clerics.

---

[*] The Sunni-Shia divide is extremely important for the entire *Islamic* world. For the purpose of this book, the theological, cultural, and political ramifications are limited to the Muslims of the *Arab* world.

Because Muhammad taught that no one stands between the believer and God, spiritual life for Muslims was delineated by the five pillars of faith, and Muslim society was ruled by Islamic law derived from the Koran—the word of God—and by the Hadith—the sayings and actions of the Prophet as recorded by his companions. Together they constitute the Muslim scriptures.

The Sunnis are the lawyers of Islam. By the tenth century, the great religious scholars in Mecca and Medina, Baghdad, Damascus, and Cairo had molded a whole body of Islamic law that detailed what obedience to God means in daily life. These rules of correct religious practice came to be called the Sharia, Islamic law that in principle covers every possible human contingency.* Making no distinction between the religious and the secular, Sharia constitutes an entire legal system. Under it, there is no room for grappling with the enigmas of theology or exploring the mists of mysticism. There is only the law.

Those who teach, interpret, and administer Sharia comprise the ulama, or "those who know." Holding an important place in Muslim societies, the ulama, in theory, acts in the interests of the faithful. Preserving the sense of a divinely guided community, members of the ulama historically have pursued the ideal of holding themselves apart from government and society. Yet those of the ulama have always been called on to issue opinions that uphold religious law while at the same time sanctioning what might be called secular law that is essential to the administration of government. This has become increasingly tricky in the modern era as governments need religious sanction for decisions on issues that did not exist in seventh-century Arabia. Many of these issues involve technology, others economics. For example, in the 1970s the

* In Sunni Islam, *ijma*, consensus of opinion of Islamic scholars, and *qiyas*, reasoning by analogy as to which principles or rules clearly laid down in the Koran or the Hadith are applicable to matters that seem similar, are secondary sources of Islamic law. There are four schools of law under which the Sharia is interpreted.

Egyptian government, with the agreement of at least some of the ulama, allowed alcohol to be sold in tourist hotels even though Sharia would seem to ban it. The reason: the state-owned breweries, wineries, and distilleries provided jobs for thousands of Egyptians who were producing a product targeted to non-Muslims.

Despite the tradition that members of the ulama declare independence from government, individual clerics often make quiet alliances with government. The most infamous of these contemporary alliances was the lavish support the government of Saudi Arabia gave to the blind cleric Sheikh Abdul Aziz ibn Baz. A major power in the religious establishment of the Wahhabi sect, the most conservative sect within orthodox Islam, Baz rendered rulings needed by the government, and the House of Saud endured his religious pronouncements on other matters, including his 1966 claim that the sun rotates around the earth that is "fixed down by mountains lest it shake."*

It was the Prophet himself who established in Medina the model Islamic community that made no distinction between the spiritual and the secular. The first test of that unity of faith and leadership came with the death of the Prophet in 632. Although he made no claim to immortality, Muhammad died without leaving instructions as to who was to succeed him as the leader of the fledgling Islamic state or how that leader should be chosen. Since he left no male heir, the Prophet's closest companions drew guidance from the rudimentary political structure of pre-Islamic Arabia—the tribe. Traditionally tribes selected their leaders from among themselves, choosing the man who by consensus commanded the most respect—the essential requirement for confirming authority and holding the allegiance of the tribe. Embracing this custom, those the Prophet left behind selected Abu Bakr, one of Muhammad's first converts and by common consent the most respected man in the

* Quoted in David Holden and Richard Johns, *The House of Saud* (London: Holt, Rinehart and Winston, 1981), p. 262.

small Muslim community. Gathering around him, they clasped the hand of the first caliph—the commander of the faithful in carrying out God's will—in the time-honored ceremony of *bayah*, or oath of loyalty.

In Abu Bakr's two-year tenure (632–634), governance in the Islamic community remained tribal and patriarchal. It was with the second caliph, Umar (634–644), that Muhammad's successors began to confront the problems associated with administering an empire that had rapidly expanded beyond all expectations. By the third caliph, Uthman (644–656), Islam's theology could no longer contain the strains rising out of empire or the old family factionalism of the Arabian Peninsula.

Unlike Muhammad, who lived an austere life of self-denial, Islam's leadership was living like an idle aristocracy on the booty of war. Yet the pleasure palaces, the wine, and the questionable sexual activities were only symptoms of the underlying stresses within the empire. The quest for personal power, prestige, and position among Islam's leaders was eating at the vitals of a Muslim society theologically constructed on the concept of the equality of all believers. Questions of how to govern an empire, what its mission should be, how its leadership would be chosen, and how its resources would be distributed not only stoked the family and tribal divisions among the Arabs that predated Islam but also pulled in new groups and new ideas that competed against each other in the large, diverse empire. It all came together in a devastating series of civil wars that severed Islam.

Uthman, the mild-mannered and pious third caliph, was a member of the powerful Umayyad family, part of the aristocratic Quraysh tribe of Mecca. Although seventy years old when he ascended to the position of caliph, Uthman pushed forward the frontiers of Islam's empire and secured its power. But he could not break the bonds of kinship. High office and the spoils of war went disproportionately to his Umayyad relatives. Thus, only a dozen years after Muhammad last preached the social, economic, and political equality of all believers, the leader of Islam had reverted to the old order of Arab society dictated by relationships of blood.

Far and wide across the empire, malcontents fed on stories and rumors about the growing power and wealth of Uthman's family. In 656, dissenters laid siege to the caliph's residence in Medina. At the end of several months, they stormed the house and seized the helpless caliph. With Abu Bakr's son raising the first dagger, the insurgents hacked him to death, leaving Islam once more without a leader. Out of the anarchy that resulted, Ali, the son-in-law of the Prophet and his closest male kin, emerged as caliph.

Distinguished by his part in the early conquests and esteemed for his piety, Ali was generally accepted across the empire. The exception was Syria, where an Umayyad still held on as governor.* Leaving Islam's capital in Medina, Ali headed toward Kufah, a garrison town manned by Bedouin two hundred miles to the northwest, where men waited to go into combat for the man they regarded as the rightful caliph.

Although the caliph held off his enemies, elements in Kufah came to dislike Ali as much as the Umayyads. In 661 when he left his house to go to the mosque for the sunset prayers, an assassin hidden in a doorway on the narrow street came out of the shadows and drove a knife into the disputed caliph. According to tradition, the mortally wounded Ali whispered to his companions that he wished to be placed on a camel and laid to rest wherever it knelt. Najaf, now in Iraq, became his burial site.

Ali's oldest son, Hassan, surrendered all claim to the title of caliph and retired to Medina. Yet the success of the Umayyads in wooing Ali's heir into retirement failed to settle the issue of how the caliph should be chosen—through qualifications of leadership or by blood descent from the Prophet? The Umayyads stood behind Muawiyah, their claim-

---

*This was not the only challenge to Ali. Muhammad's favorite wife, Aishah, led a revolt against Ali fueled by her belief that he had planted suspicions of her infidelity in the mind of the Prophet. The revolt is known as the Battle of the Camel because Aishah commanded her troops from a curtained litter, designed to protect her modesty, that was mounted on the camel's hump.

ant chosen by consensus in the family. But the followers of Ali rejected him on the grounds that Muawiyah possessed no authority because he was not related to the Prophet. It was in this context that Hussein, the second son of Ali and the grandson of the Prophet, placed himself at the head of an insurrection against Umayyad power. When warned that his meager numbers and simple weapons could not win against the Umayyads' well-manned and well-armed forces, Hussein echoed Ali's dedication to social justice for all Muslims: "He who sees an oppressive ruler violating the sanctions of God . . . and does not show zeal against him in word or deed, God would surely cause him to enter his abode in the fire."*

The Umayyads, now led by Yazid, answered. On the second day of October 680, his troops met Hussein and his followers at Karbala. The site provided a perfect stage set for tragedy. On a flat, salty plain south of what is now Baghdad, Karbala is buffeted by wind that is either hot or cold. Dust and sand swirl over a landscape where a sense of desolation ignores the presence of buildings and human beings. In 680, Karbala was nothing but an empty desert—except for Hussein's force of seventy-two, including women and children, and the Umayyad army, which numbered four thousand. In the ensuing battle on what is now known as the "Plain of Sorrow and Misfortune," the Umayyads butchered Hussein along with the rest of his coterie.† His severed head went to Damascus, where Yazid slashed it across the mouth with his cane. In the appalled silence that followed, an old man raised his voice: "Alas that I should have lived to see this day. I who saw those lips kissed by the Prophet of God."‡ Islam had ruptured into what would become its two great branches: the orthodox Sunnis and the breakaway Shia, the followers of Ali and Hussein.

---

* Quoted in Manocher Dorraj, *From Zarathustra to Khomeini: Populism and Dissent in Iran* (Boulder, Colo.: Lynne Rienner, 1990), p. 50.

† The only survivor was Hussein's infant son.

‡ Quoted in Wilfred Theisger, *The Marsh Arabs* (London: Longmans Press, 1964), p. 43.

———

TWO SHRINES IN Iraq reign as the theological centers of Shia Islam: Ali's at Najaf and Hussein's at Karbala. To stand in the *haram*, the courtyard, at Najaf is to feel the passion of the Shia. It is always crowded with men and women wrapped in black who quietly contemplate this sacred spot. From time to time, the calm suddenly breaks when a group of men carrying a coffin bursts through the gates, separates the crowd, and enters the mosque. There they circle Ali's tomb with their burden before erupting once more into the courtyard to load the coffin back on the top of a taxi for transport to the vast cemetery on the edge of Najaf, where every Shia yearns to be buried while awaiting the day of judgment and resurrection.

After Ali and Hussein met their tragic ends, the Shia continued to hold fast to the belief that only members of the Prophet's family possessed special knowledge of religious matters that set them above all others. From this hereditary premise, an elitism developed in which one man came to be regarded as the source of religious truth. He was the Imam, the ultimate spiritual authority. In life, he was, in the eyes of believers, the repository of all truth and knowledge. Representing the importance of authority in Shia Islam, the Imam linked Allah with his people on earth. As the vice-regent of God, he interpreted His will and guided the faithful toward the completion of that will. With him there was salvation; without him there was only damnation. The first of the Imams was Ali; the second, Hussein; and the last in the line from Ali for the majority of Shia was the twelfth one, Muhammad al-Muntazar, who disappeared in the ninth century.

Among the Shia who define themselves as "twelvers," al-Muntazar will return as the *mahdi* (the awaited one) to preside over a just society until the day of judgment.* Until then, a cleric in a precisely defined

* Although Najaf in Iraq is the spiritual center of Shia Islam, the majority of the roughly ten percent of all Muslims who are Shia live in Iran. There ninety-five percent of an estimated population of sixty-eight million is Shia.

hierarchy determined by scholarship, piety, and the ability to collect a group of followers acts as the spiritual guide to those who accept his authority. Unlike the Sunnis, who place no intermediary between the believer and God and who look to their clerics as scholars, lawyers, and preachers, the individual Shia chooses a man within the clerical hierarchy to act as his or her conduit to God. Regarded both as an arbiter of good within society and as the passageway through which to petition God, the Shia religious leader commands more respect and obedience than the tribal leader. At the same time, Shia religious authorities have traditionally maintained a high theological wall between the spiritual and the secular that leaves politics to others. That was until Musa al Sadr in Lebanon in the 1960s, Ayatollah Ruhollah Khomeini in Persian Iran in the 1970s, and Hassan Nasrallah in Lebanon in the 1990s joined together the spiritual and the secular in the political arena."*

THE SHIA HAVE never been alone in the camp of unorthodox Islam. The Arab world is pockmarked with Druze, Sufis, Alawites, and a smattering of obscure sects and practices. The Druze, long a significant player in the Levant, originated in the Ismaili sect, a group within Shiism known as the "seveners." According to their theology, the line of succession of religious authority established by Ali extended only to the Seventh Imam, Ismail al Sadiq. In the eleventh century, a group within the Ismailis splintered from the main body in Egypt and trekked northward into the mountains of the Levant. There those now known as Druze developed an elaborate set of rituals and a pattern of life distinctive from that of other Muslims.†

While identifying themselves as part of Islam, the Druze reject some of its basic practices. They shun two of the five pillars of the

* See chapter 6.

† Today there are perhaps five hundred thousand Druze living in these areas.

Islamic faith honored by both Sunnis and Shia: the practices of praying five times a day and making the pilgrimage to Mecca. The reason
comes out of Druze attitudes that consider a person to be in constant
prayer and Mecca to be found within the individual, not in Saudi
Arabia, the physical location of Islam's holiest site. The Druze also
adhere to their own scripture, which was codified into six volumes in
the fifteenth century. Drawing heavily on mysticism, Druze believe
in reincarnation from one life to the next, which they call "changing
the shirt." In what the Sunnis and Shia regard as perhaps their greatest
heresy, the Druze claim Jethro, the father-in-law of Moses, as their
chief prophet. Yet it is difficult to decipher just what the exact beliefs
encompassed by Druze theology are, since secretiveness is one of the
distinguishing characteristics of the faith.

The sect is divided into two distinct groups: the initiated and the
uninitiated. The initiated—about ten percent of the community—
can be seen in Druze communities scattered in the mountains of
Israel, Syria, and Lebanon wearing a ruby-red fez banded with a wide
strip of white cloth. They are the ones who hold the authority to
pass knowledge of the faith to their sons and chosen men. The other
ninety percent of the Druze, including all women, are the noninitiates. Although important members of the community as individuals
who are expected to lead moral and upright lives, the noninitiates
bear no responsibility for perpetuating the religion. In reality, what
a Druze actually believes is less important than the role the faith
fulfills in maintaining group cohesion. Ultimately, communal identification, not theology, has made it possible for the Druze to survive
a thousand years of turbulent Levantine history. Legendary for their
solidarity and ruthlessness in defense of their interests, the Druze
over the centuries have proved themselves willing to enter any alliance with any ideology perceived as beneficial to the group in either
the short term or the long term.

THROUGHOUT THE ARAB world, the Sunnis, the Shia, and the Druze are divided into families which form clans that operate within sects. In their competition with each other, these sects assume some of the basic characteristics of tribes. There is no better example than Lebanon of how confessional computes to tribe. There, families, religions, and sects create a complex mosaic in which "every village, every patch, every bend in the road house[s] another family, another clan, another way of looking at the world."*

Lebanon's particular form of tribalism is portrayed in sculpture and architecture throughout the country. Atop a mountain rising to 1,950 feet behind the harbor at Jounieh, a northern suburb of Beirut, stands a twenty-ton bronze statue of the Virgin Mary, within sight of the ferry that crosses the eastern Mediterranean from Cyprus docks. Erected in the nineteenth century, it was christened the "Queen of Lebanon" by a group of Christians known as the Maronites. In central Beirut, the soaring minarets of the venerable al Omari mosque, originally built in the thirteenth century on the foundations of a Byzantine church, dominate what is the political and emotional heart of Lebanon. Farther south, a simple mosque of undistinguished architecture or history sits at the core of a small village populated by Shia. Like hundreds of other Shia mosques, its stucco walls support a squat dome set with a few blue and turquoise ceramic tiles. These churches and mosques, joined by the other churches and mosques occupying every neighborhood and village, are symbols of a tribalism that asserts itself through religion and sect—Christian versus Muslim, Sunni versus Shia.†

Christians reside within almost every Arab country. But only in Lebanon have the Christians claimed the numbers and influence to function as equals, or at times superiors, to the Muslims. The origins of that

---

* Albion Ross, quoted in *Aramco World*, September–October 1982, p. 17.

† The Lebanese state officially recognizes seventeen different religious groups, some Christian, some Muslim, within its four thousand square miles of territory.

Christian power are deposited on the Mountain, Lebanon's magnificent snow-covered roof. This stunningly beautiful area, which runs south and west from the northeast corner that abuts the Syrian border to the northern edge of Beirut, was once ruled by warrior societies whose leaders interacted in a feudal system exhibiting some of the characteristics of the twelfth- to seventeenth-century samurai of Japan. Some were Druze, others Shia, and still others adherents to the Maronite sect of Christianity.

The Maronites owe their name to Maron, a priest in the Eastern Orthodox Church of Syria during the fourth century. Dwelling in the wilderness between Antioch in present-day Turkey and Cyrrhus in Syria, Maron broke with his own order to found a group of ascetics. Shortly after his death, his followers, suffering persecution by the church of Antioch, picked up the relics of their saint and carried them into the mountains of Lebanon.

Although they initially found safe refuge, Maronite insecurities intensified in 517 when their Christian rivals slaughtered thirty-five hundred monks at the Qalat al Madiq monastery on the Orontes River. The survivors fled even deeper into the mountains, where they "[s]ettled . . . on the outskirts of the wild cedars, in hostile climate and barren nature."* There they became a tribally based community within Eastern Christianity. Yet when the followers of Muhammad swept through the Fertile Crescent in the seventh century, carrying Islam to the east and to the west, the Maronites, like most people of the Levant, adopted the Arabic language, embraced most of the social mores enshrined in Arab culture, and slid into the Arab tribal system as a non-Muslim confessional.

Under the Islamic Empire that followed the Muslim conquest, the Maronites, along with other Christians, were accorded the status of *dhimmi,* or "people of the book."† This designation ensured that they were left alone to farm their land and worship in their churches. Although

---

* Maronite tract.

† Jews received the same designation, the same privileges, and the same obligations as the Christians.

the central authorities levied *jizya*, a special tax on non-Muslims, the Christians also escaped military duty. But the *dhimmi* system began to erode quickly, as early as 685 when new decrees appropriated existing churches for conversion to mosques; forbade Christian religious groups to recruit new members, even among non-Muslims; and punished apostasy by death. Between 847 and 861, the caliph, the spiritual and secular ruler of the Islamic Empire, went even further by decreeing that Christians and Jews affix wooden images of devils to the exterior of their houses; level the graves of their dead; wear belittling colored patches on their sleeves; and suffer the humiliation of riding only on mules. The Maronites who inhabited the rugged and isolated terrain of the Mountain escaped enforcement of most of these rules simply because their masters were men of the lowlands who abhorred snow and fielded no skills as mountain warriors. Thus the Maronites stayed ensconced among the cedars that still grow in the high mountains.

It was not until Pope Urban II in 1095 issued the call to the knights and peasants of Europe to reclaim "Jerusalem the Golden" from "an accursed race, wholly alienated from God" that the Maronites established contact with the Christians of Europe.* In 1097 when Norman crusaders, carrying wooden staffs topped with a crude cross, moved along the ancient coastal invasion route between Byblos and Batrun, jubilant Maronites streamed down from the Mountain to meet them. After generations of self-imposed isolation, the Maronites hailed the Europeans as heroes who had come to deliver them from the Muslim menace. But by 1302 the Crusaders were gone—victims of arrogance, greed, and the economic/cultural conflict between the European West and the Arab East. Yet some of the Crusaders had chosen to stay in the east. Constituting a frayed string to Europe, they pulled the Maronites toward Western Catholicism.

The twisting of that string actually began at the dawn of the Crusades. Pope Urban's motivation for sending the magnificently mailed knights

---

*Will Durant, *The Age of Faith* (New York: Simon and Schuster, 1950), p. 587.

and the barefoot peasants toward the "holy land" was to reclaim Eastern Christianity, which had been lost to Rome in the fifth century. Despite the wooing, the Vatican was rebuffed. Churches that followed the patriarch of Antioch were of the East, which was distrustful and wary of the West. But the Maronites proved different. At odds with Antioch since the time of Maron, they sensed in the Western church a powerful ally not only against the Muslims but also against their eastern Christian rivals. From the perspective of Rome, the Vatican beheld its own interests in the Maronites. Having failed to win back the Eastern Orthodox, Rome embraced the Maronites as its best opportunity to establish the Western church in the East. Thus, the seduction began as the Maronites and the Vatican each played the role of seducer.

By 1521, this budding romance between the Roman Catholic Church and the Maronites had advanced to the point that Pope Leo X designated the Maronites "a rose among the thorns" in a thicket of heretic Christians and infidel Muslims. In 1736, the Maronites formally accepted qualified union with Rome. While recognizing the authority of the Pope, they preserved their own identity by retaining their own liturgy conducted in Syriac, their own saints' and feast days, and their own patriarch, who is confirmed rather than appointed by the Pope. More than theology, the Maronites joined Rome to protect the specific interests of their community and the families within it. Consequently, what is now Lebanon became synonymous with Maronite history. Instead of identifying with the Arabs through blood, history, or society, they proclaimed themselves culturally as Europeans and ethnically rooted in ancient Phoenicia.*

---

* In 1717, a segment of the Greek Orthodox Church also surrendered to the missionary activities of the Holy See in Rome. Assuming the name Greek Catholics or Melkites, they, like the Maronites, became part of the Roman Catholic Church yet stayed apart from it. Because of their limited numbers compared with the Maronites, the Melkites have never impacted the politics of Lebanon to the same extent as Lebanon's other Roman Catholics or the Greek Orthodox.

It was in this realm of identity that the Maronites set themselves apart from the Levant's other large group of Christians: the Greek Orthodox. They came out of the Great Schism of 451, which severed Constantinople in the eastern half of the Roman Empire from Rome in its western half. Inhabiting the lowlands and pursuing their talents in commerce, most families among the Greek Orthodox sheathed themselves in the Arab identity that came with the Islamic conquest. During the Crusades, they so vigorously rejected the Europeans that one group in Jerusalem openly prayed for a Muslim victory. As the Crusaders took possession of the Levant and divided it into the fragile Crusader states, Greek Orthodox identity, accompanied by family and communal interests, placed them alongside the Muslims in the resistance to the Europeans' greed for territory and wealth. Thus the pattern within the Levant's Christian community was set: The Maronites were mountain people segmented into tough, patriarchal families presiding over ancestral lands and networks of lesser families. The Greek Orthodox were of the coastal plains, their families were urban, and their interests commercial.

Remnants of those tough mountain people remain. Although the usual worshippers at the Maronites' soaring cathedral at Harissa typify the urbane, educated Maronite of today, occasionally a weathered mountain man personifying the Maronite past arrives on the doorstep of the great cathedral. Sporting a full beard, draped in the head cloth of a shepherd, shod in sandals, wearing a large cross strung on a coarse braided cord around his neck, carrying the staff of a shepherd, and praising the Virgin Mary in a loud voice, he is an embarrassment to his fellow confessors. Yet he is what so many of the Maronites were in the middle centuries of Ottoman rule of the Levant.

THE POWER RELATIONSHIP between the Christians, Sunni Muslims, Shia Muslims, and Druze of the Levant crystallized during the Ottoman Empire, which claimed for four hundred years (1517–1918) the title of "protectors of the holy cities." The Ottomans appeared in the thirteenth century when the glorious Islamic Empire, which had preserved the art and learning of the Greeks and Romans and wed it to that of Persia and India, was in the last stages of disintegration. The causes of the Islamic Empire's demise were multiple: overexpansion in the seventh and eighth centuries; cultural strains between the Arabs and Persians in the tenth century; and death and destruction delivered by the Mongols in the thirteenth century. Smelling the rotting flesh, Oghuz, a tribal leader of western Anatolia, assembled an amalgam of Turkish-speaking tribes that began to weave a new empire on the loom of Islam.

During its golden age in the sixteenth century, the Ottoman Empire sprawled from the Dniester River through the Balkans, across Anatolia into the Fertile Crescent, down the coasts of the Arabian Peninsula and across North Africa to Algeria. Its borders encompassed twenty to thirty million people, a staggering array of languages, and the adherents of the world's three major monotheistic religions.

The Ottoman Empire was ruled from Istanbul's Tokapi Palace, a sprawling complex that hugs a hill overlooking the Sea of Marmara.* From there, the Ottomans ruled what was a vast empire, but with a minimum of armed manpower. Instead of installing battalions of soldiers to enforce law and order, they employed the leaders of various religious communities to keep the peace among their own people. In what was known as the millet system, every inhabitant of Ottoman territories inside and outside the Arab world was slotted into a communal group labeled by religion and sect. Under the system, one's sect determined one's social and political identity regardless of that individual's personal position or beliefs. The leader of each of these confessional groups, not the individual, commanded access to

* Istanbul was called Constantinople until 1453, when the city passed from Byzantine Christian to Ottoman Muslim rule.

Ottoman officials. And it was the confessional group, not the local Ottoman government, that directly governed the individual through personal status laws enforced by its own courts. While providing the Ottomans with a cheap, relatively efficient administrative system, the millet structure essentially turned confessions into institutions of unequal power for the purpose of governing the state. Thus rather than mitigating the existing confessional cleavages in the Fertile Crescent, Ottoman rule deepened them. In an order for which the Arabs are still paying the price, tribalism dressed in the regalia of confession divided group from group. In what is now Lebanon, this form of tribalism manifested itself most clearly on the Mountain.

A magnificent geographic area, the Mountain is the site of the cedars used to build Solomon's Temple and provide refuge for the Maronites in the fourth century and the Druze in the eleventh century. It was also home to some Shia, the historically persecuted of Islam. For generations, the Mountain was largely controlled by what were essentially tribal authorities, either the patriarch of a family or the sheikh of a clan. They competed for territory and influence in a martial culture where men of honor battled each other in the name of family, clan, and confession.

By the beginning of the seventeenth century, the influence of the Shia tribal leaders had been eclipsed by that of the Maronites and Druze. The Ottomans appeased both by appointing all sixteen of their warlords to positions as cabinet ministers and top administrators in what was known as the *mutassarifate*. It was not enough to reassure the Maronites, however, who harbored fears of annihilation by Muslim assimilation. To the outsider, Maronite anxieties bordered on the paranoid, for it was the Maronites in their contest with the Druze who commanded superior education, advanced skills, religious ties to the Vatican, and commercial relations with France. Nevertheless, the Maronites' great dread was realized in a war with the Druze in 1860.

The conflict actually began twenty years earlier in the 1840 revolt in which Maronites and Druze joined together to challenge the Mountain's feudal economic system. But cooperation quickly gave way to what was essentially a tribal war fought under the banners of confession. Although the Maronites were hard, fierce, and ruthless mountain people, the Druze would best them. With twelve thousand fighters, the Druze routed sixty thousand armed Christians in what the Maronites called "a dark design . . . to throw their whole race into a state of abject servitude by letting loose upon them the ferocious passions of the Druze."*

With the Maronites on the defensive, alarms sounded by the ringing of church bells sent Christians fleeing from isolated villages toward larger towns that promised some protection from the marauding Druze. Those who straggled behind fell into the hands of an enemy who slew them, severed their ears from their heads, and nailed the bloody skin and cartilage to the nearest barn wall. As the tribal war continued to unfold, plunder and massacre also fell on the towns to which those making an early escape had fled. No one was exempt. At the Maronite monastery of Ameek, rampaging Druze warriors murdered the superior in his bed and slayed priests praying at the foot of their altars. Refusing to become compliant victims, the Maronites retaliated with their own campaign of death and destruction in a war between equally vicious communities.

The civil strife of 1841–1861 defined brutality in Lebanon until the civil war of 1975. Out of a population of 500,000 people, 33,000 died by the sword: 17,000 Maronites, 5,000 non-Maronite Christians, 9,000 Druze, and 2,000 other Muslims. Suffering death at a ratio of two to one, the Maronites came out of the conflict seared by what they regarded as a never-ending wrong.[†] As a result, "the events of 1860 became the touchstone of Maronite psychology, and when the question of security from

---

* Charles H. S. Churchill, *The Druzes and the Maronites under Turkish Rule from 1840 to 1860* (London: Bernard Qaritch, 1862), p. 137.

† Maronite fears and resentments were stoked by events elsewhere. Only three days after formal peace came to the Mountain in Lebanon, eleven thousand Christians died in Damascus when their quarter of the city was attacked without provocation.

'the Muslim threat' arose in Maronite minds . . . 1860 became a potent symbol of what could not be allowed to happen again.'* From that point on, the Maronite psyche wrapped around a visceral fear of a Christian minority in the Islamic Arab world and an innate sense of moral and cultural superiority over Muslims.

BELOW THE MOUNTAIN, others lived under Ottoman rule. Along the Mediterranean coast, in the hills of the south, and eastward into Syria, they segmented into family, religion, and sect. Each pursued its own interests, held its own attitudes, and harbored its own fears. In this demographic mix, the Sunni Muslims, sharing orthodox Islam with the Ottomans, held a privileged position and exerted the greatest influence. Unlike the Mountain communities based on warrior societies and clan loyalties, the Sunnis were urban, the result of a long tradition in commerce and administration under whatever occupying power held the Levant at a particular time. In the Ottoman era, the Sunnis, in possession of needed business and administrative skills, parlayed religion and sect into political and economic advantage over Christians and other Muslims. They brought the Christian Greek Orthodox along as junior partners.

Having amassed large fortunes and high levels of education, the Greek Orthodox reigned as the nineteenth-century aristocrats of the Ottoman lowlands. Gathered in largely merchant or professional families, they protected their position and their assets by cultivating and protecting relationships with the Sunni notables of the city. In essence it was a partnership based on commerce. Like a well-drilled team, the Orthodox oiled the economic machinery and the Sunnis, publicly acknowledged as the superior partner, greased the political wheels within the Ottoman administration.

* David McDowall, *Lebanon: A Conflict of Minorities* (London: Minority Rights Group, 1983), p. 9.

———

BY THE MIDDLE of the nineteenth century, the geographic chasm between the lowlands and the Mountain began to narrow. Decade by decade, the people of the Mountain drifted down toward Beirut and the city crept outward to the low hills that sloped toward the harbor. In the harbor area where the small city centered itself, Ottoman buildings sat on top of the ruins of structures built by the Phoenicians and the Romans. On the promontory at the tip of the bulge of land known as Ras Beirut, the American University of Beirut added its own flavor to the mix. Founded in 1866 by Presbyterians of the United States, it promised a Western education to all religions and sects in this piece of the Levant. As the century closed, Ottoman Beirut, resting between the sea and the Mountain, cradled all the family and confessional tribes of what would become the state of Lebanon.

These religious and sectarian tribes of the Levant resembled the Bedouin tribes of the Arabian Peninsula in that they were pulsating organisms. As one clan grew in wealth and influence, other clans allied themselves to it. But when the dominant clan could no longer contribute to the strength and interests of the lesser clans, the power relationships within confessionals, as with tribes, shifted as the inferior clans forged new, more beneficial alliances with others.

Within the parameters of every religion and sect, the interests of the all-powerful family superceded the emotional and theological power of faith. And it was as families carrying names that extended back into the shadows of time that the Lebanese competed against each other within their larger confessional tribes. The Maronite families of the Mountain were named Edde, Franjieh, Gemayel, and Chamoun; in the Chouf Mountains south and east of Beirut, Chehab, Khouri, and Bustani. Greek Orthodox families were called Bustros, Takla, Faraoun, Tueni, and Chiha. The Druze families claimed the names of Erslan and Jumblatt. The families among the Sunnis called themselves Karami, Sohl, and Salam. The Shia families, their power somewhat eclipsed by the religious leaders, were known as Hamadeh and Berri. Within each community, these families were rivals first. Only if family interests proved compatible did they function as allies, even within the boundaries of religion. For the family was not only the cornerstone of society, it was the basic building block of what has proved to be the elusive nation. This is not only Lebanon. It is the Arab world, where families, tribes, religions, and sects jockey for position in fragile states most often contrived by powers beyond their borders.

Chapter 2

THE HOLLOW STATE

One of our men was just killed. We have to wait for
three Maronites, two Sunnis, two Shiites . . . , and one
Druze to be killed before we can start fighting again.

— GREEK ORTHODOX SOLDIER
OF LEBANESE ARMY,
National Geographic, December 1946

The two great rivers, the Tigris and the Euphrates, trace their
separate courses across the flatlands of central Iraq, draw near
at Baghdad, separate again, and finally come together in the
Shatt al-Arab to flow into the Persian Gulf. Along them lie the markers
of Iraq's ancient past—the walled expanse that was once Nineveh, the
arch of the Sasanid Palace of Ctesiphon, fabled Babylon, and finally the
crumbled ziggurat at Ur of the Chaldees. Each fell to influences and
invaders as often from the east as from the west.

To wander from Iraq's mountains in the north to the marshes of the
south is to see, to hear, and to feel the magnetic pull of lands and cultures beyond the Arab world. Here the domes of the mosques are a little
taller and a little slimmer, representing the classical architecture of Iran
more than Egypt. Hallowed Arabic is a little different, resonating with
words from Turkish and Farsi. Even Islam is more variegated, reflecting
a population that is Shia as well as Sunni. It is as if Iraq is somehow labor-
ing to stay within the sphere of the Sunni Arab world.

Iraq's empty western deserts touch the Arab lands of Syria, Jordan,
and Saudi Arabia. But its heavily populated eastern region, the region

fed by the Tigris and Euphrates, fronts two giant non-Arab countries—Iran and Turkey. Within Iraq's population, only twenty percent are Sunni Arab, the ballast of the Arab world. Almost all of the remainder belong either to the dissenting Shia sect of Islam or to the Indo-European Kurds. Constantly challenged by a sixty percent non-Sunni majority and a non-Arab minority that equals in number the Sunnis, Iraq developed an identity that is at the same time Arab and not Arab. Although included in the Arab world, Iraq does not quite fit into the Arab matrix largely shaped by the orthodox Sunni branch of Islam. Patched together by imperial fiat at the end of World War I, Iraq is constantly strained by powerful centrifugal forces within a population sharing neither a common identity nor mutual ideals. Nor did Iraq develop any institutions that functioned in the interests of all the people living within its contrived boundaries. Only the steel will and spiked heel of Saddam Hussein kept the country's component parts from ripping apart.

On April 9, 2003, Saddam Hussein's rule of Iraq ended in the symbolic sense when a man in a jubilant crowd in Baghdad's Tahrir Square swung a sledge hammer at the plinth holding a bronze statue of the Butcher of Baghdad. In the ensuing frenzy, others looped ropes around the sculpture and began to tug. Battle-clad American soldiers coming across the Jumhuriya Bridge stopped, attached the ropes to their armored vehicle, and pulled. The figure broke from its base and bowed toward the crowd, which broke into the chant of the Hussein era, "With our blood, with our soul, we'll defend you," to which they added, "Bush! Bush! Bush!" The soldiers of the United States joined them.

On that day, the American liberators envisioned Baghdad as Paris in August 1944 when Allied troops rolled through the Arc de Triomphe and down the Champs Elysees. The wide boulevard in the heart of Paris was lined with thousands of people tossing flowers and screaming their welcome. For the administration of George W. Bush, Iraq promised the United States the opportunity to revisit the post–World War II successes of reconstruction and democratization of Germany and Japan. Those who promoted this Wilsonian vision saw Iraq placed under U.S. military rule, handed a constitution, and infused with political and economic expertise that would transform it into the model for all countries of the Arab world.

The quick surgical war that Washington anticipated was supposed to end Saddam Hussein's threat to American interests in the Persian Gulf; instill unilateralism at the center of American foreign policy; establish the policy of preemption against perceived threats to American security; protect Israel without forcing Tel Aviv to address Palestinian rights; and ensure access to Iraq's rich trove of oil. Instead, the occupation of Iraq opened a Pandora's box that the United States could not close.

Almost immediately, Iraq began to spiral downward. Looting by Iraqis of the antiquities of their own country and the offices and installations of their own government unfolded in broad daylight with the cameras of the international press documenting the plunder. It was not long until an insurgency began in which the American military provided the main target. Further into the occupation, sectarian strife inched closer and closer to civil war. Outside the Sunni triangle north and west of Baghdad, the U.S. military was no longer the primary target. Depending on who was perpetrating the violence, it was Shia or Sunnis or Kurds. Before the fourth anniversary of the fall of Saddam Hussein, it seemed that the force of 130,000 American troops was all that stood between Iraq's rival communal groups. The Iraqi government elected in the much-touted elections on January 30, 2005, could not contain the insurgency and would not move to disarm the militias that fed so much of the violence. The police and security services into which the United States had poured vast amounts of energy and money refused to assume responsibility for their own country. Instead, the Sunnis attacked the political order put in place by the election. The Shia and the Kurds plotted to gut the central government at the least and to dismantle the country at worst. And Washington desperately searched for an exit strategy that would provide some semblance of order on the strategically critical Persian Gulf while the American people asked how it had all gone so wrong.

The answer is that the post–World War II scenario in which Iraq, like Germany and Japan, would move from a brutal totalitarian government responsible for unspeakable acts to a functioning democracy ignored the reality that both the Germans and Japanese were products of homogeneous societies. As such they possessed a strong sense of common identity that manifested itself in genuine nationalism. It is from the foundation of identity and sense of nation that the institutions crucial to successful government come. Those components are absent or anemic in most Arab countries.

In the Arab world, government is constructed on family and personal relationships rather than institutions. The reasons are multiple and reflect no set order of importance from country to country. They include the cultural imperative of the family; the tribal nature of societies; four hundred years of Ottoman rule that operated through communal leaders rather than civil organizations; and colonial ambitions of European nations that drew boundaries around divergent ethnic and sectarian groups subscribing to no common identity. These basic conditions were compounded when these contrived countries were thrust into statehood with no preparation in how to govern themselves through improvised governments based on models alien to the history and culture of the people they ruled. Furthermore the elites who grabbed power in these states assumed no responsibility for governing in the interest of the common good. The result is an Arab world in which individual states, with varying success, are searching for political stability and economic advancement, dragging with them elements of their culture, history, and religions and accompanied by a collection of human frailties that are the reality of every society. In what is proving an excruciating process, the West as well as the Arabs bear a major responsibility.

WHEN THE PARIS Peace Conference convened at Versailles on January 18, 1919, to write the final end to World War I, the victors, moving through receptions, dinner dances, and weekends at rented chateaux within easy motoring distance from Paris, decided the future of the Arab world. Within the conference itself, politicians and diplomats, bankers and oilmen, bondholders and missionaries circled like birds of prey over the territories of the Ottoman Empire and Imperial Germany. The American president, Woodrow Wilson, was perhaps the only honest broker present. While the other victors schemed for land, Wilson argued for peace based on his visionary Fourteen Points, which the Allies had embraced during the heat of war. But with peace, David Lloyd George, the British prime minister, and Georges Clemenceau, the French premier, jettisoned Wilson's ideals to aggressively pursue the interests and power of Britain and France. Later, Felix Frankfurter, part of the American delegation, recalled, "My months at the Paris Peace Conference in 1919 were probably the saddest of my life. The progressive disillusionment of the high hopes which Wilson's noble talk had engendered was not unlike the feelings that death of near ones brings."*

The white-thatched Lloyd George considered Egypt, Mesopotamia, Arabia, and Palestine as legitimate prizes in the Arab world for victorious Britain. The fat, partially deaf Clemenceau hungered for Syria. Ignored were the pledges made to the Arabs in 1917 that their revolt against the Ottoman Empire would secure an Arab state extending from Egypt to Persia and Alexandretta to Aden united by the Arabic language and Arab culture. Instead, Faisal, the son of the sharif of Mecca who had called the revolt, was grudgingly allotted twenty minutes in which to argue the Arab case to the conference.

Accompanied by the blond, legendary Lawrence of Arabia wrapped in the exotic robes of the Arabian Peninsula, the stately Faisal asked for the right of self-determination for the Arabs and recognition of an Arab state as an independent geographic and political entity. But Brit-

---

* Quoted in David Fromkin, *A Peace to End All Peace: The Fall of the Ottoman Empire and the Creation of the Modern Middle East* (New York: Henry Holt, 1989), p. 399.

ish and French mapmakers were already huddled behind closed doors drawing the boundaries of what would become the Arab states of Syria, Jordan, Iraq, and Lebanon. They tinkered with other boundaries here and there—Egypt, Palestine, Kuwait, and the other sheikhdoms of the Persian Gulf. In every instance, the boundaries drawn met the needs of European colonialism. In the pursuit of Western interests, ethnic groups, tribes, and religions from Iraq to Lebanon were thrown together in political entities often void of logic.

All that is left of the Arab Revolt that thrust before the Arabs the concept of a Arab nation lies in the desert north of Mecca. There, blackened remains of three passenger coaches protrude at angles out of drifts of red-orange sand. From time to time a violent windstorm brings to the surface a segment of track of the old Hijaz railroad that once ran from Damascus to Mecca. To touch the hot metal heated by the midafternoon sun is to touch history and failed Arab expectations. The sensation is one of hearing the cry of the rebels as they swept down out of the dunes: "Death has become sweet, oh Arabs." In a profound sense, the Arabs did die at Versailles. Rather than achieving an Arab state, they changed masters from the Muslim Turks to the European Christians.

Technically, Britain gained stewardship over Iraq, Transjordan, and Palestine and France took Syria under the auspices of the nascent League of Nations. Under the provisions of the League's mandate system, a "politically developed" democracy was charged with preparing the people of territories under League supervision for independence and self-government. In reality, the mandate system in the Middle East simply erected a screen behind which Britain and France hid traditional colonialism.

In Iraq, the British, gathering the Sunni and Shia Arabs and the non-Arab Kurds, exhibiting blindness to cultural realities, and ignoring the issues of identity, took charge of a schizophrenic state. In Palestine, London operated under the illusion that the Palestinian Arabs would embrace Zionists arriving from Europe to establish a Jewish national homeland. In each case, British colonial interests fed the conditions, conflicts, and resentments toward the West that today feed the many angers of the Arab world. The French did no better.

Perhaps there is no better example of a mandated territory required to be a state than Lebanon. Between 1920 and 1975, Lebanon erected the outer walls of a beautiful house. But like many in its neighborhood, it built no interior supports. That the carpenters of the house included a major contingent of Christians not found elsewhere in the Arab world altered the design but not the product. For in Lebanon, as elsewhere, a layer of elites pursued their own interests and those of their clients within a shell designated a nation.

AFTER THE 1919 peace conference at Versailles, the colonial surgeons at the Qais d' Orse, in pursuit of French national interest, laid out the French mandate of Syria, amputated its western reaches including the Bekaa Valley and the coastal plain, and sewed them to the Christian enclave on the Mountain north of Beirut. This remains the tormented country of Lebanon in which the Lebanese have never found a common identity nor an equitable political system.

On September 1, 1920, when Greater Lebanon was launched, General Henri Gouraud, resplendent in his blue French military uniform hung with brightly striped battle ribbons and golden medals, stood ramrod straight on the steps of the French headquarters in the center of Beirut. As a French military band positioned on a red carpet sounded its first chord, the dapper general snapped to attention to salute the unfurling flag of the new Lebanon—bold red stripes bordering a white field emblazoned with a cedar tree.

The cedar tree, the emblem of the Maronites, signified the degree to which the Lebanese state created by Paris was the political and cultural embodiment of a myth. The French had embraced the illusion that they could cultivate an eighteenth-century alliance with the Maronites to promote France's national interests in the Levant while placating the other groups now incorporated into the mandate. The Maronites, for their part, embraced this alliance with France as a protective weapon to wield against the Muslims who surrounded them. In their collective imagination, the Maronites saw Lebanon as a never-changing utopia of Christian villages nestled among the mountains, protected by French ships standing guard off the coast. This vision was given voice in December 1920 by the Maronite patriarch: "And now has the noble French nation given us . . . a new and brilliant proof of her love for us and our welfare . . . Her righteous policy . . . has offered to our cherished Lebanon her independence, extended her boundaries, and reestablished for her people a living nation which, God willing, will stand with honor among the civilized nations."* It was not to be. The Lebanon that the French had created was little more than a precariously balanced collective of economically and politically linked autonomous societies living in a weak, schizophrenic state.

IN LEBANON, THE attachment to the Mountain of the coastal cities of Tripoli, Beirut, and Sidon, the hills south and east of Tyre, and the valley of the Bekaa meant combining the Christian majority of the highlands with the overwhelmingly Muslim, largely Sunni, population of the lowlands. Unlike the Ottoman Empire, this new occupier could not draw on Islam to defend its legitimacy. Ignorant of the depth of communal suspicions and hostilities, the French fantasized that under their rule Christians would accept Lebanon as an Arab country speaking the Arabic language while the Muslims would submit to Lebanon's continued cultural ties with the West. Yet not even the Christians signed on as a bloc to the French version of a Lebanese state. The Greek Ortho-

* Quoted in Robert Brenton Betts, *Christians in the Arab East* (Atlanta: John Knox Press, 1978), p. 10.

dox shared culture, if not religion, with those in Lebanon who defined themselves as Arab.

No segment of the population felt more disquiet about the establishment of Greater Lebanon than the urbanites rooted in Beirut, Tripoli, Sidon, and other cities that, under the Ottomans, had been controlled by the Sunnis. Now those who had formerly wielded influence and power for themselves and their Greek Orthodox allies were slotted below the Maronites in a new political entity imposed by French colonialism. Although necessity forced the elite Sunni families and their clients into the newfound state, most failed to truly identify with Lebanon as a nation.

As for the Shia, they stayed to themselves. In 1920, adherents to Islam's major dissenting sect represented perhaps only eighteen percent of the population. At the time, they congregated in largely agricultural communities in the Bekaa and the south, where their loyalty remained where it had always been—with their traditional tribal and religious leaders, who perceived little for the Shia in the new Lebanese state.

In this atmosphere of Muslim alienation, the Maronite clan chieftains of the Mountain moved to Beirut to take advantage of their newly acquired political and economic power bestowed by the French. Almost overnight, the centuries-old Levantine fabric from which Beirut was woven acquired a new texture applied by feudal warlords out of the old tribal rivalries on the Mountain. Together the Maronites and the French moved forward.

Greater Lebanon was so new, yet so very old. With little real awareness of the state, the Lebanese continued to move to the rhythms of the past. Caravan drovers still herded their camels through the streets of Sidon beneath tattered awnings dyed in the purple hues of the Phoenicians. The farmers of the Bekaa still winnowed the chafe from their wheat in great round reed trays. The peasants of Jebel Amal still lay metal and muscle to yet another boulder to clear rock-strewn fields. Armed Druze with heavy ammunition belts slung over their chests still stood guard over their communities buried in the hills. And on the Mountain, priests wearing black robes and silver crosses still ministered to their congregations. Only Beirut seemed to grasp the reality of a new state almost equally divided between Christians and Muslims. Optimism about the future ran so high that the Beirutis cast the vision of a nonsectarian Lebanon into a statue set in Martyrs' Square. Memorializing Lebanese soldiers who had died in World War I, the bronze figures of two proud women, one veiled and one unveiled, their hands clasped in unity, faced the harbor. But metal shaped by an artist could not change the dynamics of Lebanese politics, which had already been set in a fateful mold. Patterns of identity based on blood ties, shared religion, geographic loyalties, and various external ties already had produced a political system in which politics and communalism were inextricably linked.

Although the annexed territories held huge economic potential for the new state, French investors owned the railways, public utilities, and banks, and French industrialists and traders swamped the market with their own products at the expense of an equitable Lebanese economic system critical to the process of nation building. Even more important to the future of the Lebanese state, France imposed its own culture on this contrived entity. Even though the majority of the people were Arab, French became the official language. As a result, the Maronites, who chose to speak French as a first language, gained an enormous advantage over Arabic speakers. Just as a command of English today means access to a range of opportunities in all Arab countries, the command of the French language in Lebanon opened the entry door to French colonial officials, government positions, and a wide range of business opportunities. Separating themselves even further from the other Lebanese, the Maronites refused to acknowledge their Arab origins. Instead they created a new identity called "Phoenician."

The still-enduring notion among the Maronites that they are the direct heirs of the ancient Phoenicians sprouted in the blood of the massacre of 1860. In the 1920s, the Christian intellectual Michel Chiha spun words around the idea of Lebanon as the successor to the ancient Phoenician state—a merchant republic, a bearer of a Mediterranean culture, and an interpreter of the West to the East. For the Maronite disciples of Chiha, the inconvenient facts that ancient Phoenicia included many city-states outside Lebanon's borders, that the Phoenicians spoke a Semitic tongue, and that the Maronites were migrants from Syria became lost in romanticism and self-interest. The Maronites so eagerly embraced the myth of a Phoenician heritage because it clearly differentiated them culturally from the Arab Muslims of Lebanon. From this perspective, the Maronites, utilizing their privileged position in the French Mandate, promoted as the defining characteristic of Lebanese national identity the idea that Lebanon's soul was to be found in the Phoenician ruins in Byblos.

Yet the greatest deficit under the mandate was not the feeding of a separate identity for the Maronites but the failure to administer Lebanon as a whole. The fault did not lay totally with Paris, for religious organizations promoting their own sectarian viewpoint provided seventy percent of all education. Consequently it was the norm rather than the exception that a Lebanese child entered a private school and emerged twelve years later barely having met a child of another confessional and ignorant of the multifaceted history, geography, and particularity of his or her own country. With patterns of identity based on blood ties and shared religion, there was more than folklore attached to the parable that any Lebanese returning to his or her country of birth after fifty years abroad would still demonstrate three basic characteristics: the accent common to the village of birth, a mentality that was sectarian, and the political vision of the leader of the communal group with which the individual identified. Ignoring perhaps the only commonality among the inhabitants of the mandate—the love of Lebanese food—the French failed to plant any seeds that might germinate into a common identity because Paris ruled Lebanon through religious communities much as Istanbul had. The few efforts the French made to develop political links that crossed communal or regional boundaries were frustrated by rock-solid communal affinities and the self-interests of family and confessional leaders who held the whole system together. That system functioned by common consent of the Lebanese, who benefited from the highest standard of living in the Levant, the best schools, and a developing system of interconnected roads. Modern medical care had arrived in the towns. And an American-style soda fountain in Beirut served up authentic chocolate milk shakes. But below the benefits of the French colonial system, the birth defects of infant Lebanon remained.

In 1925, the Druze grabbed their rifles and ammunition belts and stormed out of their mountain strongholds to demand greater autonomy. In response to this and other challenges, the French in 1926 declared a constitutional republic in which all citizens technically enjoyed equal rights under the law. Attempting to address Muslim sensitivities while reassuring the Maronites, the French established a tacit understanding that the president of Lebanon would always be a Christian. Four years later, when it appeared the Muslims were poised to force the election of a Muslim to the presidency, the constitution was suspended, throwing the mandate into crisis.

It was this political crisis that produced the all-important 1932 census, the only official head count ever taken in Lebanon. According to the government poll, Christians numbered 396,746 out of a total population of 793,226. This gave the Christians a real majority of only 226 over the combined total of all other people. Yet the results of the official census, which included Lebanese living abroad, fifty percent of whom were Maronite, established that the Christians outnumbered by 54,000 the Muslims and Druze combined. The count stood in part because the Druze and Shia, afraid of being engulfed by the Sunni majority in the larger Arab world, refused to join the Lebanese Sunnis in the creation of a Muslim block. Thus on the basis of a flawed census, the French declared the ratio of Christians over Muslims to be six to five. Consequently, seats in parliament and positions in the bureaucracy were distributed by the same ratio. Tragically for the future of Lebanon, this six-to-five ratio assumed the aura of a holy writ which shielded the Lebanese political system from the demographic reality that the Muslim population continued to increase vis-à-vis the Christians.

There is a certain irony in the fact that the crisis of 1932, ignited by sectarian conflict, stoked a sense of Lebanese nationalism among certain factions within the Christian and Sunni Muslim communities. Even within the Maronite fold, the idea of an independent Lebanon that included a legitimate role for the Muslims gained ground. The interwar years were a time when Muslims looked to the West for technology and political models through which they could reform their own societies. They also accepted certain Western values as universal practices and philosophies that any people could incorporate without damaging their own culture. To the detriment of the Arabs and the West, this viewpoint would suffer in the frenzied Arab nationalism of the 1950s and 1960s and go on life support in the late 1970s as Islamic fundamentalism roused itself to confront the West. Even so, as World War II approached, a budding Lebanese nationalism nourished by those who embraced Western political thought coaxed some Christians and Sunni Muslims into a tenuously united front against French colonialism. With the Nazi occupation of France in 1940 suspending French rule in Lebanon, the Lebanese, in the interest of independence, agreed on a modus operandi for accommodating their communal differences.

The Mithaq, or National Pact, of 1943 came as an informal agreement negotiated by the colorful and somewhat eccentric Maronite president, Bishara Khouri, and the staid Sunni prime minister, Riad Solh. From the outset, the pact guaranteed the Christians their accustomed dominant role in government. Employing the flawed 1932 census as its basis, the two leaders and a majority of the Lebanese accepted the existing six-to-five ratio of Christians to Muslims as the formula for the distribution of parliamentary seats, cabinet offices, and positions in the bureaucracy. The president, to be elected by the parliament, would always be a Maronite Christian. He, in turn, would choose the prime minister, who would always be a Sunni Muslim. The position of speaker of the parliament was reserved for a Shia Muslim, who gave recognition to the despised step-children of a state grounded in a Maronite-Sunni alliance. To win the support of the Druze, Greek Orthodox, and other Christians, each confessional was guaranteed special preserves of political power and patronage. Regardless of an individual's worth or qualifications, his confessional determined particular positions in government. Thus rather than eliminating confessionals as the basis of the political system, the Mithaq provided a formula through which religious groups with basically different political orientations and frames of reference could coexist in terms of access to power and control over resources. It was in this milieu that the Sunni and Maronite elites, like predatory animals, quickly co-opted the confessional system as their special reserve, thus retaining for themselves control of a toothless national government.

In a sense, the National Pact would prove workable precisely because it acknowledged that Lebanon was a country of deep religious antagonisms. A British tourist in Lebanon at the time spoke this truth better than the Lebanese: "I haven't yet come across one spark of national feeling: it is all sects and hatreds and religions."* In later years Nabih Berri, an urbane leader among the Lebanese Shia, gave a brutal yet accurate assessment of the grand compromise of 1943: "We [Lebanese] behave like tribes instead of like people of one country. The 1943 Pact . . . helped make us build a farm, not a country."†

Incredibly, the National Pact, the accord over which the Christians and Muslims would shed so much blood, was never committed to writing. Instead it was accepted as an understanding among Lebanon's elite. They agreed not because the pact defended a particular religious

---

* Quoted in Hilal Khashan, *Inside the Lebanese Confessional Mind* (New York: University Press of America, 1992), p. 9.

† Quoted in Augustus Richard Norton, *Amal and the Shi'a: Struggle for the Soul of Lebanon* (Austin: University of Texas Press, 1987), p. 80.

doctrine or promoted a political doctrine on which to build a nation, but rather for narrow political considerations of competing groups. The National Pact continued to work after Lebanon wrested independence from France in 1946 because it was sustained by politicians who were masters at the art of flexibility and compromise in protecting the only two fundamentals on which they all agreed: a free economy that served their commercial interests and a political system that abetted the patron-client relationships on which their power rested.

From the time the borders of Greater Lebanon were established, the men who kept the peace or led the violence were a coterie of political bosses known as the *zuama*. Unique to Lebanon's particular culture, these sometimes flamboyant creatures provide a vivid portrait of a specific type of Arab elite who in grand style or from the shadows operate the politics and economics of most Arab countries. Other Arab elites can come out of traditional tribes; long-established urban families; monarchies in which a tribal leader has created a kingdom or a king has been placed on a throne built by a foreign power; military officers who seize power by way of a tidy coup d'etat or a bloodstained revolution; or officials in a republic put in place by an invading military force of a foreign power. They defend their legitimacy through tribal power; or tightly knit alliances between families; or religion and sect; or military force and internal security services; or distribution of economic resources belonging to the state; or a deft combination of two or more of these elements. In Lebanon prior to the civil war of 1975, the elite was composed of the *zuama*, who were to Lebanese society what the feudal lords were to medieval Europe and the ward heelers to American politics.

A *zaim*, with some exceptions, reigned as the unquestioned leader of a community tightly knit together by family, religion, or confession. Reflecting the centrality of personal relationships in Arab culture, a *zaim*'s link to his followers was personal, not ideological or programmatic. Nor was it necessarily rational.

The *zaim* ascended from one of two sources. Either he was the eldest son of one of the powerful families entrenched in Lebanon's feudal past or he held power within his communal group through his position as a rich businessman or banker or, on rare occasions, the spokesman for a political ideology. The common denominator of all *zuama* was their ability to operate as merchants of influence in a system where democracy was a real if flawed concept. The feudal lords, like the Franjiehs within the Maronites and the Jumblatts among the Druze, were a constant in the political arena, gaining or losing a bit of power to their rivals from time to time. The *zuama* who emerged from business or political movements came and went depending on how much they were able to deliver for their clients, for a *zaim*'s follower was a client in every sense of the word. Newly emerged or well seasoned, the *zaim* worked his district like a ward heeler. Reeking of expensive cologne, he attended births, weddings, and funerals, planting kisses on the cheeks of men and washing women in elaborate flattery. When a new shop opened in his district, he and his entourage arrived in a fleet of cars laden with flowers, fruit, and chocolates. From his office, which functioned like the members' room of a men's club, he found a job for an unemployed father of four, paved the way to a university admission, pulled strings for a beleaguered businessman in need of a loan, and snared government contracts for his clients. When in trouble, a client never called a lawyer—he called his patron.

In gratitude for past favors and anticipation of future ones, clients pledged their loyalty to the *zaim*. Once the relationship was established, the *zaim* sustained it through a combination of charm and authoritarian displays that protected the size of his clientage and demonstrated his own competence in dispensing personal favors—the essential ingredients of his position and power.

Lacking any commitment to the common good, a *zaim* stood for public office as an inherent right. Consequently in the months before an election, newspapers announced one after another the names of the reigning *zuama* who intended to hold office once again. The privileges that came with those offices included the accumulation of power and money as well as pandering to individual egos. That is why between 1950 and 1970 almost all of the main thoroughfares in Beirut proudly bore the name of some reigning *zaim*.

The whole elaborate system worked because the Lebanese, largely a product of Arab culture, possessed no clear sense of institutions. Instead personal relationships were, and are, enshrined in the place of legislative bodies elected by the people, public officials confined within the boundaries of prescribed powers and duties, and legal systems codified and enforced by written law. For generations, it has been a person, not an institution, in which an individual has invested his personal and political loyalty. As a result, bureaucracies respond only to men in power. And government most often functions to appease individuals of power, not necessarily to ensure the public welfare.

As elsewhere in the Arab world, the elite of prewar Lebanon all but ignored ideology or public policy. Rarely did anyone within this elite step forward to take a stand on a specific issue or problem crucial to Lebanon's stability. So poorly developed was the concept of government as an extension of the corporate body of citizens that the Lebanese paid little attention to a political crisis in 1969 that left the country without a government for seven months. In the perpetual disconnect between the citizen and the state, public debate amounted to nothing more than "the personalized pragmatic politics of patronage, transaction relations and changing factional alliances in which the prize to be won was not victory for one set of values over another, but the achievement of high political office and personal gain."*

Since a *zaim* held his position only by delivering for his clients, the *zuama* within their respective communities were intense and often ruthless rivals. In this context, the Franjiehs battled the Gemayels inside the

---

* Michael Johnson, "Fractional Politics in Lebanon: The Case of the 'Islamic Society of Benevolent Intentions in Beirut,'" *Middle Eastern Studies* (January 1978), p. 72.

walls of the Maronites; the Sohls, Salams, and Karamis vied with one another among the Sunni Muslims; the Jumblatts outmaneuvered the Erslans within the Druze community; and so on through every confessional. Elections frequently degenerated into mini-wars as the *zuama* marched out their hired thugs and their militias to intimidate the opposition. Playing the political game for keeps, the *zaim* who lost to another proved to be a master of revenge. Yet as competitive as they were, the *zuama* stood shoulder to shoulder against any force that threatened to erode their power. Labor unions, benevolent associations, merchant groups, and student organizations were all channeled through confessional organizations under the watchful eye of the respective *zaim*. With no competition from governmental or private agencies, only the *zaim* effectively provided services, goods, and favors for his clients.

Although they skimmed the cream off the economy and paralyzed the development of any alternative to their personal rule, the *zuama*'s government-by-patronage was not entirely bad. It provided a measure of political integration among the widely divided and hostile confessionals. It maintained a modicum of stability and harmony in an otherwise fractured social structure. And with the exception of the Shia, it gave individuals and groups some leverage in securing benefits, services, and a more equitable distribution of resources. But the system was rife with cataclysmic flaws. The *zuama* ran Lebanon like a private club, swapping cabinet offices, government contracts, positions in the bureaucracy, and favors in the private sector. Plagued with endemic corruption, nepotism, and favoritism, the entire political process amounted to little more than squabbles over political spoils and the boundaries of each *zaim*'s territory and influence.

That the *zuama* controlled Lebanon was a symptom of a society and political system crawling with the same nepotism, bribery, opportunism, and petty rivalries. Lebanon was corrupt, at least in the Western understanding of the term, from top to bottom because the people themselves did not expect a politician to be honest or tend to the interests of the state. They demanded only that he be a fixer and doer in pursuit of his clients' interests. And since the Lebanese held in admiration anyone who could turn a fast dollar, activities of public officials that would have been highly questionable or downright illegal in the West escaped general condemnation in Lebanon. The *zuama* were tolerated, even held in esteem, because they reigned as the kings of the shady deal in a highly permissive, laissez-faire economy, one that a majority of the population believed gave them, as individuals, a small piece of the action.

If the Lebanese understood the nuances and mechanics of the system, foreigners did not. In the 1940s, a Belgian economist dispatched to study the Lebanese economy expressed shock at the way business and government were conducted but voiced pleasure with the prosperity it produced. His observation has become enshrined in the annals of Lebanese wisdom: "We don't know how or why, but if it works, don't touch it."*

In this atmosphere, critics of the elite were ignored. When Bishara Khouri was president (1946–1952), the Maronite archbishop Mubarak wrote to him, "[I]n Lebanon there is no peace, justice or happiness—only graft and injustice and murder, robberies and thefts committed by men in office, and government intervention to prevent free elections and make easy the victory of a group which has sacrificed every public interest for its personal profit."† The exertion of influence to move money became so pervasive by the 1950s that virtually every politician was on the take from someone—a Lebanese seeking a favor, international business interests, some foreign power, or all of the above. Lebanon was a state in which powerful individuals trumped weak institutions.

The understanding between the governing elites representing

---

* Quoted in Kamal Dib, *Warlords and Merchants: The Lebanese Business and Political Establishment* (Ithaca: Ithaca Press, 2004), p. 201.

† Quoted in Habib J. Awal, "Threat to Lebanon," *Commonweal*, August 8, 1947, p. 398.

Maronites, Sunnis, Shia, Druze, Greek Orthodox, and others that had enabled the Lebanese to proceed to independence in 1946 left undefined the state's identity and, by extension, its foreign policy. By the 1950s, the basic domestic differences that had been contained in 1943 became increasingly explosive as events outside the borders of Lebanon engulfed the Middle East—the 1948 war for Palestine, various disputes between Arab states, and the Cold War in which the United States and the Soviet Union sent their proxies in to circle each other. In the world of realpolitik, these regional conflicts often required Lebanon to side with one or another of the protagonists. That in turn widened further the fractures in the foundation of the Lebanese state. As a result, the Lebanese in 1958 stumbled into their first civil war.

The events of 1958 actually began in 1952 when the shy, reserved Gamal Abdul Nasser led a cadre of young army officers in the seizure of the government of Egypt. Before the end of 1954, Nasser's dashing good looks and his newly discovered oratory had transformed the Egyptian army colonel into the worshipped hero of the masses of the Arab world and the terror of conservative establishments. In Lebanon, Sunnis locked out of the dining rooms of the posh hotels where the *zuama* made their deals were enthralled with Nasser's blazing rhetoric. Glued to cheap radios that carried his broadcasts from Cairo over the "Voice of the Arabs," they emotionally responded to the Arab messiah's clarion call for the restoration of Arab dignity by pulling back their fragile commitment to Lebanon.

The spell Nasser cast over the lower classes and much of the middle class came from doing what no other Arab leader had ever done: molding together socialist economic doctrine with the concept of the unity of all Arabs, or pan-Arabism. Bundling economics and identity together, Nasser created a new ideology labeled "Nasserism" that stirred the masses of every Arab country from Egypt to Saudi Arabia. In Lebanon, the vision of Arab unity and economic equality elucidated by the self-declared Arab messiah seriously threatened to tip the critical balance of power in Lebanese politics achieved by the Christian, Sunni, and Druze *zuama*.* The heaviest weights on the scale of the Lebanese state were the Sunnis and the Christian Maronites. Yet many Sunnis outside the elite questioned why they should continue to accept a secondary position in a state dominated by Christians ambivalent about Arab nationalism at the very moment when Arab identity was on the threshold of its finest hour. For Christians, that same call to Arabism threatened not only to annihilate their political and economic privileges but also to obliterate their communal haven.

The Lebanese president at the time was Camille Chamoun, a typical Maronite *zaim*. He was born to a Maronite family in the hilly Chouf region, educated in law at the Catholic Université Saint-Joseph in Beirut, elected to parliament in the 1930s as the heir to his father, and appointed to several important positions in the cabinet in the 1940s. In 1952, he was elected president by the parliament. By 1957, rumors abounded that Chamoun was conniving within parliament to secure a second term as president, a move that threatened to violate all the rules of office swapping that kept the establishment united.

Whether the crisis of 1958 over control of Lebanon's domestic politics and foreign policy resulted from Camille Chamoun's devious power plays or his own stupidity is still being argued. During his first term, Chamoun had placed allies from every confession in strategic locations throughout the government. But in the prelude to the 1957 elections for the parliamentary body that would choose the president in 1958, Chamoun jettisoned his existing alliances in favor of new alignments more submissive to his ambitions. These new allies included the Douehi clan, rivals of the Maronite Franjiehs in Zghorta; Emir Majid Erslan, the Druze rival of Kamal Jumblatt in the Chouf; as well as the Shia Kazem al Khalil, who was the foe of the Shia Assads in south Lebanon. Dispersing

* The presence of Shia among the *zuama* was small and their influence slight. See chapter 6.

briefcases full of Lebanese pounds from a gold De Soto and employing the emerging power of the Phalange, the Maronite militia belonging to Pierre Gemayel, Chamoun engineered the 1957 parliamentary election. When politicians crucial to the old order such as the Sunni Rashid Karami and the Druze Kamal Jumblatt lost their seats, they struck back. Over three days, dozens of pro-Chamoun politicians felt their violent wrath. Symbolic of the ugliness that pitted one coalition of warlords against another was the brazen attack on the army's al Masna checkpoint on the Beirut-Damascus highway that was manned by five Christians and one Muslim. The attackers castrated and disemboweled the Christians and incorporated the Muslim into their ranks. As the violence continued to widen, Chamoun pleaded with General Fuad Shihab, commander of the army, to intervene. In what is probably the wisest decision any Lebanese government official ever made, Shihab refused, reasoning that intervention would destroy the army's impartiality and probably its cohesion as Christians and Muslims within the ranks would split to join one side or the other. Shihab recognized there was no such institution as a Lebanese army that possessed the power or the will to defend the state. There were only individuals whose first loyalty was to confession and clan. In the end, it was events beyond Lebanon's borders that turned communal violence into outright war.

Ever since Nasser had emerged as an Arab nationalist capable of mobilizing the Arabs across national boundaries, Britain, France, and the United States had been aggressively building alliances designed to contain his growing power. In 1957, Chamoun, unnerved by the Nasser phenomenon, dashed consensus politics in Lebanon by signing onto the Eisenhower Doctrine, the American pledge to defend friendly governments against outside threats. With a stroke of a pen, Chamoun placed himself in opposition to Arab nationalists, both Muslim and Christian. In 1958, the February unification of Syria and Egypt into a federation called the United Arab Republic (UAR) and the July assassination of Iraq's pro-Western King Faisal by Arab nationalists set off alarm bells in both Washington and Beirut. The next day two thousand U.S. Marines landed in Beirut, not to save the Chamoun government but to convince the pro-Western governments of Pakistan, Turkey, and Iran that the United States was committed to enforcement of the Eisenhower Doctrine.[*]

Except for the fact that between two thousand and four thousand people were killed, the 1958 civil war in Lebanon with its American invasion contained elements of an absurd comedy. When battle-clad U.S. Marines splashed ashore on a white-sand beach south of Beirut, they expected to meet armed hordes screaming the name of Nasser. Instead they found themselves charging through women clad in scanty bikinis sitting in the sun. Beyond the beachhead, the only encumbrance to the progress of the leathernecks was swarms of adolescent boys selling American Coca-Cola and Hershey bars. The following day when U.S. troops redeployed into downtown Beirut, they were preceded by three columns of Lebanese policemen on motorcycles, followed by children on streamer-decked bicycles and pro-Chamoun adults honking the horns of their big American cars. All the while the premier, Saeb Salam, sat in his sand-bagged command post hung with a small, decorous sign: "Appointments 9 to 1 and 4 to 7."

The mere presence of fourteen thousand U.S. Marines on the ground in Lebanon cooled what was essentially infighting between elements of the Lebanese elite. Soon the warlords "kissed each others' beards" and declared peace because the *zuama* had determined that the interruption of business, flight of capital, and drop in foreign investments caused by what they called "the Events" were intolerable to their interests. By convincing Camille Chamoun of the wisdom of resigning, they ended the little war with no clear victors or losers. But Lebanon as a state lost

---

[*] Chamoun played a role in the American decision to invade by convincing Eisenhower that the Druze goat herders who followed the socialist Kamal Jumblatt were dangerous communists.

in the sense that this brief war produced no change, much less resolution, of the issues surrounding the country's identity or the entrenched power of the elite. If the Lebanese did not see this, Sandy Campbell, the American president of the Tapline, which carried oil from the Arabian Gulf to the shore of the Mediterranean, did: "To hope that the Lebanese won't resort to violence again is like hoping dogs don't chase cats."*

NO MATTER HOW much the elite wanted to believe otherwise, Lebanon, after 1958, contained elements of change. In the decade and a half since the National Pact, new economic and financial forces had risen to exert their pressure. Non-Maronite Christians and Sunni Muslims demanded a wider democracy. And the Druze and Shia expressed their aspirations for a larger piece of the Lebanese pie. But the zuama, like most of the Arab elites today, refused to respond even to enlightened leadership.

Fuad Shihab, the commander of Lebanon's army who had rejected appeals to put the army in the midst of the turmoil of 1958, had assumed the presidency. Concentrating on building a nation rather than promoting the privileges of the elite, he put forward an ambitious economic development program designed to meld rich and poor, Christian and Muslim, into a single society. Shihab's vision of a Lebanese state stretched beyond the fragile coexistence among communal groups or the brittle association of different categories of the population. Instead the new Lebanon would coalesce around each citizen's conviction that he or she was an integral part of a single people committed to a nation rather than a confessional. Tragically for the future of Lebanon, Shihab's efforts failed. Lebanon's traditional political establishment, Christian and Muslim, lined up to block any new order that threatened to diminish their power and position. Blind to the realities that the common

* Quoted in Dib, *Warlords and Merchants*, p. 88.

welfare demanded a commonality of citizenship, the warlords and their merchant allies led Lebanon into its golden age.

IN LATE 1946, when Lebanon secured its independence from France, Beirut was little more than a sleepy village whose only claims to fame were its harbor, its scenic beauty, and the American University of Beirut. By the mid-1960s, Beirut had morphed into a glitzy Mediterranean metropolis, a Mecca for the international set, a haven for exiles of the region's political wars, and a brothel of business where ready cash transcended law and ethics. In 1966, *Life*, the slick, high-circulation American magazine, described Beirut as "a kind of Las Vegas-Rivera-St. Moritz flavored with spices of Araby."* The Hotel Saint Georges, hugging a peninsula that juts out into a quiet cove of the Mediterranean, shaded scantily clad sunbathers under umbrellas of blue, yellow, orange, and pink. Across the street, the Phoenicia Hotel, the newest and poshest hostelry in the city, flaunted a huge, round swimming pool tiled in three shades of Mediterranean blue. One end of the pool, constructed of an expanse of glass, formed the backdrop of the elaborately stocked downstairs bar, where customers lounged in the semi-darkness and watched the swimmers glide past.

While much of the Middle East pitched in the storms of the Arab-Israeli struggle or convulsed with movements fed by the emotions of Arab nationalism, Lebanon stayed aloof, reaping benefits from the disorder of others. The ability of the Lebanese establishment to position the country as a haven from the turbulence of the surrounding Arab countries contributed to Lebanon's economic allure. The advantage was maximized by the Lebanese people's own energy and commercial aptitudes. Planted in the Lebanese psyche was a drive that demanded hard work and commercial success. The literacy rate stood at eighty-eight

---

* "The West Went Thataway—East," *Life*, January 7, 1966, p. 5.

percent, far above that of most other Arab societies of the time. Above all, the Lebanese were true traders. There was nothing they would not trade at a profit. And it was profit that constituted the supreme value of commercial life, undergirded by a government dedicated to laissez-faire capitalism. Catering to the international business community, Beirut bragged that it possessed more banks than New York; transacted half of all the world's gold trade; produced more newspapers than London; and published more confidential business newsletters than New York, London, and Paris combined.

If Beirut had pulsated in the 1960s, it vibrated in the early 1970s. With the 1973 oil boom in the Arabian Peninsula, the components of the Lebanese economy dovetailed perfectly with the wildly escalating demands of the Gulf economies. Geography alone placed Lebanon at the crossroads of revenues moving from the east and goods coming from the west. Lebanese farmers in the south and water bottlers in the north sent their produce via truck to the Arabian Peninsula to sustain cadres of foreign workers flooding in to build the new elaborate infrastructure. Inexperienced Arab investors from the Gulf arrived to pour copious amounts of money into good and bad investments put together by worldly Beiruti businessmen. The Lebanese themselves, well-educated and multilingual, flocked to the Gulf countries, where they became managers, contractors, doctors, and clerks. From there, they sent their handsome wages back to their families in Lebanon, who in turn fed the money into the economy.

With thirty international carriers serving Beirut's international airport, more and more Western businessmen doing business in the Gulf made the city their headquarters. Real estate prices exploded, causing a stretch of properties on Hamra Street to become more expensive than the Champs-Élysées in Paris. These prices spoke to the widely held perception that Beirut was an oasis, a sophisticated retreat from the heat, disorder, and strict social codes of the Persian Gulf states. Attracting both Westerners and high-rolling Arabs, the Casino du

Liban, perched on a cliff on Beirut's northern perimeter, did a boom-
ing business. In its 1975 sequin-and-feather extravaganza, scantily clad
Western showgirls lacquered in gold and silver stepped off the petals of
a giant flower that descended from the casino's ceiling. But there was a
darker side to Lebanon.

Although nightclubs and mosques stood side by side in an era of shallow, flashy prosperity, Lebanese society was troubled. This most urbane
and Westernized of Arab countries was hiding a near-feudal system
where thirteen families controlled fifty percent of all large companies
and forty-seven percent of all capital investment. These same families
along with their allies and rivals produced the political leaders who acted
as godfathers defending the interests of their followers, segmented into
families, clans, religions, and sects.

The ruling families competed for status through flagrant displays of
materialism unhampered by any sense of modesty or moderation. To the
contrary, those at the top of the social and political hierarchy considered
the outward signs of wealth logical since status went a long way in seal-
ing marriages and securing financial deals that promoted the interests
of the family enterprise. Thus fleets of luxury cars, the large apartment
in a prestigious location, the elaborate Louis XV furniture (especially
in the public rooms where guests were entertained), designer clothing,
and heavy gold jewelry were all considered investments.

The sad fact is that the rituals of the upper class that can be awkward
and uncomfortable to those scattered down the rungs of the social ladder were eagerly embraced by the middle class as the standard to imi-
tate. Even Lebanese on the outer edge of the economy and the political
system seemed to watch with more wistfulness than envy. So in the
glitter of the golden age, the country, and especially Beirut, functioned
as a stage on which the Lebanese played out their fantasies.

But a detour from Beirut's showy hotel district led into ugly back
alleyways. The governing system that collected few taxes from the four
percent of the population that swallowed up sixty percent of the gross

national product also directed resources into short-term commercial credit instead of long-term investments in manufacturing and agriculture. Investments in infrastructure went to Beirut while the rest of the country languished. As a result, some villages still drew their water in buckets from wells dug by charitable organizations and wealthy individuals as long ago as 1812. At Sidon, the harbor continued to look much as it did six hundred years before when the Crusaders occupied the castle at its mouth. Unable to make a living from fishing or farming because of inadequate physical infrastructure, thousands of families migrated to Beirut, where they settled into the ring of slums known as the "Belt of Misery." Crammed into hovels often with no electricity, running water, or sanitary facilities, they struggled for survival. While at the other end of the social spectrum, the elite in their expensive clothes sat in chic coffee shops discussing lofty topics such as Jean-Paul Sartre and self-indulgences like the next trip to Paris. These were the realities of Lebanon's golden age.

At the end of 1974, Lebanon—whose borders drawn by Europeans encapsulated families identifying themselves as Roman Catholic or Orthodox Christians, Sunni or Shia Muslims, the theologically mysterious Druze, or one of a mixed collection of smaller minorities—was approaching the breaking point. The widening cracks in Lebanon's stability came from a deep discontent rooted in the social, political, and economic inequalities that had characterized Lebanon throughout its short history as a state. These primary fissures had, in turn, produced more cracks caused by conflicting interpretations of national identity, colliding ideologies, differing demands on power sharing, and dissenting views on security and foreign policy. Under the gloss of Beirut's exterior, the territory France had squeezed into the boundaries of Greater Lebanon in 1920 was nothing more than a heterogeneous collection of groups exhibiting the characteristics of tribes. Never having engaged in building a nation that would bind these tribes together, the *zuama* held no weapons and possessed no will with which to counter the ideological movements rooted in identity and economics that were rapidly spreading through the Arab world. Nor were there any governmental institutions or truly national leaders capable of repairing the damage or even sounding the alarm. Continuing to live the illusion, the elite ignored the storm bearing down on the hollow Lebanese state.

Thus three decades before Iraq approached its own crisis early in the twenty-first century, produced by the same issues of kinship, identity, anemic political institutions, and inequitable societies ruled by an elite, the Lebanese stood on the rim of another, far more destructive civil war. It only took the Palestinians to push them over the edge.

Chapter 3

THE PALESTINIANS:
VICTIMS AND VILLAINS

Not yet has there been a full history of us as a people,
not even a full record of what has been done to us,
what outrages have been done in our name,
and what we have done to others.

—EDWARD SAID,

After the Last Sky

A l Baqaa, located just outside Amman, houses the largest concentration of Palestinians in Jordan. Spread out on the floor
of a desert valley that lies below gentle hills on which are
erected the houses of wealthy Jordanians, it is, at night, an engaging
mirage of tightly compressed lights. But dawn exposes the reality of
al Baqaa—a collection of a hundred thousand people jammed into a
largely impoverished warren of cinder block houses, small, poorly
stocked shops, humble mosques, and crowded schools. Except for its
size, al Baqaa is typical of the fifty-nine Palestinian settlements containing 4.1 million refugees scattered in Lebanon, Jordan, Syria, Gaza, and
the Israeli-occupied West Bank.*

---

* The number of Palestinian refugees varies widely depending on the criteria by
which they are counted. The number given above represents those who receive direct
assistance from the United Nations Relief and Works Administration (UNRWA). Eli-
gible for this aid are those who lived in Palestine in the period from June 1946 to
May 1948 and their direct descendants. The actual number of Palestinians who live in
settlements described as "camps" is much higher.

All of these jumbled settlements trace their origins to 1948 when a war fought for the territory of Palestine between Jews and Arabs dumped seven hundred thousand Palestinians into surrounding countries. When Israel closed the gates of the new Jewish state to their return, and their host countries refused to take responsibility for resettling them, the Palestinian refugees became trapped in tents and one-room mud-brick structures hastily built to provide shelter from the hot sun of summer and the cold winds of winter. These settlements of stateless people are what became the "camps," and it is these camps that remain the ugly symbol of the Palestinian refugee.

The affluent of Palestinian society who fled the war of 1948 escaped the grasp of the camps. With resources and skills, they rented apartments in Beirut, Cairo, Damascus, Amman, and other cities, where they took up lifestyles that avoided the physical deprivation of displacement. But the small merchants, the unskilled laborers, and, most of all, the tenant farmers huddled in frail wooden structures that gradually gave way to inadequate houses assembled from raw cement blocks covered by patchwork tin roofs pounded from scrap. Sixty years later each of these camps—whether in Jordan, Egypt, Syria, or Lebanon—project a sameness that continues to speak of dispossession.

A main gate mounted with heavy iron doors opens on narrow alleyways linking a chaotic web of houses devoid of style and color except for what is provided by laundry hanging out to dry on flat roofs. Inside, the rooms are near barren boxes that hold a cheap sofa, some worn chairs, an occasional table holding a box of tissues and a vase of plastic flowers, and certificates of completion from schools across the Middle East and the West that hang proudly on the walls. In these camps, generation by generation the anger of the dispossessed of a lost land feeds a deep and abiding hatred of Israel and bitter resentment against the Arab countries in which they are resident. None of these countries is more challenged by its Palestinian residents than Jordan.

The Palestinians of Jordan are not only victims of the state of Israel but many are also villains, acting as rogues in a state that has integrated more displaced Palestinians than any other country in the world. In the 1948 influx of refugees, the population within the boundaries of Jordan literally doubled. In the wake of the Arab-Israeli war of 1967, another four hundred thousand arrived in a country always short of resources. Today Palestinians make up at least fifty percent of the population and represent one side of the profound divide that characterizes Jordan. Jordanians of Palestinian origin dominate the economy. Non-Palestinian Jordanians rooted in pre-1948 Jordan dominate the government and the military. After almost being destroyed in 1970 by the sword of Palestinian nationalism held by the most radical elements of the Palestine Liberation Organization (PLO), the Jordanian monarchy has been reasonably successful in holding its Palestinian population within the parameters of the Jordanian state ruled by the Hashemites. The young King Abdullah II, who succeeded his father, King Hussein, in 1999, and his beautiful queen, Rania, personify the balancing act. He is Jordanian; she is Palestinian. Together they carefully walk the high wire over the deep demographic divide within the Jordanian state.

The entire Arab world has been tormented for more than half a century by the stateless Palestinians and their plight. Today their dilemma entangles the West because within it are buried many of the explosive elements that fuel Arab anger against Western nations. For essentially all Arabs, the Palestinian stands as the great, boding symbol of the Arab perception of their humiliation at the hands of the West, a humiliation that Arabs see as beginning in the age of the Crusades. In what is an article of faith harbored by almost every Arab, Israel represents the modern Crusader state, a Western colony planted in the Arab world, armed with the best of Western technology and nourished by Western capital. In Arab eyes, it is only by reducing Israel to a state within the Arab Middle East rather than a tool of the West that the Arabs can spur their own renaissance.

Only by grasping the Palestinian issue in all its realities and myths can Westerners, especially Americans, begin to understand the depth of Arab passion about a population they see as victimized by the 1948 confluence of Jewish nationalism and Western collaboration that gave birth to the state of Israel. Ever since, the passionate cause of lost Palestine has fed Arab political/cultural movements from the pan-Arabism of Gamal Abdul Nasser to the Islamic militancy of al Qaeda. For the West, no so-called victory can be achieved over the chronic instability of the Arab world, which hinders genuine political and economic reform, or over militant Islam, which menaces the civilian populations of the West, without beginning with what is the essential of the region: the Palestinian issue. But there is also a side of that question that has been, and continues to be, perpetrated by the Arabs.

Originally dispossessed by Zionism and neglected by the West, the Palestinians are also the victims of Arab governments. Every Arab regime mouths the rhetoric of the Palestinian cause while, in varying degrees, oppressing Palestinians within their own countries. The reasons range from the reality of the severe social and economic burdens imposed on their own societies by the large numbers of Palestinians, to the use of the Palestinians as pawns in the power game with Israel, to resentment against the work ethic and skills possessed by many Palestinians. For their part, the Palestinians, particularly since 1967, have pursued their all-consuming agenda—the return to Palestine—by challenging the governments and people of countries in which they have found refuge. As a result, the Palestinians constitute both the touchstone of Arab unity and the verification of specific interests and identities that pit Arab against Arab. Nowhere has this duel between Arab states and Palestinian nationalists, between Israel and the Palestinians, wreaked more havoc or inflicted more damage on societies and individuals than in Lebanon. But before Lebanon, there was Palestine.

HISTORIC PALESTINE WAS a fragment of jagged geography along the eastern Mediterranean that divided the verdant coastal plain from the bare, crusty deserts to the east.* A thousand years before the Christian era, the Hebrew king David proclaimed the kingdom that still marks the high point of Jewish history. Yet it did not last. Wracked by internal dissension and assaulted by outside forces, David's kingdom served as a battleground for competing powers to the east and the west. By 63 BC, it was the Romans who possessed Palestine. For several decades, the legions of Rome enforced stability. But on the death of Herod in AD 4, Palestine once again plunged into disorder. In AD 70, the Jews staged another of their periodic revolts against occupation. The Romans responded by demolishing the Second Temple, leaving only its western wall. In the wake of yet another revolt in AD 135, the Jews scattered into their Diaspora. They left behind a remnant that took up life side by side with the rest of Palestine's indigenous population. The result was another of those human patchworks by which the Levant is defined.

By the criteria most often used to define ethnic groups—the sharing of common ethnicity, religion, language, region, and culture—the indigenous people with whom the Jews lived were an enigma. Ethnically they were the mixed product of all those who had battled over this piece of the Levant through the centuries. After the Islamic conquest of the seventh century AD, the majority became Muslims while the minority remained Christians. Although they spoke Arabic and adhered to Arabic culture, they possessed little sense of themselves as a whole. Instead each individual was a member of a family, a village, a clan set against other families, villages, and clans.

When the Ottoman Turks swept into Palestine in 1516, the Muslims of Palestine as well as most of its Christians continued to regard themselves as Arabs, culturally similar to those of Mecca, Baghdad, Damascus, and Cairo. But they also recognized themselves as an amalgam of the indigenous people of their ancient land—Canaanite and Philistine and Ammorite. In the waning years of the Ottoman Empire, during

---

* Palestine is a name derived from the Philistines of the Bible.

the late nineteenth century, they remained simply Arabs who shared
Palestine with a small Jewish population. Before the twentieth century
reached midpoint, they would be Palestinians locked in a desperate fight
for survival with Jews inflamed with the passion of Zionism.

IN 1877, THE population of Palestine included only twenty-five thousand Jews out of a total of six hundred thousand inhabitants. Almost
exclusively Orthodox, they were the descendants of those left behind
in the great Jewish migration of the first century AD. Clustered within
closely knit communities in and around Jerusalem and living side by side
with their non-Jewish neighbors, they were nothing more than another
piece in the collage that was the Levant.

In 1882, other Jews began to arrive in Palestine. Coming principally
out of Poland and Russia, they planted small agricultural communities
typical of utopian societies promoted by nineteenth-century socialists
in Europe on the coastal plain, into the hills of Galilee, and over the
western approaches to Jerusalem. Others belonged to Haluka, communities that lived on charity from world Jewry. As Zionists born of
the pogroms of eastern Europe, they sought nothing more than to live
on the ancient stones of Palestine as Jews immune from persecution. In
1903, they were joined by a second wave of Zionists who came to claim
the land of David as a Jewish national homeland.

In the beginning, Palestinian antagonisms toward the Zionists revolved
around economics. For the merchants, the Zionists, who commanded
some skill in the economic practices of industrialized Europe, threatened an indigenous economy already debilitated by the cheaper products of Europe's industrial revolution. For the *fellahin*, the peasants, the
danger was greater. The Zionist demand for land, and access to capital
with which to buy it, began to suction up fields that Palestinian families
had cultivated for generations. But the brewing contest between Zionist
and Palestinian involved, at its most basic level, a conflict of cultures.

Coming from Europe, ignorant of Arab ways, and insensitive to the local customs of Palestine, too many of the European Jews attempted to impose Western customs on an ancient and traditional society. Even within the Zionist movement, the political Zionists—those seeking a Jewish homeland—outnumbered and outflanked the Zionists who had come to Palestine for purely religious reasons. But the zeal to found a Jewish state in Palestine could not be satisfied without greater numbers of Jews.

During World War I, when the bloody stalemate on the Western Front was draining away Britain's youth and its resources, the European Zionists promised to launch a fifth column of German Jews against Kaiser Wilhelm and to provide Jewish financial resources to the struggling British war effort. In return, they extracted from the British government a public commitment to a Jewish homeland in Palestine. In a letter to the banker Lord Rothschild dated November 2, 1917, Arthur James Balfour, the British foreign secretary, issued the words that would wrack Palestine for the next three decades: "His Majesty's Government view with favour the establishment in Palestine of a national home for the Jewish people, and will use their best endeavours to facilitate the achievement of this object." The great caveat followed: ". . . it being clearly understood that nothing shall be done which may prejudice the civil and religious rights of existing non-Jewish communities in Palestine."* With the Balfour Declaration, Palestine became a thrice-promised land. Britain had already pledged Arab independence in return for the Arab revolt against the Ottoman sultan. It then determined Palestine's future as a British colony in the secret Sykes-Picot Agreement, which divided the Ottomans' Middle East territories between Britain and France. Now the British embraced the Zionist agenda.

In 1919 when Britain claimed Palestine as a mandate from the League of Nations, London began to extricate itself from the tangle of pledges

* Fromkin, *Peace to End All Peace*, p. 297.

made during World War I. The British promise of Arab independence was already dead. The British goal of acquiring the territory of Palestine was accomplished. Only the promise of a Jewish homeland remained in play. For London, the reality of Palestine's population meant that the Balfour Declaration could be finessed. After all, out of a population of 620,000 people in Palestine, 550,000 were Arab Muslims, 70,000 Arab Christians, and only 50,000 Jews, some of whom looked on political Zionism as a blasphemous assault on the teachings of the Torah. What Britain failed to recognize was that in the coming contest for Palestine, numbers were the only advantage the Arabs could field.

The depth of Arab disadvantages began with the organization of their society. Palestinians for centuries had been welded into family and place.* Consequently, a vast chasm separated the rural *fellahin* from the workers, merchants, and landowners of the towns. Rural and urban, they lived separate lives, interacting only as tenants and landowners. Within this broad rural/urban split burrowed the most basic source of being in the Arab world—the family. A Palestinian's identity began with his extended family, then reached to his village and finally to his region. What little political organization existed followed the vertical lines of family, locality, and sometimes faith. The horizontal lines of class functioned only as a by-product of the vertical forces. While the Zionist immigrants purposefully left their established social structure and tra-ditional culture behind to turn themselves into "new men" dedicated to the building of the Zionist state, the Palestinians carried with them into the mandate their "web of belonging"—the social and cultural charac-teristics that resided in Palestine. This is how the Palestinians met the combined forces of the British and the Zionists.

The Zionist organizations, creatures of the West and largely funded

---

*Although the designation of the Arabs of Palestine as specifically "Palestinians" did not evolve until after 1948, the author has chosen to use that differentiation prior to 1948 in the interest of clarity.

by Western Jews, quickly established themselves as the favored elite of the British mandate. Any outside help for Palestine's Arabs depended on their Arab neighbors, who were also under the yoke of Western colonialism. Yet during the interwar years, the Arabs of Palestine believed that the Arabs of Damascus and Aleppo, Cairo and Alexandria would join them in a stand against the Zionist interlopers to dispel the British and Zionist illusion that the whole Arab nation could be defied. But the mandatory power, the Zionist settlers, and world Jewry did just that.

In an unequal contest for dominance in British colonial policy in Palestine, the Zionist strategy centered on population and land. In their carefully devised game plan, the Zionists focused on mass migration to create a Jewish majority in Palestine in as short a time as possible. When that majority was realized, Britain would be pressed to relinquish its mandate and Palestine would emerge as the Jewish homeland. In the simplicity of this concept, the Zionists reduced politics to a mathematical formula: Jewish immigration equaled numbers of Jews in Palestine and Jews in Palestine equaled a Jewish homeland.

Ultimately, Palestine's future would not be determined by the Jews, the Arabs, or even the British. It would be determined by the realities of World War II, for it was worldwide revulsion triggered by images of the Nazi death camps that secured wholesale Western political support for Palestine as a homeland for the Jews. In the process, this turned the Palestinians into a nation of refugees and the Arabs into a people united in anger against the state of Israel and the West.

When World War II began in 1939, the Jewish population of Palestine still accounted for only thirty percent of the total. Five years later when Allied troops that had come ashore at Normandy moved closer and closer to Hitler's capital of Berlin, the Zionists were delivered a Jewish population from the hells of Auschwitz, Buchenwald, Dachau, and the other German concentration camps. But the British, still standing guard at the portals to Palestine, tried to turn back thousands of hollow-eyed, homeless European Jews. While sympathetic to the refugees, the British were also concerned about securing stability in the Middle East, which was necessary to protect the empire's communications and transportation routes to the Suez Canal and India as well as access to the oil fields of southwestern Iran. In the end, Britain could not ignore world opinion, which demanded justice for the Jews, or stem the tide of Jewish immigration. Exhausted by World War II, overextended economically, and overwhelmed by the pressure to open the gates of Palestine, the British looked for a way to dump the responsibilities London had assumed along with the coveted territory of the mandate.

In February 1947, His Majesty's Government passed the conundrum of Palestine to the fledgling United Nations. When the UN attempted to resolve the issue by partitioning the territory between the Jews and the Palestinians, the Palestinians refused. According to Arab attitudes shaped by a history of occupation and deception, no international body or other foreign power had the right to deliver Arab land to an alien people. Beyond that, the Arabs of Palestine raged against the very idea of partition, which they saw as tailored by the Western powers to meet the needs and demands of the Zionists, eighty to ninety percent of whom were Europeans. With partition off the table, the war for Palestine was on.

With most of their leadership imprisoned or exiled in the 1930s and early 1940s and lacking economic resources, the Palestinians were prepared neither militarily nor politically to confront the highly financed, organized, and motivated Yishuv, the Zionist community in Palestine. Burdened by the legacy of the mandate's misrule and crippled by the imprisonment and exile of most of their leadership as well as the fissures in their own society, the Palestinians furiously drove into war with nothing but a passionate determination to hold their land. It was not enough.

In Jaffa, Haifa, and even Jerusalem, raw fear among the Palestinians began to dismantle a whole society. The rich drew down their bank accounts, locked their imposing homes, boarded ships, and loaded into automobiles headed for Beirut, Cairo, or Damascus to wait out the war. The minuscule middle class, carrying suitcases and herding children, strung eastward to join relatives in towns a safe distance from concentrated Jewish settlements. With these greater and lesser notables went the *fellahin*'s only political identification: their allegiance to the personages of the clan. Almost overnight, the ribs of Palestinian society had broken. Soon those left behind would flee, by choice or force.

In February 1948, the Haganah, the Zionist army, emptied the ancient coastal town of Caesarea of its Palestinian citizens. Threatened by Haganah artillery and terrified by rumors of Jewish atrocities, the Palestinians surged out of coastal cities and villages.* By May 14, 1948, when David Ben-Gurion declared the state of Israel, the Palestinians had become a defeated people.

The next day, the war for Palestine between the Zionists and the Palestinians expanded into an Arab war. The Egyptians moved northward out of the Sinai toward Tel Aviv and through the Negev to Beersheba. An Iraqi force crossed the Jordan River. A few thousand Syrians came down through Galilee, perceptibly reducing the panic spreading through Palestinian villages. Even Lebanon sent a small force to join in the Arab cause, a profound symbol for a ruling elite that held as a sacred trust the determination to stay out of Arab politics. The Arab Legion of Transjordan, the only effective fighting force on the Arab side, occupied areas east of the Jordan River and held the Arab part of Jerusalem.

Although the Arab radios and the Arab press claimed victory after victory, the Arab armies were losing. Lacking equipment, leadership, and zeal, the Arab League, a loose, flabby association of independent Arab countries formed in 1945, lacked a commonly agreed objective. Its leaders had joined the fight as much to thwart any attempt by Transjordan's King Abdullah to establish his own hegemony over Syria

---

* A small percentage of Palestinians fled at the urging of their leaders, who were seeking to create chaos in Palestine's Jewish-dominated economy.

and the Levant as to save Palestine. By October, Israeli forces had driven the Egyptians from most of their positions in the Negev, cleared northern Palestine, and forced the beaten Arab Liberation Army back across the borders of Lebanon and Syria. By December, the war for Palestine was over. Seven hundred thousand people, sixty percent of an entire society, were homeless. Of the four countries on the border of lost Palestine that absorbed them—Egypt, Syria, Jordan, and Lebanon—Lebanon proved least able to contain the Palestinian refugees.

AS A STEADY stream of refugees trekked out of Palestine into Lebanon in the spring of 1948, the luminous yellows and pale purples of wildflowers dotted the valleys and clustered in the folds of gray rock on the hillsides. Above the pastoral scene, the arching sky was cloudless, allowing the sun to cast its warmth into the very bottom of the smallest ravine. Yet the tranquility of nature was counterpoised against the turmoil of man.

The majority of the forty thousand Palestinians who stumbled across the border of Lebanon went into refugee camps near the Israeli border and squatter settlements encircling Beirut. At the time, the common belief of the Lebanese, the Arabs as a whole, the West, and the United Nations was that the refugee problem was temporary. No one—not the Lebanese, the neighboring Arabs, or the Palestinians—accepted the idea of *towteen*, the permanent settlement of Palestinians in the country of refuge. But with the doors to historic Palestine closed by Israel, there was nowhere else to go.

The Palestinians, who were as motivated and ambitious as the Lebanese, gradually built their own society in the sprawling camps. Although unsightly, cramped, and bare, these patched-together communities enclosed by fences provided a semblance of permanence. And it was here that Palestinian numbers began to grow, creating yet another sizeable group within the mosaic of Lebanon.

As in Syria, Egypt, and Jordan, the haves of Palestinian society went to the cities where they expected, as Levantine traders, to be welcomed by the elite. On one level, the elite did lay out the welcome mat for Palestinians bringing capital and talent into the Lebanese economy. But on a deeper level, no amount of money or economic savvy could erase the stigma of "two-bit Palestinian" applied by the Lebanese. Although Palestinian entrepreneurs learned the labyrinthine ways of Lebanon and came to accept the sectarian balance that maintained the stability of the country, they would never secure a place for themselves in the exclusive circle of the Lebanese elite. A case in point is Yousef Beidas, the founder of Intrabank.

Like a typical Levantine, Beidas believed money was power. What he failed to appreciate was that in Lebanon money was only half of an equation in which the other half comprised the family ties and clan politics that had shaped Lebanese life for centuries. Thus as one Intrabank success built on another, the *zuama* came to detest the bank's Palestinian identity, its ever-expanding size, and its growing hegemony over Lebanese banking. Although Beidas perfected his Lebanese accent, built cordial relations with people in government, and achieved Lebanese citizenship, he never won over the *zuama*. In 1966, they destroyed the Palestinian interloper.

Intrabank, like the rest of Beirut's banks, engaged heavily in speculation. With the U.S. dollar appreciating at a rate judged to be too high to sustain, Beidas bet all Intrabank's available liquidity against the dollar. It was the wrong decision. Subsequent heavy withdrawals by some of the bank's biggest clients forced Beidas to seek help from Lebanon's Central Bank. Before saying no, Joseph Oghourlian, the deputy governor of the bank, put Lebanese prejudice into words: "Why did you invest in Lebanon? You are not Lebanese and Lebanon does not want you to control its economy."*

Consequently, on October 9, 1966, when a run on Intrabank began,

---

* Quoted in Dib, *Warlords and Merchants*, p. 114.

the government refused to lift a finger to save Beidas and his institution even though the bank still held valuable international assets. When Intrabank was forced to close its doors on October 15, the Central Bank quickly transferred ownership of the bankrupt institution to its biggest depositors. Without its Palestinian founder, it remained the largest financial institution in Lebanon for the next twenty-five years.

Lebanese attitudes toward the Palestinians also included a political side. Overwhelmingly Sunni, Palestinians of whatever class offered Lebanon's Sunnis a potential ally in their struggle for political parity with the Christians. But the Maronites beheld the Palestinians as a dire threat to the confessional balance in Lebanon and their own tenuous hold on political supremacy. For almost two decades after 1948, a sharp-edged triangle composed of the Maronites, the Sunnis, and the Palestinians hung heavily around the neck of Lebanon. It failed to rip the country open only because the Palestinians did not control their own affairs.

EARLY IN THEIR Diaspora, the Palestinians—a dispossessed people without boundaries, leadership, military power, or even the ability to negotiate on their own—were compelled to look to the governments of the Arab countries to seek redress of their grievances. The Arab leaders to whom they looked gave passionate voice to the Palestinian cause but commanded neither the resources nor the power to deliver anything to the displaced people. Then in July 1952 a military coup ended the Egyptian monarchy and with it British influence in Egypt. By June 1956, the former colonel who had led that coup was the undisputed leader of Egypt and the mesmerizing voice of the Arabs, including the Palestinians. But like other Arab leaders who have taken up the cause of the Palestinians, his agenda was his own.

The handsome, magnetic Gamal Abdul Nasser was first and foremost an Egyptian nationalist committed to restoring the dignity and self-respect of his ancient land. He was also a man who gloried in personal adoration. To the Egyptians, he was the latter-day pharaoh. To the Arabs, he promoted himself as the new Saladin who promised to vanquish the humiliation of 1948 as the original Saladin had broken the Crusaders. That required embracing the Palestinian cause. Beginning in 1956, Nasser's speeches hammered away at the theme of Western imperialism's complicity in the birth of Israel. A hypnotic speaker who sheathed neoclassical Arabic in the vernacular of the man in the street, he cast his spell over the masses with his rendition of the Arab condition. According to the Egyptian president, Britain armed the Zionists and in so doing handed Palestine over to Zionism. The United States then armed and aided Israel, enabling "world Jewry and Zionism to conquer a beloved part in the heart of the Arab fatherland, so as to be the tip of imperialism's bayonet inside the Arab nation."*

The charismatic Nasser performed on a broad stage. In 1955, a time when the world was in the grip of the Cold War, he rocked the West by announcing that Egypt would buy arms from Czechoslovakia, the major arms manufacturer of the Soviet bloc in Eastern Europe. In 1956, he nationalized the Suez Canal, bringing Britain, France, and Israel into war against him. He survived the conflict only because the United States, protecting its own interests, refused to join its allies in the assault on Egypt. But in 1958, the United States decided to act against Nasser on its own by landing Marines in Lebanon. In 1962, Nasser rebounded by turning tribal fighting in Yemen into a war in which Arab nationalism challenged a regime backed by "reactionary" Saudi Arabia.

During the years of his glory, Nasser and the Palestinians stayed entangled in a web of compatible and conflicting interests in which each needed the other and each intensely feared the other. The Palestinian cause provided Nasser the magnet that drew the emotions of the Arab masses to himself. For the Palestinians, Nasser drove the vehicle

---

* Quoted in P. J. Vatikiotis, *Nasser and His Generation* (New York: St. Martin's Press, 1978), p. 252.

with which they could pursue lost Palestine. At the same time, Nasser demanded that the Palestinians themselves neither flock into Egypt nor operate at odds with his agenda. And so from 1952 to 1967, Nasser and the Palestinians danced a duet in which they embraced and parted depending on the rhythms of the Arab world. Yet during that same period, the Palestinians were beginning to find their own identity.

In the earliest years of the 1950s, Palestinians in search of an education that might secure their future had headed toward the open doors of Egyptian universities in Alexandria, Luxor, and especially Cairo. Among them was Yasser Arafat.* At Cairo University, he mingled with other Palestinian students who zealously espoused all the reigning political philosophies of the time, from the politicized theology of the Arab Brotherhood to the socialism of Karl Marx. Regardless of which ideology the individual adhered to, each Palestinian accepted himself as a largely unspecified unit within the Arab nation. That began to change in 1952 when the small man with delicate hands stood for election to the executive committee of the Palestine Student Union, an organization of young Palestinian exiles. To a membership that thrived on complex political philosophy, Arafat presented a starkly simple idea: Palestinians possess their own identity that is unique, distinct, and separate from that of other Arabs. It was the beginning of a revolution in Palestinian thought that would, by stages, build a distinct Palestinian nationalism.

In 1957, when Nasser reigned as the high priest of the Palestinian cause, Yasser Arafat moved to Kuwait to take a job as a civil servant charged with reviewing construction plans for the Kuwaiti government. Sometime between 1959 and 1961, he put together a nebulous organization called Fatah, the "Movement for the Liberation of Palestine." Hurling aside the sacred belief that the Arab nation held the key

---

*Yasser Arafat was born Muhammad Abdul Raouf Arafat al-Qudwa in Jerusalem in 1929. The name "Yasser," meaning "easygoing," was acquired in childhood.

to the liberation of Palestine, Fatah promoted the concept that the Palestinians must assume responsibility for their own destiny. While focusing on the return to Palestine as its single goal, Fatah deliberately left undefined the social, economic, and even territorial makeup of the future Palestinian state. Nor did Fatah describe the context of Palestinian society within it. Papering over the chasms of families and clans, the religious divisions between Muslim and Christian, and the age-old hostilities between town and countryside, Fatah's only program was the development of a pure Palestinian identity within a secular, nationalistic movement.

Seeking new recruits to the cause, Fatah's founders tilled the neglected populations of the Palestinian refugee camps located in Jordan, Egypt, Syria, and Lebanon. These camps had become cages for the emotionally dead, holding pens for people suspended between the despair of the present and the hopelessness of the future. Constantly moving from camp to camp, sharing crowded slum dwellings or living out of their cars, Yasser Arafat and the vanguard of Fatah labored to lift the Palestinian cause out of the hands of Arab governments and Arab intellectuals and place it in the arms of the Palestinian masses.

Little by little, Fatah built an organizational skeleton and set a leadership structure in place. Unaided and uncontrolled by Egypt, Fatah posed a growing menace to Nasser's domination over the Palestinians. In 1964, an alarmed Nasser acted to neutralize the threat. At the invitation of the Arabs' great charismatic leader, thirteen kings, emirs, and presidents gathered in Cairo for the First Arab Summit. At Nasser's direction, they sewed Fatah and more than forty other Palestinian groups into the Palestine Liberation Organization (PLO).

For the next three years—1964 to 1967—the PLO chased the Palestinian cause at the end of Nasser's leash. Fatah survived by sending its own commandoes on guerrilla raids inside Israel. Nothing more than attacks by mosquitoes, they nonetheless played to the emotions of the Palestinian masses. With Fatah hitting the theme of Arab dishonor day after day in 1966, the cult of the *fedayeen*, the "men of sacrifice," grew among the Arabs. Soon the masked, fatigue-clad freedom fighter over-shadowed the PLO and everything else except Gamal Abdul Nasser. Then in 1967, Nasser stumbled into war with Israel.

In the spring of 1967, Nasser's fiery rhetoric combined with guerrilla attacks on northern Israel and Israel's tough threats of retaliation stoked the coals of another Arab-Israeli war. In June, a swaggering Nasser trained his big Egyptian guns positioned on the heights above Sharm al Sheikh on the narrow Tiran Strait and declared the Gulf of Aqaba closed to ships headed for Israel's port of Eilat. Rattling its own sabers, Israel angrily responded that the blockade constituted an act of war. In Amman, King Hussein of Jordan, fearing revolt among his own people if he failed to act, swallowed his abhorrence of Nasser and entered a military pact with Egypt, dated June 1, 1967.

Five days later, as the morning sun crested over the Moab hills, a string of Israeli fighter planes streaked down long ribbons of runway, peeled off to the east and to the west, turned over the Mediterranean, and screamed back toward land. Dropping low, they unloaded their explo-sive cargoes on the airfields of Egypt, wasting Nasser's Russian-supplied planes; on al Mafraq and the air base near Amman, destroying the Royal Jordanian Air Force; and on Syria's lone airfield for fighter planes just north of Damascus. Three hundred and fifty MiG-16s, Hawks, and a col-lection of other aircraft were reduced to twisted metal.

With the air power of the Arab states destroyed, armored columns under the blue-and-white Israeli flag plunged south into the sands of the Sinai and pushed toward the Suez Canal. A secondary force curled north to seal off the Gaza Strip. To the northeast, Israeli artillery laid a barrage on Syrian gunners perched on the commanding heights of the Golan above the Huleh Valley. In the east, tanks rolled across the seventy-mile-long border of the West Bank of the Jordan River, where they met King Hussein's Arab Legion. After six days of fighting, Egypt had lost the Sinai and Gaza; Syria, the Golan Heights; and Jordan, the West Bank and east

Jerusalem. On June 9, Gamal Abdul Nasser, the great charismatic figure of pan-Arabism, acknowledged defeat.*

Another hundred thousand Palestinian refugees from Gaza and the West Bank trudged out of historic Palestine. They carried with them the crumbs of an entire era of Arab political thought and practice. The long-promised liberation of Arab land through traditional military action by the Arab states had proved an illusion. Now it was the commando, the martyr against Zionism, who in the dark shadows of 1967 became the symbol of the Palestinian cause.

From across the Arab world, millions emotionally joined the *fedayeen*. Thousands among them flocked into the ranks of the commandoes operating from bases along the borders of Israel. Those who came were not only teenagers from the camps vowing to liberate Palestine with rifles and grenades but also the cream of Palestinian youth, who abandoned their universities to enter the armed struggle. With this ground-swell of recruits, Fatah prepared what it termed the "second launching" of the armed struggle to recover Palestine. Never seriously believing that the Palestinians alone could retake their lost territory, Yasser Arafat intended to make the guerrilla movement into a fort within which Palestinian identity would solidify and mature to the point that neither the Arab regimes nor the international community could ignore the Palestinian problem.

IN FRAGILE LEBANON, rising Palestinian nationalism added yet another element to the existing collage of competing identities and

---

* Prior to 1967, the area east of Jerusalem that fronts on the Jordan River and was part of the Kingdom of Jordan generally was referred to by its geographic name, the west bank. After 1967, when this area became territory occupied by Israel, it took on its political name, the West Bank. Part of it held by Israel and the rest by the Palestinian Authority created by the Oslo Agreement of 1993, it remains that today.

interests within the Lebanese state. Although no more than half of the Palestinians in Lebanon lived in camps, the strength of the PLO came from al Baqaa, Ein al Hilweh, Nabatieh, Shatila, and other collections of the dispossessed. From small clusters of dusty faded tents hidden in southern Lebanon, PLO commandoes ran raids into Israel. Holding the Lebanese government responsible for the actions of the Palestinians, the Israelis hit back.

The fatal flaw in the Israeli strategy was that Lebanon was a country only in that it possessed defined borders. It was not a state capable of exercising a national will or mobilizing either police or military power sufficient to clamp the hand of Beirut on the Palestinians. Deeply fearful that Palestinians on Lebanese soil were undermining the political balance enshrined in the National Pact, the Maronites regarded the Palestinians with increasing consternation and anger. In contrast, the Sunnis openly embraced the Palestinians in order to strengthen their own stance against the Christians. There was also a third faction composed of the Palestinians' "fellow deprived"—the poorer Sunni and Shia Muslims, joined by the Druze—who shared the revolutionary aspirations of the Palestinian movement. Grabbing the tail of the Palestinian tiger enraged by dispossession and rejection, they hoped to ride it toward the eradication of massive social inequalities in Lebanon perpetuated by the corrupt practices of its political elite. And so emerged a symbiosis between the Palestinians and segments of the Lebanese political spectrum, particularly nonestablishment Sunnis. To attack one was to attack the other. Succumbing to the Lebanese propensity to see things only as they wish them to be, the Sunnis failed to taste the unsavory reality that the Palestinians were serving up their own agenda. Neither the redistribution of political power in Lebanon nor the ideologies of the leftists could compete with the Palestinians' determination to return to Palestine. Thus instead of embracing a role in the Lebanese political structure, the Palestinians became arrogant and contemptuous of the Lebanese state.

In 1969, when Jordan began to exercise better control along its border with Israel, the *fedayeen* increasingly relied on southern Lebanon
as a staging base for raids into the lost Palestine. Although the commandoes exacerbated tensions with Israel, the Lebanese government,
as weak and divided as ever, could do nothing to control the Palestinian
swashbucklers. So the men of Beirut tried to compromise. The resulting Cairo Agreement ceded sovereignty over a seven-square-mile area
in southern Lebanon from which the commandoes could prosecute
their guerrilla war against Israel. Elsewhere in Lebanon, the Palestinian
refugees won the right to carry arms and patrol their own camps. But
instead of subduing the Palestinians, the Cairo Agreement produced the
watan badil, the alternative Palestinian homeland in Lebanon.

Regarding themselves as autonomous, the Palestinians took pride in
their commandoes, swaggering through the streets of Lebanese towns
brandishing guns and defying authorities to stop them. Palestinian
neighborhoods in Beirut often refused to pay for electricity, telephone
service, garbage pickup, and other public services. In southern Lebanon, where their numbers were the greatest, the Palestinians collected
protection money from the poverty-ridden Shia and defied community
elders who opposed their presence around their villages. While many
Palestinians continued to live as model citizens within the Lebanese
state, too many others were willing to sacrifice Lebanon in the interest
of the elusive Palestine.

LEBANON WAS NOT alone in facing the escalating power of the Palestinians. The Arab-Israeli war of 1967 had barely ended when the
fedayeen began to eat away at King Hussein's Jordan, weakened by the
loss of east Jerusalem and the west bank of the Jordan River to Israel.
Erecting heavier fences of barbed wire around their camps and placing
guards armed with automatic weapons at the entrances, the commando
organizations shut out Jordanian officialdom. Ignoring Hussein's impas-

sioned reminders that Jordan had given the displaced Palestinians vastly greater opportunities than they enjoyed in other Arab states, the *fedayeen* mounted a virulent propaganda campaign against the king's attempts to subject them to Jordanian rule. By the beginning of 1968, Hussein faced twenty thousand armed commandoes in a Jordanian population of which fifty percent were Palestinian.

As the king struggled to hold his authority, commandoes with their automatic weapons stalked the streets of Amman and other towns throughout Jordan. The king reacted to their audacity by throwing up roadblocks and instituting vehicle searches, which ignited *fedayeen* accusations that he intended to stop commando operations against Israel. Undeterred, the king sent press gangs of Jordanian soldiers to remove Palestinian youths from the streets and dispatch them to remote desert camps in order to keep them out of the ranks of the guerrillas. He could do so because, unlike the embattled Lebanese government, Hussein commanded a well-trained army committed to his person and his government.

If the *fedayeen* movement had been a unitary bloc, perhaps King Hussein and Yasser Arafat, the commander of the largest faction in the PLO, could have struck a compromise. But the guerrilla movement was split between personalities and ideologies. While Arafat was content to coexist with Hussein, the destruction of Hashemite rule lay at the very core of the leftist ideology of other factions—the Popular Front for the Liberation of Palestine (PFLP) and the Democratic Front for the Liberation of Palestine (DFLP). Thus a confrontation with Hussein—the "reactionary," the "slave to Western imperialism," the "Zionist puppet"—was not only desirable but an ideological necessity for those who combined Marxism with the cause of Palestine.

Increasingly Hussein and the commandoes circled around each other, throwing exploratory jabs. In December 1969, commandoes stopped the king's wife, Princess Muna, as she was driving through Amman and held her until urgent appeals from the royal guard secured her release.

On February 10, 1970, Hussein tried to tighten his grip on his kingdom by issuing an eleven-point decree banning *fedayeen* weapons in the towns and requiring the commandoes to license their vehicles and carry identity cards. The move was enough to ignite a four-day riot, which left eighty people dead and the guerrillas in control of half of Amman.

In late June 1970, Hussein's army and the *fedayeen* clashed again when a guerrilla shot a Jordanian army officer of the Saiqa regiment, a unit especially faithful to Hussein. The next day, the well-trained, well-equipped, and well-commanded Arab Legion within Jordan's military structure wreaked its revenge against fortified guerrilla encampments. With the commandoes dug into their positions, violence erupted across the landscape as combat between Hussein's army and the *fedayeen* spread toward Amman. On July 9, 1970, the crisis escalated to the point that the king evacuated his summer villa outside Amman and raced toward his capital. Rounding a bend in the road, his motorcade of six armored Land Rovers and his personal Mercedes drove into an ambush of Palestinian commandoes firing automatic weapons and a Russian 50-mm machine gun. Although he escaped death, Hussein had lost control of his kingdom.

In the escalating violence, the PFLP invaded Amman's imposing Intercontinental Hotel and seized sixty-two foreigners as hostages, including the youngest son of Lebanon's former president, Camille Chamoun. In rapid-fire actions, the leftist commandoes grabbed another fifteen hostages in the Philadelphia Hotel; seized the first secretary of the U.S. embassy on his way to a dinner party; and murdered the U.S. Army attaché when he answered the door of his apartment. On September 6, 1970, commandoes jumped out of seats on TWA's around-the-world flight number 741 as it flew over Germany and ordered the pilot to turn toward the Mediterranean. Hours later the Boeing 707 circled in a black night sky over the desert of Jordan before setting down on a rough landing strip lighted with flaming oil drums and jeep headlights. Forty minutes later, a Swissair DC-8 seized in the air west of Paris rolled to a stop a mere fifty yards from the 707. The two airliners were joined on "Revolution Airstrip" three days later by a BOAC VC-10 hijacked between Bahrain and London. In the ensuing crisis over the fate of three planes and 439 passengers, it was as if the Jordanian government no longer existed, for it was Red Cross negotiators who sought to free the hostages by dealing directly with the commandoes. On September 12, the PFLP, the perpetrators of the perilous circus, released all but fifty-six of the passengers. Those freed went to hotels in Amman while the remainder disappeared into Palestinian camps. In the final act of the drama, the hijackers ignited the explosives packed into the planes, turning them into balls of fire in an unclouded sky.

Four days later, King Hussein went on Jordanian radio to declare martial law. The capital of Amman shut down as the airport closed; buses and taxis parked; police abandoned their posts; and shopkeepers rolled heavy shutters down over their storefronts and hurried home. Just before dawn broke on the seventeenth, fifty tanks of Hussein's Arab Legion and scores of armored personnel carriers pulled out from the multimillion-dollar sports stadium at the eastern edge of Amman and began rolling toward the city's center. Within minutes, the long dusty columns were rumbling into narrow streets that wound through the seven dun-colored hills of Amman. In a city built of limestone, the mechanized army cleared its path with a blistering hail of artillery shells that smashed into the Palestinians' entrenched positions and leveled entire buildings. The outgunned *fedayeen*, fighting from sandbagged buildings and street barricades, retaliated with hails of machine-gun fire and antitank rockets.

Hussein expected his lightning thrust to produce a victory within hours. From the king's perspective, the war had to be short because a long conflict against the *fedayeen*, the reigning symbol of Arabism, threatened to bring united Arab opinion down on his head. But instead of capitulating, the guerrillas holed up behind the thick stone walls of a hundred buildings throughout Amman and other towns. Using its superior firepower, Hussein's army slowly blasted its way from house to house. The commandoes held out by merging with the Palestinian population. Consequently, the camps became prime targets of the Jordanian assault. Still the commandoes did not break. In what has become known in the annals of the Palestinians as "Black September," no Arab government came to the defense of the scruffy, resolute guerrillas of the *fedayeen* for fear of becoming the next target of Palestinian zeal. The Arab nationalists in charge of Iraq vacillated and then decided to hold back troops ready to enter northern Jordan. Syria's defense minister, Hafiz Assad, who had never liked or trusted the PLO leadership, did nothing. Finally Nasser, the enfeebled godfather of Arab nationalism, proved the most emblematic of official Arab attitudes toward the Palestinian "freedom fighters." He simply stated, "I am not prepared to send troops to Jordan."*

IN THE AFTERMATH of Black September, the withered PLO, carrying all of its internal divisions, withdrew into Lebanon, the only remaining field of operations still available. Having surmounted his leftist rivals, Yasser Arafat established PLO headquarters in a crowded one-square-mile area of Beirut's Fakhani quarter, adjacent to the sprawling Shatila refugee camp. From there, he and his lieutenants began to coax into life what amounted to a Palestinian government. The importance of cross-border attacks into Israel declined. A new strategy focused on planting in Lebanon a political, diplomatic, and cultural center where Palestinian institutions could develop and Palestinian decision making could be exercised relatively free from the tutelage and interference of Arab states. Without this territorial base, the PLO with Yasser Arafat as chairman and guide could exist only by playing one Arab leader against another while holding in harness Palestinian splinter groups mutually hostile to each other. Thus from 1971 to 1975 the PLO would live the

* Quoted in Vatikiotis, *Nasser and His Generation*, p. 245.

"Ayyam Beirut"—the Beirut era, the time in which the Palestinians not only planted a political capital but also cultivated their own intellectual and spiritual life. As Palestinian numbers grew to almost twenty percent of the population, the fragility of Lebanon increased. With the Sunnis and the leftists utilizing the Palestinians in the old game of political demography, and the Palestinians and Israelis employing Lebanese territory for their contest with each other, the politics of Lebanon spun toward greater polarization.

The schism in Lebanese society between those who detested the Palestinian presence in Lebanon and those who supported it imposed itself on the longstanding, unresolved issues that had divided the Lebanese since independence: Lebanon's identity, its position in the Levant, and the extent of its "Arab" obligations. As Lebanon moved through the early 1970s, the governing elite faced two mounting challenges: rising political, social, and economic discontent within the Lebanese population and increasing disruptions caused by external forces headed by the Palestinians and Israel. The pressures proved more than Lebanon's fragile political system could manage.

The challenge that the Palestinians and their cause posed to the Lebanese government is much the same as that posed to all governments of the Arab world. Prior to 1975, the passion that surrounded the Palestinians as victims of the unequal relationship between the Arabs and the West and the real and perceived position of Israel as the godchild of Western military, economic, and political support coexisted with the anxiety within Arab states that the Palestinians' own agenda and talents would overpower them. This was the right side of the Palestinian equation containing the particular interests of states and societies that began to gain weight against the left side of the equation—the emotional power of the events of 1948 and 1967. In Lebanon, before the equation tipped enough to reorder the state, the Maronites, Sunnis, Druze, and Shia; the Christians and the Muslims; the leftists and the rightists; and the non-Lebanese Palestinians went to war.

Chapter 4

WOE BE TO THE STATE

Here am I, the wretched city,
lying in ruins, my citizens dead
. . . you who pass me by bewail my fate,
and shed a tear in honor of Berytus
that is no more.

—UNKNOWN SIXTH-CENTURY POET

The citadel of Kirkuk in Iraq rises out of an ancient tell where some claim the Biblical prophet Daniel is buried. At its base, a city of roughly seven hundred thousand fans out on a flat landscape in north central Iraq. It is a monotonous collection of dusty stucco buildings interspersed with the turquoise-tiled domes of undistinguished mosques and short, square spires of ordinary churches. All stand against a backdrop of orange flames shooting skyward from the towers of oil-processing facilities. Kirkuk, straddling perhaps ten billion barrels of oil reserves, is the grand prize for the area's competing ethnic and sectarian groups: Arabs, Kurds, Turkomans, and Assyrians.

Following the American invasion in March 2003 that toppled Saddam Hussein and the elections of December 2005 that chose a government charged with pulling Iraq's competing groups into a nation, a palpable tension gripped Kirkuk's streets. By the early weeks of 2007, it had escalated into acute anxiety underwritten by fear. Trucks mounted with high-efficiency machine guns shielded every government building. Guards wearing blue shirts and maroon berets nervously manned gates constructed to thwart attacks by a range of agitators labeled "insurgents." Elsewhere in the city, the Pesh Merga, the tough, battle-hardened Kurdish militia, dressed in traditional pants, short vest, and checkered turban, patrolled its own sections of the city. In the enclaves where the Sunni Arabs lived, snarling tribesmen in *dishdashs* and *gutras* spit out their hatred of the Kurds and vowed to kill ten for every one of their own that died at the hands of the Pesh Merga. In the Arab Shia sector of the city, a cleric and his followers shouted into telephones connected to the Mahdi Army, the militia of black-clad Muqtada al Sadr headquartered in eastern Baghdad. In their area of this segmented city, the Turkomans whispered warnings to their Turkish cousins in Ankara of the dire threats facing them. While behind the walls of some of the finest houses of Kirkuk, prosperous Assyrian businessmen dressed in Western-style suits set off by large, expensive gold wristwatches pleaded with visiting Westerners to sound the alarm that the Christians of Iraq were facing annihilation. At this moment, the Iraqis stood at the crossroads. They could take one of two directions: political accommodation or civil war. Unless they proved capable of coming to terms with each other over conflicting identities, longstanding grievances, differing interests, and corrosive suspicions, they, like the Lebanese of 1975, would descend into chaos.

Iraq and Lebanon, representing the eastern and western frontiers of the Arab world, differ significantly. Iraq is oriented as much to the Persian Gulf as the Arab heartland. Lebanon looks west as well as east. Geographically, Iraq is expansive and possesses the black riches of petroleum. Lebanon is small and resource poor. Lebanon is coated with a deep patina of sophistication applied by centuries of history at the gate between Christian West and Muslim East. Although generation after generation of Iraqis provided the Arab world with scholars, writers, and artists, large numbers of tribesmen from the Arabian Peninsula who arrived as late as the end of the nineteenth century and the beginning of the twentieth kept alive the ingrained traditions of tribalism. Yet contemporary Lebanon and Iraq share profound similarities: highly diverse populations, a large Shia presence, a history of an inequitable political and economic system dominated by a minority, and the absence of state institutions in which the majority is willing to invest its security and welfare. In the late twentieth century, these factors threw Lebanon into the clutches of anarchy. The question in the early years of the twenty-first century is whether the Iraqis will follow.

Although its condition is the most critical of any country in the Arab world, Iraq is not alone on the endangered list. Syria follows closely behind. With a disparate population, it is a ragged patchwork of families, sects, ethnicities, values, and economic interests. With no institutions capable of governing, Syria is kept functioning and reasonably stable by the authoritarian nature of a sectarian minority operating through the army and a ruthless internal security system.

To the south, the borders of Saudi Arabia encompass a brittle network of regions, tribes, towns, and cities cobbled together for the last eighty-plus years by Wahabbism, one of Islam's most conservative sects, and tribal alliances built and maintained by the House of Saud. The cohesive strength of both is deteriorating, leaving the kingdom open to geographic fragmentation, tribal competition, religious and sectarian strife, and generational conflict between those who want to establish institutions of government in which the people have a voice, those willing to allow Saudi Arabia to remain in the hands of the ruling family, and those who reject any form of government other than the model drawn by the Prophet Muhammad in the seventh century.

Perhaps only the population of Egypt is homogeneous enough to call itself a nation. But there is no state machinery to bridge the wide chasm between the haves and have-nots. That leaves Jordan and some of the sheikhdoms of the Persian Gulf. They have succeeded in developing some institutions in limited areas that function for the benefit of citizenry. But all remain governed by an elite that keeps the political process tightly gripped within its own hands.

None of the countries of the Arab world exactly replicate Lebanon in either the period leading to the civil war or the war itself. The relevance of Lebanon's history from 1975 to 1990 is not in the specific groups who did battle but in how easily Lebanon descended into chaos; the inability of a government lacking institutions to control that chaos; and the damage inflicted by a range of militias and their foreign supporters, both of whom looted the state and the society. With all countries within the Arab world currently whipped by winds of change, the counter winds of tradition blowing within their own populations, the interests of outsiders in the geographically strategic Fertile Crescent, the realities of fragmented societies, and governments that rule through personal relationships, there are lessons to be learned in the brutal Lebanese experience. War came to Lebanon because there was no political structure capable of mediating between the predatory strong and the unshielded weak. Thus for fifteen years the clash of family, clan, community, ideology, theology, private armies, and foreign money and manpower nearly extinguished the Lebanese state.

AS LEBANON ENTERED the 1970s, few inside or outside the country believed that anything could shake, let alone pulverize, the jewel of the Levant. On the surface, Beirut was as luminous as ever. But beneath a surface buffed with the money of the oil boom, the underlying flaws widened. Decades of communal competition had gutted every institution necessary to the maintenance of social cohesion and political unity. Even the loyalties of the army and the police, those entrusted to enforce the order and security of the state, were segmented between contending communities and leaders. In April 1975, the "pearl of the east" crumbled.

In retrospect, the final collapse of the Lebanon that had enchanted so many began in 1970 with the choice of a new president. On the day of the election, Suleiman Franjieh, the godfather of the mountain town of Zghorta, the man who claimed to be a direct descendant of a Crusader, arrived at the Chamber of Deputies accompanied by four thousand

Zghortan militia men. They stood outside while Franjieh's supporters inside battled with those backing Elias Sarkis, the candidate of the
critical reform movement begun in 1958. On the third ballot Franjieh
won by one vote. But when the speaker of the chamber announced that
Franjieh's fifty votes (out of a possible ninety-nine) did not constitute a
majority, mayhem erupted. Deputies jumped to their feet to drive their
fists into the faces of their opponents while others whipped ever-ready
guns out of their desk drawers. Outside, the Zghortan militia as well as
private militiamen hired by several political chieftains nervously waited
for orders. In the melee, the speaker backed down and reversed his ruling. Suleiman Franjieh was the new president of Lebanon by one vote.
The reform movement that had begun twelve years earlier died on the
tines of a pitchfork plunged into the Lebanese state. Oblivious to the
ramification, Franjieh's militiamen careened through the streets, reck-
lessly firing rifles and pistols in the air in noisy celebration.

Among his first acts as president, Franjieh ordered the Lebanese army
to crack down on the Palestinians who were building their state-within-
a-state inside the boundaries of Lebanon. But the army, like every other
institution of the Lebanese government, conformed to strict confessional
lines.* Thus when the Christian president issued his order, the Muslims
in the ranks refused to act against their political ally. With the army
paralyzed by confessionalism, the Phalange, the militia of the Maronite
warlord Bashir Gemayel, entered the void. Organized by Bashir's father,
Pierre, in 1936 as the Social Democratic Party, Phalangists did claim a
vague ideology of Lebanese nationalism. Yet what most set the Phalange
apart from other Maronite militias was the predominance of its members drawn from the poorer echelons of Maronite farmers who lacked

---

* An exact confessional profile of the Lebanese was not public or even easily
determined. The best guess was that there was roughly a 60/40 split favoring the
Muslims among the enlisted ranks and a 60/40 split favoring the Christians among
the officer corps.

roots in the traditional feudal families. Even though the Gemayels themselves had long sat at the table of the political elite, they had never been
considered the equals of the prestigious families of Lebanese history.
Lacking the same status as the Chamouns and others planted at the pin-
nacle of the social pyramid, they increased their power by linking some
farmers of the Mountain with lower-middle-class Maronite families of
east Beirut under the motto "God, fatherland, and family."

The prominence the Phalange achieved by the 1970s was a symbol of
the seismic shift occurring in Lebanese society. When the decade began,
the *zuama* still ran Lebanon. But the old political bosses, particularly
those among the Muslim communities, were losing their clientele to
more radical leaders demanding political and economic equality. These
same stresses between the haves and have-nots of Lebanese society
racked the Maronites. In the shift, the art of consensus through which
the elite had kept Lebanon functioning was disappearing. Still the same
zuama who were proving incapable of corralling the threats to the political system remained powerful enough to block the emergence of a new
order. By 1972, this erosion of the old order accelerated as the Lebanese
Muslims linked up with the Palestinians, the beneficiaries of subsidies
and arms delivered by Arab regimes employing the Palestinian cause for
their own purposes.

As the pressures on the existing social and political system mounted,
the Maronites continued to cling to their cardinal belief that no matter how large or how powerful the Muslim-Palestinian alliance became,
Christian security would be guaranteed by the Christian West. That illusion vanished in October 1973 when the Organization of Petroleum
Exporting Countries (OPEC) withheld oil from international markets
in order to force up prices and the Arabs completely embargoed oil
shipments to Israel's major allies. With oil prices quadrupled, frantic
motorists lining up at gas stations, and ordinary consumers fearful of
dwindling supplies of heating oil, the Western nations were in no mood
to buttress the Maronites' vision of "petite Liban." That left the Maroni-

tes facing a coalition of Lebanese Muslims linked to the Palestinians and energized by the new wave of Arab consciousness that had awakened when the Arab petroleum producers unsheathed the oil weapon against the West.

The other threat confronting the Maronites was numbers. Population estimates for 1973 put the Lebanese Christians at 1,525,000, including 175,000 non-Lebanese Armenians. Of this number, 900,000 were Maronites. The Sunnis and Druze together with the alien Palestinians equaled 950,000.* Outnumbering any other single group were roughly a million Shia Muslims who chose to stay outside the Muslim alliance.[†] The Maronites knew as well as anyone that their hold on the politics and economy of Lebanon could no longer be justified by a demographic majority. Gripped by a visceral fear of extinction, the Maronites vowed to fight for their own version of order and civilization in Lebanon. Unlike in 1860, when they were saved by the French, the Maronites would save themselves.

The fateful year of 1975 began with a classic dispute. The Maronite Camille Chamoun, the malefactor of 1958, lay claim to the fish off Sidon for his protein supplement company. Muslim fisherman registered a counterclaim based on history and equality. Ignoring the lessons of 1958, when Fuad Shihab refused to inject the army into a dispute with Christian-Muslim overtones, General Iskander Ghanem brought in the army to break up Muslim protests. A fishing dispute quickly escalated into a showdown between all religious factions as well as the political right and left over issues that had simmered in Lebanon for decades. The line was drawn. The Maronites stood on one side and the Sunnis, Druze, a representation of Shia, and the leftists stood on the other. Gone was

* Although not counted in their numbers, the Sunnis and Druze benefited from some support from the 100,000 Syrians, Kurds, and other Muslim minorities scattered throughout Lebanon.

† See chapter 6.

the luxury of 1958, when the *zuama* could patch up alliances across confessional lines. In 1975, everyone was armed and ready. It was the Palestinians, ironically from outside the Lebanese mosaic, who put the match to civil war.

On the peaceful Sunday morning of April 13, 1975, in the predominantly Christian Beirut suburb of Ain al Rummaneh, a Peugeot sedan, its license plates wrapped in dingy cloths, drove toward a Maronite church where Pierre Gemayel, the founder of the Phalange, had just emerged from mass. As the car pulled even with the entrance, the occupants opened fire and sped away on squealing tires. Gemayel escaped injury, but four other people, all connected to the Phalange, sprawled lifelessly on the sidewalk.

Convinced that the assassins were Palestinian commandoes, Phalange militiamen quickly gathered to deliver retribution. Within an hour, they saw a busload of Palestinians singing Palestinian songs and chanting PLO slogans, threading its way through the narrow streets of Ain al Rummaneh, en route from the camps of Sabra to Tel Zaatar. The Phalange opened fire in a fusillade that lasted twenty minutes. When it ended, twenty-seven passengers aboard the crowded bus were dead and nineteen others wounded.

As the news of what happened in Ain al Rummaneh spread, Lebanon erupted. For four days in the streets of Beirut, Tripoli, and Sidon, Palestinians joined by Lebanese Muslims battled the Phalange, reinforced by Chamoun's militia, the Tigers. While the Maronites laid Palestinian camps under a barrage of fire, the Palestinians and their Lebanese allies blew up Maronite-owned offices, shops, and factories. The war was on, and there was no force capable of stopping it. The Lebanese government was too enfeebled by its own history of placing the interests of sect above those of the state to wield authority. The army, reflecting the same deep-rooted communalism, was fracturing. And the leadership, nothing more than a clique of ambitious, quarreling tribal chieftains, was unable to rise to the crisis with an organized plan of action.

With no government and no army to stand for Lebanon, each group within the Lebanese mosaic launched its own war for its own interests. The Druze and some Lebanese leftists fought for power in the Lebanese system. Other Lebanese Muslims fought for radical reform and a Lebanon stripped of its Western identity. The Palestinians fought for their own nationalism. Some Christians fought for political reform and Arab identity. The Maronites fought for their vision of Christian Lebanon. Among the Maronites, only the Phalange militia was strong enough to bear the brunt of the fighting. So after years of quiet preparation, the Phalange openly proclaimed itself the armed protector of Christian Lebanon. For the militia, this was a new Christian Crusade. But before the war ended—fifteen years later—Lebanon would become a multi-layered battleground on which Christian fought Muslim, the political left combated the political right, Lebanese engaged Palestinian, Syria sent in its army, Israel ravaged the PLO, a covey of Western countries blundered as peacekeepers, and Iran further politicized the Shia.

When the war began, the Lebanese combatants stood inside an ideological framework in which a status quo coalition faced a revolutionary alliance. The status quo coalition was backed by the military muscle of the Maronite militias of Bashir Gemayel, Camille Chamoun, and Suleiman Franjieh—the Phalange, the Tigers, and the Zghorta Liberation Army. The revolutionary coalition was leftist in its economic orientation and largely Muslim. Known as the Lebanese National Movement, it was a loose association of Kamal Jumblatt's Progressive Socialist Party (Druze), the Syrian National Party (Greek Orthodox and Sunni), the Amal (Shia), two secular Baath Socialist parties (one allied with Syria, the other with Iraq), and the Lebanese Communist Party. Most possessed a militia, or at least arms.

Through the summer of 1975, the fury that is civil war mounted as Lebanon continued to polarize, leaving moderates of all persuasions nowhere to go. With Lebanon's deep-seated communalism at full throttle, wealthy Muslims reluctantly threw in their lot with the radicals, and moderate Christians grudgingly moved into the arms of the Maronite militias. It was then that ideology began to vanish into the deep pools of communalism as the Lebanese took psychological and physical refuge in sectarian ghettos defended by same-sect militias.

By September, violence was jumping from locale to locale. This was not a war in which a central government defended the state. It had become a war of opposing militias defending their own self-defined turf. There was no front line, no confrontation between organized armies. Instead citizen soldiers who wore sneakers as often as combat boots fought each other with rifles and mortars from behind barricades erected on street corners. Violence ratcheted up in November 'when most of the Maronite militias, calling themselves the Lebanese Forces, moved out of their strongholds in eastern Beirut into Muslim and neutral areas in western Beirut. Their prime target was the hotel district on the beachfront, the stone and glass symbol of Beirut's golden age.

On December 8, 1975, the Saint Georges, the Phoenicia, Excelsior, and Palm Beach hotels all came under attack by competing militias. It took armed men only one day to storm the elegant Saint Georges and burn down the showy Phoenicia. When the Phalange seized the newly completed Holiday Inn, the forces of the National Movement took the forty-story Mour tower, the tallest building in Beirut. From there, they rained down fire from twenty-millimeter cannons, Katyusha rockets, and .50 caliber machine guns. When the fighting ended with a truce on December 15, the Holiday Inn was a nearly windowless shell streaked with smoke. Less prestigious establishments suffered a similar fate. Hotel Urabi, frequented by low-income foreign workers, had been burned down, roasting thirty-seven guests trapped inside.

Immediately the "battle of the hotels" gave way to the "battle of the thieves." Over several weeks, hordes of armed men from competing factions stripped Beirut's most exclusive shopping area. Without any police or military power to defend law and order within the state, the frail Lebanese government could do nothing but watch militiamen fill trucks with expensive furniture, designer clothing, 18k gold jewelry, and fine perfumes. When the inventory was gone, window frames, doors, flooring, light fixtures, electrical wiring, and anything else that was portable disappeared from the grand hotels already looted. What was left was put to the torch. The destruction was not only physical but also societal. Among the many casualities were the Empire, Rivoli, the Capitol, the Byblos, and Le Grand, theaters that had long hosted people of all backgrounds. They, like much else in the commercial and cultural center of the Middle East, had been reduced to a heap of rubble.

This assault on the center of Beirut's commercial and cultural life served as an introduction to the real savagery of the war as both sides moved to eliminate hostile populations within their own enclaves. There is no measure of humanity by which to judge the most brutal of the warring militias. The Phalange and the Tigers laid siege to the Karantina section of Beirut, slaughtered a thousand people, and piled their bodies in the street before moving on to Maslakh, where they murdered five hundred Palestinians, Shia, Syrians, and Kurds. In response to the slaughter at Maslakh, the Palestinians officially ended their quasi-isolation and joined the National Movement. Between them, Lebanese Muslims and Palestinians forced several thousand people to evacuate the Christian town of Damour before massacring the three to four hundred villagers who had stayed behind.

As centuries-old attitudes, resentments, and hatreds joined the Palestinians' defense of their territorial base in Lebanon, dreadful acts of brutality became the norm. Muslim militias broke into houses and massacred whole families on the knowledge—or often the assumption—that they were an awful enemy. Phalangists burned crosses on their victims' bodies and stuck severed testicles into the mouths of the dead. Druze reverted to the tactics of 1860—nailing the ears of their Christian victims to barn walls. This style of communal warfare struck at the roots of personal honor, imposing shame by cutting away at the manhood of the "other" by raping his women and defiling his religious icons and places of worship. In the carnage, terrified people shifted from west to east or from north to south seeking safety among those of their own confessional. The result was that the Lebanese left even further behind the socioeconomic issues that underlay the demands for reform of the Lebanese political system to pursue the dragons of communalism.

In this initial phase of the war—April 1975 to March 1976—no outside force appeared to impose order. Unlike in past centuries, no Greek, Roman, Ottoman, or French occupation forces came to "pacify" this strip of the Levant. Not even the U.S. Marines who had stormed ashore in 1958 turned up. The Lebanese were alone. But not for long. This time the foreign power would be Syria.

Ever since it was severed from Damascus in 1920, Lebanon has been considered a vital component of Syria's national interests. For the Syrians, Lebanon is their front yard. It is the conduit through which trade and information flow from the Mediterranean into the Arab hinterland. In the Syrian psyche, Lebanon constitutes part of Greater Syria. And to Hafiz Assad, the military leader who seized power in a military coup in 1970, Lebanon was something more—a vital part of Syria's front on Israel.*

During the initial months of the war when Christian forces were being pushed back into their enclaves, Assad became acutely aware that a victory by an alliance of the Muslim left and the Palestinians would bring Israel into Lebanon to check the rise of Palestinian power. The Israelis, sitting on the southern border of Lebanon, were already within striking distance of the Bekaa—Syria's soft underbelly, only eighteen miles from Damascus. If Israel did choose to move into Lebanon to squelch the Palestinians, Syria would be faced with two equally unappealing choices: to engage Israel militarily or to suffer the humiliation of standing aside. The wily Assad created a third alternative: a Syrian military intervention to stabilize Lebanon.

---

* See chapter 7.

Initially Syrian maneuvers in Lebanon were cautious. In early 1976, Hafiz Assad approached the factions with a peace plan that balanced power between the Christians and Muslims slightly more equitably and hinted at an improved status for the Palestinians within Lebanon. The Muslims rejected the plan as inadequate. The war continued, causing the outnumbered Maronites to revert to past behavior by frantically casting around for a foreign protector. The United States, burned by the fall of Vietnam, and Europe, tied to Arab oil, were no longer viable possibilities. Suleiman Franjieh, the eviscerated Lebanese president with long ties to Syria, provided the conduit through which the needs of the Christian Maronites met the goals of Muslim Syria. Thus, in October 1976, Hafiz Assad, in a last-ditch attempt to control events in Lebanon and armed with the blessing of Western powers, saved the Maronites by sending thirteen thousand troops reinforced by T-55 and T-62 tanks into Lebanon to block a Muslim victory.

With Syria patrolling central Beirut, the Phalange moved back to fortified positions north of the Place des Martyres. The old Beirut-Damascus Road became the "Green Line" that effectively divided Beirut between the Christian east and the Muslim west.* On each side, the opposing forces dug into fixed positions that more or less held for the next fifteen years.

Of all the areas of Lebanon subjected to the violence of war, Beirut suffered the most. Tourists no longer arrived seeking pleasure. Instead the foreigners registered in the surviving hotels were mostly foreign reporters and businessmen, many of whom were arms dealers from Europe. But what was most changed about Beirut was the decentralization of the city, which resulted from massive population shifts. Except for the boarded-up National Museum, which served as the only mutually accepted crossing point from western Beirut to eastern Beirut,

---

*The term "Green Line" came from the shrubs and weeds that sprouted through the broken asphalt of one of Lebanon's main highways.

public thoroughfares, crossroads, bridges, hilltops, and other strategic intersections that had served as links between communities were now treacherous barriers that divided them. And the once-gracious squares, busy traffic terminals, and inviting pedestrian shopping arcades were reduced to a series of desolate "no-man's lands."

On each side of the Green Line, schools, universities, banks, trading companies, and even travel agencies served their own sectarian communities. Most of those communities possessed their own broadcasting stations, newspapers, periodicals, and publishers. Through them, each group produced pamphlets, slogans, symbols, and motifs to promote its own ethnocentric version of the social and political history of Lebanon, its own interpretation of the war, its own public and private concerns, and its own perceptions of the basic issues in a society being drastically reshaped and redefined. In contrast to the prewar years when Beirutis were compelled to traverse communal boundaries to secure public services and use amenities, the proliferation of self-sufficient urban enclaves extinguished the need for any business, governmental, or social intercourse. Gradually even the desire to cross over boundaries drawn by communal groups died. In the new reality, Lebanese lived, worked, shopped, went to school, received their medical care, and found their entertainment within constricted communal circles. Within them, a generation of children and adolescents grew up thinking that their social world did not, and could not, extend beyond the confines of the communities within which they were entrapped.* More anguishing to observe was how ties of trust, intimacy, benevolence, and just simple caring among neighbors disappeared. Instead angry combatants

* Despite massive population shifts, neither west nor east Beirut experienced total communal cleansing. West Beirut remained a mixed area where some Druze, Sunnis, Shia, and Christians, including a scattering of Maronite warlords opposed to those in east Beirut, lived. Muslim warlords, rivals of those dominant in the west, took refuge in the east.

flung themselves, often irrationally, into recurring episodes of violence that erupted, faded, and resurfaced later for no recognized or coherent reason. The Lebanese of Beirut lived like this because most communal groups fielded their own armed force.

Militias had been a fact of life in Lebanese politics before the creation of the state. The Maronites and Druze sent their militias against each other in 1860. The *zuama* employed militias against each other in the mini-war of 1958. In contests for political and economic power, rival families used private armies to promote their individual interests in the early 1970s. But when the government could no longer field an army and the state ceased to function as the arbiter between competing factions, the militias divided Lebanon between themselves.

Holding sway over territory defended by their own militias, warlords out of the old elite established local authority with all the trimmings of government. Operating in the void created by the collapse of state authority, each presided over its particular group through the intricate web of rules and obligations of the old feudal patron/client system. Beside them were new warlords created by the realities of civil war. Booty delivered by raiding the state and cantons belonging to other confessionals provided a bountiful windfall to the warlords. But the perpetrators of the looting, the vandalizing of private property, and the robbing of banks were not all warlords or even Lebanese. Professional pillagers came from adjacent countries. Some came from Europe, possibly courtesy of the Mafia. Among these foreigners were specialists in particular types of crime, such as the leader of a Syrian-sponsored faction of the PLO nicknamed the "Persian" because of his expertise in collecting quantities of valuable Persian carpets. Alongside the old feudal warlords, the new warlords, and the criminals were foreign governments that funneled inordinate sums of money to their clients. They all held a vested interest in the status quo of belligerency.

In Beirut, militiamen with ammunition belts hung across their chests strutted on streets where expensively clad women, smart-suited businessmen, and chattering students had walked before the war. What had begun as a contest between the old order and the new had degenerated into a series of localized turf wars between militias vying to eliminate adversaries or to extend territory. Although thousands of people died in shoot-outs, the ultimate victim was the Lebanese state. In a war now characterized by fixed trenches, long-range artillery exchanges replaced frontline battles as each militia protected its separate canton. To do so, militias drew young men into a macho culture disconnected from civil society.

In the early stages of the war, the militiaman bearing arms and engaging in combat assumed the aura of romance that enticed legions of young recruits from both the old feudal clans and the disenfranchised urban masses. The tragedy for Lebanon is that even the sons of stable, middle-class families could transmute from gentle schoolboys to calloused, heartless killers. The question is why. Perhaps the only answer is the charisma projected by the macho militiaman. All over Lebanon young men watched jeeps stop with a screech of brakes to allow a lithe young man to jump out, adjust the position of the Kalashnikov rifle slung across his shoulder, and extend a confident handshake to a brother in arms manning a checkpoint. For a teenager, the urge to belong to these men, to emit the same air of confidence, to feel as powerful as they felt, was irresistible. Often ignoring their parents' pleas to stay removed, they flocked to join a militia as regular fighters or subsidiary recruits. In doing so they did their part to drain the life blood of the Lebanese state.

As early as the first year of the war, the militias, through a variety of means, began to acquire weapons heavier than the assault rifle. When the Lebanese army split into communal factions early in 1976, both Christians and Muslims seized the military's large arsenals, including tanks and heavy artillery. In addition, the militias spent an estimated $1 billion each year to import arms. Of the Lebanese, the biggest spender was the Phalange, who took the hundreds of millions of dollars looted from warehouses in the harbor in 1975 or stolen from bank vaults to buy weapons. Their purchases were supplemented by Israel, whose interest was to weaken the PLO. For its part, the PLO used an estimated $8 to $13 billion held before the war in Beirut banks plus transfers from Arab governments opposed to Israel to build its own arsenal. On all sides, sizeable revenues poured in from foreign governments pursuing their national interests in the Levant; individual Lebanese living abroad; illegal taxes; a drug trade that generated a half a billion dollars a year; Syrian foot soldiers who sold their rifles; and Syrian officers who, for a price, opened the doors of their arsenals. Most went directly into the hands of the militias. The remainder flowed into the street markets, where pistols and hand grenades took their place alongside apples and bananas. Beckoned by demand, arms dealers from all over the world descended on Lebanon—the West German Gunther Leinhauser, the Armenian Sarkis Soghanalian, and the American manufacturer Colt. It was Colt that held a press conference publicized by the U.S. embassy in Beirut to announce a sale of three thousand shiny chrome-plated pistols.

By the fifth anniversary of the start of the war, there was no longer an army or a government in anything but name. There were only the militias. In every sector of Beirut, militiamen crouched behind barricades built of broken, discarded furniture, ruined refrigerators, and the debris of bombed-out buildings, holding their fingers on the triggers of the guns provided by their militia chiefs. When they fired at the perceived infringement of territory by another militia, civilians were left to protect themselves. Like a drill called by the first sound of shots, shopkeepers pulled down the iron shutters over their storefronts, mothers scooped up their children, and vendors ran with their carts behind whatever structure might provide a shield. The lovely city on the Mediterranean had become a nightmare. In 1982, it turned into a living hell.

The illusion of the Lebanese state clung to the office of the president.

As the time for the 1982 election approached, the Maronites were nervous. While for the moment they did not fear annihilation because of the presence of Syria, they did not trust the Syrian commitment to their protection. Instead they saw Syrian policy moving more toward the Muslims, which Damascus now judged necessary to retain its control over Lebanon. Once more, Christian Lebanon needed a savior. Instead of searching for another foreign protector, Bashir Gemayel, the twenty-eight-year-old son of Pierre and the leader of the Phalange, sounded the bugle for "Marounistan," Maronite land.

Within the Phalange, Bashir Gemayel was the leading proponent of Christian military might as a basis of Christian political power. He forcefully argued that the fragmentations and divisions that had characterized the Maronites throughout the first phase of the war had become a luxury that a beleaguered community, fighting for its survival against numerical and political odds, could no longer afford. Although his opponents saw him as erratic, restless, and willing to do anything to further his ambitions, for the Maronites of the Mountain, Gemayel personified an integrity and idealism that starkly contrasted the corruption of most Lebanese politicians. In this, Gemayel touched a deep longing for a clear, unequivocal leader capable of bringing order out of nearly a decade of chaos. Declaring the Christians "a small population . . . fighting alone for liberty, democracy, for the dignity of man against peoples and groups that deny these values," he won over many of the non-Maronite Christians.* Burying their socioeconomic contempt for the Phalangists, many, perhaps most, Maronite as well as non-Maronite Christians were ready to join Gemayel at the barricades.

More than a year earlier, in December 1980, Gemayel had published his manifesto: "The Lebanon We Want to Build." The points he

* Quoted in Itamar Rabinovich, *The War for Lebanon, 1970–1985* (Ithaca, N.Y.: Cornell University Press, 1985), p. 91.

had argued were clear, decisive, and appealing to the Christian community. Shrinking Christian percentages in the population had rendered
the formula at the core of the National Pact no longer valid. But since
the Christians had played a vital and constructive role in Lebanon, they
should retain a special position regardless of the percentage of the population they constituted. If the Christian ethos and the Christian place in
the power structure could be preserved, Lebanon would stay unified. If
not, the Christians, particularly the Maronites, would opt for a smaller
Lebanon created by partition or cantonization. As a last resort, Greater
Lebanon of the last sixty years would be jettisoned for a Christian Lebanon composed of east Beirut, the northern part of Mount Lebanon, and
the coastal areas north of Beirut.

Through the Phalange, Bashir Gemayel developed the infrastructure
of an embryonic Christian state. Its future rested on three presumptions:
that recruits for an army could be raised by tapping the mentality of
Christianity under siege; that financial resources could be garnered from
the Christians of the Lebanese Diaspora; and that a foreign sponsor—this
time Israel—could act as arms supplier and military advisor.

For Israel, Bashir Gemayel's vision of "Fortress Lebanon" created a
natural ally in its struggle against the Palestinians. Furthermore, a relationship between Israel and the Maronites was not new. Even before
the Lebanese civil war began, Israel had operated as a major arms supplier to the Phalange via nighttime deliveries to isolated coves along the
coast. Now the Phalange offered an open alliance to the Jewish state.
Thus the sides joined—the Israelis believing Bashir Gemayel could be
molded into a wedge against the Palestinians, and the Maronites convinced they had found yet another foreign rescuer eager to protect the
Maronites' special position in Lebanon. All the pieces had fallen in place
for another major assault on the Lebanese state.

With the Phalange burrowed into eastern Beirut in defense of Christian Lebanon, Israeli tanks on June 5, 1982, broke through the barbed-
wire fence dividing Israel and Lebanon. What lay ahead in the minds of

Israeli military planners was nothing less than the destruction of the Palestinian presence in Lebanon.*

On the second day of the invasion, Israeli forces reached Damour just south of Beirut. To the north, the city was quiet. Suddenly the stillness broke. Israeli planes streaked low to drop leaflets warning the PLO and the Syrians to withdraw or subject Beirut to its impending fate. The Syrians hastily evacuated their checkpoints, leaving them vacant for the first time in six years. But the PLO stood firm.

With the Palestinians trapped inside vowing to turn Beirut into the "Stalingrad of the Arabs," Israel had two choices: to empty Beirut of the Palestinians through negotiations or to clean them out by force. To soften the city for either option, the Israeli army threw a blockade in front of Beirut that cut off water and electricity and stopped the flow of fresh fruits, vegetables, and bread from the south. Aware there was no protection from their government, Beirutis hunkered down for a siege that would kill eighteen thousand people.

For seventy days, the Israelis pounded Beirut with bombs and mortar rounds that destroyed buildings and infrastructure as well as much of the umbrella of pines planted by the Romans around 64 BC. Thousands of people, their homes destroyed by the intense bombing and exploding munitions stores, were living in basements, stairwells, the lobbies of damaged apartment buildings, and the collapsed ruins of commercial structures while health officials from the United Nations worried about a pending plague of typhoid and cholera.

By the end of July, all sides—the PLO, Israel, and the Lebanese—looked for a way to end the siege. It was to the United States that they turned for a negotiated settlement.[†] It was brokered at a time when the tattered and depleted Lebanese parliament once again faced the perilous task of electing a new president.

* See chapter 7.
† See chapter 7.

The Phalange intended to anoint Bashir Gemayel, but he faced opposition from the old Sunni *zuama* and the Gemayels' archrivals, the Franjiehs and former Lebanese president Camille Chamoun. However, the political plan attached to Israel's initial invasion of Lebanon demanded Gemayel as president. And so the Israelis set about guaranteeing his election. Parliamentary delegates in Israeli-controlled areas were delivered for the election with instructions on how to vote. For the remainder, the Gemayel forces themselves reverted to the time-honored tactics of Lebanese politics. Chamoun was bought off with political promises and cash. The rest of the deputies Bashir needed were just bought off, at a cost of about two million Lebanese pounds apiece. Thus, on August 23, two days after the PLO began to evacuate Beirut under American protection, Bashir Gemayel was elected president of Lebanon in an east Beirut military barracks surrounded by armed Phalangists. When his election was announced, exuberant Phalangists uncorked champagne bottles and killed five people in a fusillade of celebratory bullets.

For the next forty-five days, the thirty-five-year-old Bashir Gemayel prepared Lebanon for his assumption of the presidency. Through his control of the information services, he created an image of stability by announcing detailed plans to reconstitute the bureaucracy and re-create the trappings of what a former Chamoun supporter called "a proper country." Radiating the aura of authority, the handsome, dashing Bashir convinced most Christians that he held the defense of Christianity in the Middle East in his hands. It all proved an illusion.

On September 14, Gemayel traveled to the Ashrafieh branch of the Phalange Party. At 4:10 p.m., while vowing to his audience that the Muslims would learn to accept the new order in Lebanon, a two-hundred-pound bomb planted in the ceiling above the president-elect's head detonated. The entire building collapsed. At 9:45 p.m. his body, his head all but blown away, was identified at the Hotel-Dieu Hospital.

While the Phalange buried Bashir Gemayel, the Israeli Defense Forces (IDF) moved into the heavily populated Palestinian neighborhood of

Sabra and the camp of Shatila to flush out any remaining Palestinian guerrillas. Originally intending to send in elements of the reviving Lebanese army, the Israelis instead stood aside at sundown on September 16 to allow the Phalange militia to enter an area in which eighty thousand Palestinians were encircled. As darkness descended, squads of Phalangists crept into the streets of Sabra and scaled the earthen embankments around Shatila and disappeared into the narrow alleyways. For two days and two nights, the Phalangists gutted their victims with bayonets, trampled infants to death, and slaughtered whole families in a frenzy of revenge for Bashir Gemayel, for Lebanon, and for Christendom. Its end marked the beginning of another phase in Lebanon's tortured political history.

The vacant presidency was filled by Bashir's older brother, Amin. By common agreement, he was more attuned to the Levantine character of Lebanon than his brother ever was. Therefore, he was at least reasonably acceptable to the old-line politicians, if not to the radicals. "To Muslims, Amin Gemayel represented a compromise. It was like the class of 1943 rising from the grave. Innocent of ties with Israel, convinced of the need to get along with the Muslims, and involved in business like any self-respecting Lebanese, Amin represented a return to the past."* Yet a bewildering array of domestic and foreign adversaries drove the war on. In 1983, Maronite and Druze militias fought in the Chouf in a repeat of 1860; US warships shelled the Druze village of Souk al Gharb before losing 241 American Marines to a bomb attack on their barracks in Beirut; the politically energized Shia took control of west Beirut in 1984, the same year the United States withdrew from Lebanon; militant Islamic groups inspired by the Islamic Revolution in Iran began to seize Western hostages off the street; in 1985 the Shia Amal attempted to drive the Palestinians out of southern Lebanon in a

---

* Jonathan C. Randal, *Going All the Way: Christian Warlords, Israeli Adventurers, and the War in Lebanon* (New York: Viking Press, 1983), p. 149.

long, brutal series of sieges called the "camp wars"; in 1987 Syria sent more troops into Lebanon; Iran, as it had done since 1979, continued to pump money and influence into militant Islamic organizations; and two Shia militias belonging to Amal and Hezbollah battled for control of Beirut's southern suburbs. At one point it was estimated that no fewer than 186 warring factions representing contending communal identities and ideologies, splinter groups within these larger blocs, and foreign governments pursuing their own interests were battling within a country seven-tenths the size of Connecticut.

In the long years since 1975, violence in Lebanon had become normalized. There remained no public ethic, no sense of what it meant to destroy the state. Instead the cruelty of one group against another acquired the patina of moral legitimacy and cultural sanction. In this milieu, the grotesque became the mundane. Newspapers casually reported discoveries of bodies in the trunks of abandoned cars, in destroyed buildings, in the debris of churches and mosques, in the quiet forests of mountains and hills. Too often, simply killing a victim had not been enough. Necks were slashed, fingers cut off, and eyes gouged out. Those who escaped physical harm learned to survive in an incomprehensible, totally changed world. Like robots, they got up in the morning, went to work, did the shopping, ate dinner, and made love. Yet they did so in an environment that bore no relationship to the halcyon days of the 1950s. Symbolic of the new reality was the antiaircraft gun placed at one of the old, elegant apartment buildings along Hamra Street. It was on the roof, above the penthouse. By 1988, Beirut from the air still retained its natural beauty. But on the ground, militias held streets lined with pockmarked buildings, dogs roamed like hyenas, and wild vegetation grew out of the broken asphalt of an urban landscape. In this realm of the surreal, two local militias engaged each other in a firefight adjacent to the Summerland Hotel, where guests continued to sip martinis and whirl around the dance floor. Everyday the front pages of newspapers printed photographs of the bombed-out carcasses of cars and slaughtered civilians above ads for expensive nightclubs and performances by Ragheb Alami, the Lebanese Madonna.

Although the communal cantons that coalesced in the first two years of the war acted like separate governing entities, none could operate as a self-sustaining economic unit. To survive within them, the princes of Levantine business could function as entrepreneurs only by securing sources of financing, markets in which to sell goods, and transportation to move those goods. Still, none of the warlords would put down their weapons even to promote trade. With no government commanding enough legitimacy to pull the country together and no army capable of quelling the violence, the famed Lebanese economy, like the Lebanese state, became the tortured victim of civil war.

During the first five years of the war—1975 to 1980—a country that was tearing itself apart floated in cash. In addition to the nefarious means by which the militias financed themselves, money came ashore from Lebanese employed in the Persian Gulf whose high salaries supported their families in Lebanon; Lebanese in the West who not only sent money to their families but also contributed to their favorite militias; and foreign governments that transferred millions to the war chests of their client militias at the rate of $15 million to $50 million a month. There was also the construction industry. In the early stages of the war when large-scale population shifts occurred, Beirut mushroomed in every direction. Like a giant squid, it swallowed up villages named Dbaye, Sinn al-Fil, Forn Chebak, Dora, Bourj Hammoud, Chiyah, Ghodeiri, Quzai, Kahlde, and Bir Hasan. In the transfers of populations resulting from the cantonization of the city and the physical destruction of the country, developers, contractors, and construction workers all derived profits and wages. It seemed only the state lost money.

Imports of everything from cars to bottled beer delivered through illegal ports controlled by militias cost the government millions of dollars in lost taxes. At the same time, the warlords within their individual cantons exercised taxing authority and erected tollbooths at every major crossing, starving the Lebanese government of more revenue. By the mid-1980s the tax structure built by the warlords within their cantons had become so elaborate that fees were imposed on everything from customs to real estate transactions to social services. At the same time, the national Social Security Fund was running deficits and defaulting on the payment of benefits to Lebanese citizens. Without enforcement from a central government, some employers continued to deduct government-required contributions from their employees only to pay them into the coffers of the militia of their choice. The Beirut airport, another critical source of government revenue, never recovered from the drastic drop in the number of travelers passing through the facility before 1975. Central authorities could not even collect utility bills. Individuals not only defaulted on their bills, but also ran wires off the main lines in order to steal subsidized electric power from their own government.

Eventually everyone, not just the government, began to suffer. As early as 1981, the inflow of remittances began to fall as Lebanese lost their jobs in oil states when a global oil glut plunged those economies into recession. In 1982 the shoot-out between Israel and the Palestinians inflicted $2 billion worth of economic damage on Lebanon. In its forced exit from Beirut, the PLO took its militiamen as well as its political, economic, and social structure. That deprived Lebanon of what had been an estimated fifteen percent of all economic activity in the country before the war.

As a result of this accumulation of woes, Lebanon needed massive amounts of money for the legitimate needs of government. But instead of applying Lebanon's limited resources to the needs of the nation, the regime of Amin Gemayel bought $880 million worth of weapons, which in the ebb and flow of fighting gradually disappeared into the arms caches of militias of every color and stripe. Even the celebration of the new year of 1985 in a financially starved state devoured $5 million worth of bullets fired into the air by simple merrymakers.

The crumbled Lebanese government became so economically and institutionally weak that after 1985 the cabinet failed to present a budget. What government there was functioned by way of allotments of scant public funds from the Ministry of Finance. Under the arrangement, the Central Bank provided to the various departments what amounted to a purse of money. Although practical in terms of keeping a semblance of government running, it gave free rein to senior officials to spend the money as they chose. Not surprisingly, some ministers served only the interests of their clients and their own egos, using their allotments to build entire new office blocks equipped with expensive furniture.

By 1987, the major remaining asset of the Lebanese government was 9.22 million ounces of gold bullion stored in the basement of the Central Bank on Rue Massraf Lubnan. It remained intact because the governor of the bank, Edmound Naim, physically stood guard over it. Among the few heroic figures in the governmental structure of Lebanon, he worked at his desk during the day and slept on a couch in his office at night.

With the 1989 economy further crippled, the minimum wage at $75 a month, and most families struggling to survive, the militias were still spending $9,500.00 for a 240-millimeter shell and $0.30 for every Kalashnikov bullet. An attempt by the debilitated central authority to exert control over some of the seaports ruled by the militias only triggered a battle that cost 1,400 lives. A subsequent move to seize control of the fourth and fifth basins of the Beirut harbor touched off another bloody battle that cost another 1,000 lives and inflicted almost $1.5 billion in damages to the economic infrastructure. Despite sending in nineteen thousand troops armed with artillery, the Lebanese army failed to reclaim that portion of the Beirut harbor controlled by six thousand heavily armed militiamen of the Lebanese Forces. For fifteen years, there had been a blank check for violence in which every horror seemed to have been allowed. The 150,000 who died seemed victims of an abstract, quasi-biological fate determined by militia chieftains who claimed to be the indispensable champions of national reconciliation, even as they dismantled the state. The only two remaining symbols of central authority were the presidential palace in Baabda and the prime minister's office in west Beirut. With yet another presidential election approaching, the Lebanese were preparing for the last act of the Lebanese civil war. It would produce the question: To what extent must Lebanon be degraded before the Lebanese themselves accepted the changes that would allow civil society to make peace with itself?

Chapter 5

IDENTITY IN PURSUIT
OF A NATION

Lebanon is a great trading post.
It didn't ask to be a model nation.

—ELIZABETH WARNOCK FERNEA

Fingers of the Nile slowly wander through the wide delta that
begins north of Cairo and ends at the edge of the Mediterranean.
Small rivers in themselves, they feed moisture and nutrients into
a triangle of rich soil that has been a vast farm since the time of the pha-
raohs. Today it is worked by the *fellah*, the peasant, who is a descendant
of the ancient Egyptians and the heir of those who adopted Arab culture
when Egypt yielded to Islam. Day after day, year after year, the *fellah*
scratches the dense, black soil with the same crude hoe devised by his
ancestors, and milks the water buffalo that powers the same primitive
apparatus that dips water from the river and pours it into the narrow
channel that runs into his field. Like those from whom he is descended,
he lives in a village of small, mean, mud-brick houses centered around
the mosque and the coffee shop. In the coffee shop, men clad in the
age-old *galabia* smoke the *naghile* while two among them play musical
instruments of age-old design, the *oud* (lute) and the *nai* (flute). Reclin-
ing on crude wooden platforms embedded with years of dust, they lis-
ten to the professional storyteller recite the adventures of Sultan Baibur
as told and retold without variation for a thousand years. On occasion

they watch an Egyptian dance in which not one new movement has been added since the days of Ramses. This is life in rural Egypt, where the power of tradition welds together the past, the present, and the future.

For all Egyptians, tradition comprises the well from which the individual draws the first bucket of his or her identity. And tradition provides the framework for other basic elements of identity: family, religion, and sect. Each fills its own place in the psyche of the individual to create a total identity that separates one group from "the other." Absent in that same psyche is the overarching sense of belonging to a commonly defined nation in which all individuals share a stake.

The sense of identity in any society is complex. Among the Arabs, the Egyptians perhaps possess the greatest sense of oneness. All relate to their ancient history and share traditions that came with Islam so many hundreds of years ago. But they also differ among themselves about Egypt's particularity, especially its relationship to its geographic region. Outward-looking Egyptians, principally those educated in English, place their country at the edge of the Mediterranean and at the gateway of both Europe and north Africa. The inward-looking—usually those unschooled or educated solely in Arabic—place Egypt firmly in the Arab world. These two concepts have long lived in tension with each other. Today the current pro-Western leadership of Egypt strains at the bonds of tradition, which it sees as constraining the implementation of its own definition of Egyptian identity, while Saudi Arabia's House of Saud continues to anchor its legitimacy in the preservation and defense of traditional society.

The politics of tradition as practiced by the House of Saud was evident on a hot August day in 2005. The afternoon sun was pounding Riyadh like an anvil when the body of Fahd ibn Abdul Aziz, king of Saudi Arabia, arrived by ambulance at the central mosque. Draped in a brown *bisht*, the cloak worn for centuries by the Bedouin sheikh, it was carried inside for prayers. A short time later, the king's male relatives lifted the litter on which his corpse lay and bore it to the humble al Oud cemetery. Before the sun set, the man who had ruled this wealthy kingdom for almost a quarter of a century was lowered into a simple unmarked grave.

With the approval of the major clerics within the ultraconservative Wahabbi sect of Islam, Fahd's half brother, Abdullah, assumed the position of Saudi Arabia's grand sheikh. Like his father and four brothers before him, the newly designated king traveled the kingdom to forge again the link between the tribes and the House of Saud. On the desert, in dancing light created by the flames of a campfire, tribal men wearing the traditional costume of the Arabian Peninsula, their chests crossed with swords, circled the tall, bearded Abdullah, chanting the same oath of allegiance heard by the new king's predecessors.

But beyond the common cemetery and the humble ceremony of *bayah*, Saudi Arabia's royal family lives according to its own description, as "a highly privileged tribe that permeates every corner of the country."* At the upper levels of the family, hundreds of princes and princesses live in opulence. Marble palaces fronted by multi-tiered fountains stand behind elaborate wrought-iron gates set in high stucco walls. Behind some of those walls, the reigning King presides over salons in which dozens of ornate chairs upholstered in thick cut velvet line the walls. But those who sit in them are most often men of the desert and Wahabbism who have come to seek favors from their sheikh, whose official title is "Custodian of the Two Holy Mosques" of Mecca and Medina, which lie within the boundaries of Saudi Arabia. They are welcomed by a servant carrying a shiny, golden, four-legged vessel filled with burning incense who moves from chair to chair flicking his wrist to direct the fragrant smoke toward each guest. He is followed by a tea boy offering small cups of overly sweet tea or even smaller cups of strong coffee laced with cardamom to the herders of goats, sheep, and camels; farmers who plant the oases; minor

* From an advertisement paid for by Saudi Arabia in the *New York Times*, April 25, 1983.

tribal leaders; and taxi drivers whose roots dig deep in Bedouin culture. All regard themselves as worthy clients of the House of Saud. Even though they are there to petition their leader for loans, grants, and gifts that come out of state resources, their identity remains in family, tribe, and faith, not in a nation labeled Saudi Arabia.

All Arab states—for reasons and degrees that differ from one to the other—are plagued by populations lacking the sense of common identity that is the essential foundation of a true nation. Among states that are cohesive nations, Japan embraces a people whose identity developed over many centuries on islands largely isolated from outside influences. European countries took form as nations whose populations shared a common ethnicity, language, religion, history, and culture. The United States, a collection of immigrants, gathered around a set of commonly respected principles fed by economic opportunities. Today all of these nations possess a history of at least two centuries, some many more. They stand in stark contrast to most Arab states, which are both contrived political creations rooted in short national histories and aged vessels holding centuries of rigid tradition. For it is tradition that has held their people in place over centuries of absent or oppressive governments, foreign invasion and occupation, economic hardship, and political disorder. Individuals survived by huddling within communal walls sunk in the firm foundation of tradition. Even today those foundations remain thick, deep, and resistant to destruction by the forces of urbanization, mass communication, and accelerating globalization.

The resistance to change is universal. No person, no group, no society welcomes interruptions in their comfortable patterns of tradition, perception, and identity served up by a changing social order or delivered from outside by rival societies, alien cultures, competing economies, and advancing technology. Yet some societies, no matter how reluctantly, have proved willing to modify deeply rooted beliefs, values, and practices in order to advance economic growth and political tranquility. In contrast, most societies that are tightly bound to tradition have proved profoundly afraid to modify, alter, or re-create themselves because it is tradition which provides the anchor to which the individual has tied his or her identity for centuries. In Arab societies specifically, individual identity reposes in the genealogy of families claiming long histories, and in religions and sects that themselves reenforce the continuity of tradition and therefore identity.

Yet despite their deep fears and resolute defiance of the unknown, Arabs have been subjected to enormous thrusts of change since the end of World War I. Beginning before the collapse of the Ottoman Empire and increasing with the imposition of contrived borders and Western colonial rule, the pressures intensified in 1948 when the largely Western Zionists wrest Palestine from its Arab inhabitants. In 1967, Jordan and Syria suffered the effects of territorial loss and population alterations as a result of a lightning fast war. In 1973, the explosion of petroleum prices produced a series of seismic shifts in the Gulf oil states, which ranged from a cascade of sudden wealth to a flood of foreign workers. During the 1991 Gulf War, xenophobic Saudi Arabia experienced another onslaught of foreigners who arrived wearing military fatigues and riding in vehicles driven by women. More widespread and invasive change came to every Arab country during the 1990s via satellite dishes and the Internet. In 2003, Iraq entered what would prove to be a hell of change when American military force removed from them the nailed boot of Saddam Hussein and unleashed the repressed energy of the Shia. Underlying it all has been the unrelenting challenge to Islamic societies to find their own path to modernity within the realm of Arab culture.

While Westerners assume modernization requires the Western model, Arabs generally fear secular Western institutions. To an Arab, relationships within faith and tradition provide the very foundation of Arab society and government. Individual freedom, the golden chalice of Western political thought, demands the questioning of assumptions, which implies to an Arab the most dreaded of ends—the breakdown of community.

Unlike the West that glorifies the individual, Arabs define self in personal relationships with others. And it is mutual obligation of one to the other that knits Arab society together. Consequently institutions are inseparable from those who occupy them. In the realm of Arab politics, a person who holds a political or legal position is seldom if ever capable of separating himself from his relationships within his family, community, or web of indebtness in order to exercise an impersonal, institutional role. To the officeholder as well as those he represents, any act of independence is the equivalent of splitting the social atom, risking the release of unknown and uncontrollable forces that threaten order. Therefore, to most Arabs, it is better to live in tyranny than risk chaos. This is the dilemma of Arab governance.

Even defined in terms of Arab culture, modernization challenges Arab societies because it requires them to surrender their various forms of tribalism to the common identity required by a nation. Because the nation-state comprises the system on which the twenty-first-century world functions, no society can achieve political stability and economic advancement without first molding its diverse factions into an authentic nation in which almost all are willing to buy a share. In this failure to find a common identity, which can be achieved only through altering the patterns of the past, the Lebanese serve as a mirror of the Arabs.

For a decade and a half, Lebanon suffered destruction, brutality, and terror inflicted by religious bigotry accompanied by political and economic inequalities among confessional groups that multiplied in the presence of private militias and foreign armies. During those savage years, the violence was most often characterized by those on the outside of the conflict as a religious war between Christians and Muslims. The reality was far more complex. This was a war of identity to determine whether Lebanon is a part of the West or a part of the Arab world. How an individual Lebanese answered the identity question was not solely determined by whether he or she was a Christian or a Muslim. Perceiving the stakes as their very survival in a country with an Arab character, the Roman Catholic Maronites not only rejected an Arab identity but desperately fought to weld Lebanon to the West. Many other Christians, most commonly those of the eastern rite, accepted themselves and Lebanon as Arab by culture. The Muslims, fractured into Sunnis, Shia, and Druze, never doubted Lebanon's Arab identity. But within that Arab identity were sectarian conflicts over the definition of the state, which carried with it the formula by which political and economic power would be distributed. If this contest of definition and distribution had stayed confined to the Lebanese, perhaps the violence could have been contained within some tolerable parameters. But each group—Christian and Muslim; Sunni, Shia, and Druze—called forces outside Lebanon to join in the attack on each other. And together Lebanese and foreigners turned this tiny territory at the gate of the Arab world into an inferno. When the fires diminished, the remaining foreigners carved out spheres of influence while the Lebanese themselves refused to significantly alter the basic patterns of their society and the political rules that had brought Lebanon to the edge of suicide. Fractured still by the same issues on which the war had been fought, the Lebanese state remained hostage to the myriad factors of religion, psychology, politics, and economics that had taken them into war.

AFTER YEARS OF savage warfare, Lebanon in 1989 was broken. Militiamen standing guard over their respective enclaves outnumbered the army. A twenty-five-thousand-man Syrian army of occupation spread out over the north and east; Israel claimed its "security zone" in the south; and Hezbollah, provided bone and muscle by Iran, plotted the destruction of Lebanon as a secular state.* Lebanon remained a country only through the symbolism of a sitting president accepted by all the

* See chapter 6.

major factions within the intricate Lebanese mosaic. Repeating the pattern in which the choice of president in 1970 began the slide toward civil war, it was the choice of president in 1988 that finally wrung down the curtain on that war.

The six-year term of Amin Gemayel—selected in 1982 to fill the place of his assassinated brother, Bashir—was due to end in September. Even though the civil war had shorn the presidency of most of its power, it was still the emblem the Maronites required to confirm their existence in Lebanon and the laurel the Muslims demanded to place on the head of Lebanon's chief of state. Thus before the war-weary Lebanese could end the war, pick up the pieces of a shattered society, and reconstitute the state, a president had to take office.

The problem was that the mechanism under which a president was chosen had been structured by the reigning *zuama* forty-five years before to accommodate a unique political system. But the crafty men among the Maronites, the Sunnis, and the Shia who made that mechanism work were no longer there. During the course of the war, some had fallen to assassins or simply died. Most of the other *zuama*, as well as their descendants, were in exile or dethroned by the militias. And in the chaotic bloodletting of the civil war, the Lebanese political base had broadened vastly as young men with guns contested the authority of the old political leaders. Eventually it was they who harvested a meaningful measure of power in a crumbling social order.

In the realm of realpolitik, the distribution and exercise of power could no longer be determined by the Lebanese themselves. Any president, Christian or Muslim, had to satisfy Syria's Hafiz Assad, whose army stood ready to intervene between the militias. Even so, the last remaining deputies of the 1972 Lebanese parliament rejected the choice of Syria—seventy-eight-year-old Suleiman Franjieh, the last tottering lion of prewar politics. Only the absolute need to reach an agreement on another choice could seduce the skeleton of the Chamber of Deputies into the old parliament building in west Beirut on September 21, the day before Gemayel's term was to expire. It was in this desperate atmosphere that Prime Minister Selim Hoss, surrounded by bodyguards, cautiously emerged from his apartment fortress to undertake the nostalgic journey to the once-sparkling center of Beirut. Elsewhere in the Muslim sector of the city, Hussein al Husseini, the Chamber's speaker, crept from his office and climbed into his car surrounded by his own covey of gunmen nervously holding their fingers on the triggers of automatic weapons. But the Chamber of Deputies did not convene. The Maronite deputies refused to leave the security of the Mountain. Without them, there was no quorum and no president. The day ended appropriately when a twilight barrage of artillery shells arched across the Green Line.

At the stroke of midnight on September 22, 1988, Amin Gemayel's term as president expired. Lebanon was without a president, the last symbol of its unity. Drawing on the precedent established by a presidential resignation in 1952, Gemayel named an interim government headed by Michel Aoun, the Maronite commander of the Lebanese army. Lebanon's Muslim factions immediately denounced the move, claiming that in the absence of an elected president, the interim government should be headed by the Sunni prime minister. Consequently, as the sun rose on the morning of September 23, Lebanon found itself with not one but two governments: the Muslim-led government of Prime Minister Selim Hoss and the Christian-led government of General Michel Aoun. Neither claimed the allegiance of all the factions in their respective communities. Nor were the Lebanese as a whole yet ready to raise themselves above their communal identities, their family squabbles, their long-fixed attitudes to sign on to a new order in Lebanon underwritten by a shared identity.

On the Mountain, the Maronites, protected by the Christian elements of the thirty-seven thousand-man Lebanese army and an estimated twenty thousand members of the Lebanese Forces, had lived through the war somewhat removed from the violence of Beirut and the south.* They occupied what they called "Marounistan," where the Lebanese Forces fulfilled the role of government. The militia collected taxes and ran a sophisticated system of kickbacks and payoffs that substituted for the old patronage system of prewar Lebanon. But there was opposition to the Lebanese Forces' heavy hand and corrupt rule, stoked by personal ambitions and rivalries, competing interests, and the ever-present family vendettas that had stalked the Mountain for generations. Overlying it all was a profound ideological difference between the leading factions within the Maronite confessional.

During the war years, the stark realities of declining numbers and power had split the Maronites into two opposing camps. At issue was how to respond to their reduced status and influence. One camp favored turning their Christian-held enclave into a ministate protected by foreign guarantors—almost a return to the old *mutassarifate* of the Ottoman era. The other sought to salvage what was left of the Maronites' eroded position and shape it into at least a semblance of Maronite power within a unified Lebanon.

Samir Geagea, a member of a minor Maronite warlord family and the leader of the Lebanese Forces since December 1985, clearly stood for a Christian canton in a unified Lebanon. Michel Aoun, the appointed head of the interim Lebanese government, did not fit precisely into either group. Aoun was a self-proclaimed nationalist who believed Lebanon's whole existence was gravely imperiled by the presence of Syrian forces within its borders. But Aoun, unlike some Maronite nationalists, showed

---

*The Lebanese Forces date back to 1976, when several Maronite militias including the Phalange integrated to achieve a higher degree of independence from the more moderate, traditional Maronite political leaders. In 1978, Bashir Gemayel, leader of the Phalange, moved a step further by incorporating the other militias into his own organization. Those who resisted—the militia of Suleiman Franjieh and the Tigers of Camille Chamoun—were forcibly subjugated in 1978 and 1980.

no interest in accommodation with the Muslims, a basic necessity if the Lebanese state were to be restored.

As 1989 dawned, General Aoun, vowing to reestablish central authority and Lebanese sovereignty, brazenly moved to brace the enfeebled Lebanese presidency. Lacking support outside the part of the Lebanese army he controlled, Aoun's mandate was his own. In his grand scheme, he envisioned unifying Lebanon's diverse elements by exploiting Lebanese antagonism toward Syria; wrapping himself in the image of a leader of an oppressed people fighting against foreign occupation; and attracting enough outside support to offset Syria's daunting military superiority over Lebanon.

In command of only twenty thousand men, Aoun was emboldened by Iraqi arms flowing in to his forces as part of Iraqi president Saddam Hussein's own grand design to claim leadership of the Arab world.* The greatest obstacle in Hussein's path was Hafiz Assad, the Syrian autocrat who was the only Arab leader to support Iran during the 1980–1988 Iran-Iraq War. In Michel Aoun, the tyrant of Baghdad saw a battering ram he could aim at the whole Assad regime and Aoun saw a foreign ally.

To Samir Geagea and the Lebanese Forces, Michel Aoun was a megalomaniac embarking on a suicidal course. Rather than protecting the Christians within Lebanon, his actions threatened the Lebanese Forces' strategy of preparing the Christian enclave for a federal system that Geagea and his supporters believed could be put into place through negotiations with the Druze and perhaps some of the Shia. Thus the coming carnage among the Maronites involved not only Aoun's confrontation with Syria and the Muslim militias but also the showdown between Aoun and Geagea for the right to determine the Maronite vision of postwar Lebanon.

Rather than negotiating with the Lebanese Forces or the Muslims,

* See chapter 7.

Aoun announced in February from the presidential palace at Baabda that he would restore the authority of the Lebanese state by seizing control of all ports in the hands of the country's various militias. On March 19, the general-cum-president proved he was serious. On his orders, Lebanon's debilitated military forces threw up a blockade around several of Beirut's ports. In laying claim to the exit points of Lebanon's marijuana crop, Aoun threatened the profits of both Muslim and Christian militias.

Politically and ideologically, the Lebanese Forces were willing to swallow their losses in the name of Christian power in Lebanon. But for the Muslim militias, the seizure of their ports on the sole authority of a Christian president meant not only lost revenue but also an alarming rebirth of Maronite power and influence. In essence, the confrontation between the acting president and the Muslim militias reeked with the odor of the prewar political system they had fought so long to over-throw. As if it were again 1975, Walid Jumblatt and his Druze militia picked up the gauntlet. Other elements of the original alliance against the Maronites joined in. With the reluctant support of his Maronite rivals in the Lebanese Forces, themselves approximating the Christian side of 1975, Aoun ordered the thirty thousand troops of Hafiz Assad out of Lebanon. With them would go the precarious balance between Christian and Muslim forces.

But instead of expelling Syria, Aoun changed the pattern of war within Lebanon. Aside from the bloodletting of 1975–1976 and 1982, the long conflict had produced a well-understood and commonly accepted system of sectarian cantons policed by private armies. Under it, the Druze repelled any force that threatened to encroach on their mountain fortress, yet they seldom moved on the lowlands. Amal and Hezbollah engaged in bloody struggles for power among the Shia, but carefully kept their battles confined within west Beirut and south Leba-non. Now Aoun, in the name of central authority, broke the rules by trying to push his power beyond his own enclave. In the end, his gamble to reconstitute the Lebanese state by disarming the militias and driving out Syria plunged Beirut and areas to the north into a new and bestial round of death and destruction.

For forty straight days and nights during March and April of 1989, Syria's 240-millimeter mortars—capable of slicing through three floors of a building—dueled the Lebanese army's multiple rocket launchers across the hills north of Beirut. On April 13, the fourteenth anniversary of the outbreak of the war, approximately ten thousand mortar shells and rockets fell on the Christian enclave at the foot of the Mountain, until now spared so much of the wartime fighting. Hospitals and grain silos exploded in flames; power grids incinerated; food distribution ceased; and oil from the Dora storage facilities burned. In Jounieh, previously unscathed streets filled with the debris of war. Over the next days and weeks, prices on depleted stocks of food and goods soared within the Christian enclave. Dazed people not used to carrying jerry cans lined up at communal pumps to collect precious water. In the onslaught, some elements among the Maronites, including the leadership of the Leba-nese Forces, wondered if the Christian-led defiance of Syria could suc-ceed. But Aoun, ignoring reality, refused to waver from his plan. For him and his supporters, there was no alternative to soldiering on.

As August unfolded, renewed fighting drove more than a million Bei-rutis out of the city. They left behind two hundred thousand others who had nowhere to go. As the month wore on, the fierceness of the bom-bardments reached levels that shocked and terrified even the most war-hardened Lebanese. And again the formerly sheltered Christian enclave took the brunt of the fighting.

As a wide swath of the population descended to a level of desperation not experienced before, the Arab League resumed an attempt begun in the spring to mediate the seemingly endless conflict. In retrospect, Aoun had precipitated a crisis so destructive and so brutal that Lebanon's war-ring factions seemed at last ready to accept a new, if imperfect, plan of accommodation. It was in this atmosphere that the committee composed of King Fahd of Saudi Arabia, President Chadli Benjedid of Algeria, and King Hassan of Morocco appealed to all parties to end the bloodshed. This time the combatants agreed. The reasons were multiple: Lebanon's economy was in free fall. Several key leaders who had held onto their maximal demands for much of the war no longer occupied center stage. Some militias, weakened and exhausted by fractionalization and infighting, had lost their foreign sponsors. Finally, most Lebanese realized that no single group or coalition was capable of imposing its will on the others. Faced with widespread domestic disenchantment with the militias, the men who had kept the war going so long could no longer sustain themselves. Therefore, on September 13, 1989, the troika appointed by the Arab League presented the warring parties with a proposal that called for an immediate cease-fire and summoned the parties to discuss a document of national reconciliation. Eleven days later, the guns fell silent.

In October, sixty-two deputies remaining from Lebanon's 1972 parliament—the only remaining legitimate constitutional organ of the Lebanese government—assembled in Taif in the southwestern mountains of Saudi Arabia. A few still resided in Lebanon. But most came out of exile, principally in France, Switzerland, and Iraq. This bastion of the old order represented neither power on the ground nor the current demographic profile of Lebanon. Within it, individuals held widely divergent and intensely passionate views on everything from constitutional reform, to the preservation of Maronite prerogatives, to the replacement of proportional confessional representation with a system of one person one vote. Most of all, they held diametrically opposed positions on three issues crucial to the Lebanese state: the distribution of power, political reform, and national identity. Minus the Palestinians, these were the same issues that led to war in 1975.

These veterans of Lebanon's prewar politics expected to remain in Saudi Arabia's summer capital for three days. They stayed twenty-three. Under the guiding hand of the Saudis, a committee of seventeen containing the usual communal representations drafted a document of national reconciliation that satisfied no one but was acceptable to all. It opened by explicitly stating the one clear result of the war: "Lebanon is an Arab country, both by kinship and identity." With this one statement, competing definitions of Lebanon's identity, which had deployed Lebanese against Lebanese since the creation of Greater Lebanon, seemed to end. The 1943 National Pact was, at last, officially put to rest.

On the operational level, the new pact cut away Christian dominance by gutting the once-vast powers of the Christian president. While the presidency continued to be the preserve of the Maronites, the president himself no longer controlled the central government but symbolized the authority of the state. The actual management of government belonged to a Council of Ministers led by a Sunni Muslim as prime minister. The newly created 108-seat parliament dispensed with the six-to-five ratio of Christians to Muslims in favor of a half-and-half split between various Muslim and Christian sects. Yet despite the alterations in the political contract between the Lebanese, only a small minority of those called to Taif would accept radical political change.

The Taif Accord confirmed only that Lebanon was a country of various sectarian communities that wished to live together. Ignoring the core problem of Lebanon—the conflicting definitions of Lebanese identity—the Taif pact did not constitute a paradigm shift or even a radical departure from earlier attempts at political reform. Nor did it lay out strategies that might breach the walls of communal loyalties and perceptions that formed bases of Lebanon's torment. Instead it embraced many of Lebanon's deeply ingrained political traditions. In the final analysis, the agreement at Taif rejuvenated the very system that had caused the disintegration of the country in the first place. Consequently leaders possessing neither the ability nor the incentive to rebuild what they themselves had destroyed were given the lead in restoring the state. As for the Lebanese people, they embraced an end to the war while ignoring the inescapable need to build a nation.

So it was that on November 4, 1989, the aging "foxes" of prewar Lebanese politics assembled in the tiny mountain town of Qlailaat, less than ten miles from the Syrian border. There they ratified the Taif Accord and elected as president the sixty-four-year-old Maronite Christian Rene Moawad, who, as a longtime member of Lebanon's prewar parliament, epitomized the cultivated, astute *zaim* trained in the old school. In his role as president, Moawad was to serve as confirmation of the absolute need to compromise and the grim necessity of accepting Syrian acquiescence to any negotiated settlement. It was in this atmosphere that Moawad on November 21 gave his first official speech. It rang with words of optimism and ended with an emotional plea to all Lebanese: "Let us come together, rejoice, reunite, and rebuild the country." But disappointment came quickly for those who thought the Lebanese people were at last on the road to genuine accommodation with each other.

Rene Moawad lasted only seventeen days as president. On the forty-sixth anniversary of Lebanon's independence, a four-hundred-pound bomb under Moawad's armor-plated Mercedes limousine exploded, hurling his body fifty yards and killing sixteen others, including thirteen of his security guards.* Every radio station in Lebanon dropped its regular programming to honor "the martyr of the promise of a better future." Only the television station controlled by Michel Aoun, the man who continued to claim to be the legitimate president of Lebanon, ignored the event by continuing its regular programming.

Yet those who killed Moawad failed to stop the process begun by the Taif Accord. The parliament quickly assembled to elect Elias Hrawi to fill the void. He would face the challenge of making the historic compromise at Taif work. In his initial address, the new president struck an optimistic tone: "To all those who are skeptical and doubtful I say:

---

* There was never an investigation into Moawad's death and those responsible remain a mystery.

do not worry. Lebanon, with the will of all, is a final nation for all the Lebanese. It is too solid to melt and too shiny to be eclipsed."* It was in the name of Lebanon that Hrawi dismissed Aoun as commander in chief of the army and gave him forty-eight hours to evacuate the presidential palace.

In his adamant refusal to accept the Taif Accord, Aoun acquired the aura of a cult figure, rebelling against the old *zuama* and the new warlords. Ignoring the direction from both their traditional and religious leaders, tens of thousands of young Maronites gathered in front of the presidential palace at Baabda to acclaim the defiant Aoun. Over the following weeks, speakers, singers, poets, and musicians wove together politics and entertainment. Absent was Aoun's bitter rival, Samir Geagea. The Maronites, who had fought for fifteen long years against the Lebanese Muslims, the leftists, and the PLO, were now poised to exhaust their remaining communal strength in a war between themselves.

The fighting between Michel Aoun, allied with those who rejected the Taif Accord, and Samir Geagea and the Lebanese Forces who accepted it would prove to be the most intense and bitter fighting since the outbreak of the war in 1975. Within the Christian enclave on the northern edge of Beirut, heavy artillery, tanks, and rockets commanded by the dueling chieftains pounded their fury on the most densely populated part of the country. With manpower claimed to be three to four times that of Aoun's army, the Lebanese Forces demonstrated utter disregard for what the Maronites had always considered their sacred community. The hard core of the militia deployed in Beirut was composed mostly of lower-middle-class refugees from northern Lebanon who fought as if they were in a foreign land. Conducting a scorched-earth policy against their "own," they fired their

---

* Quoted in Theodor Hanf, *Coexistence in Wartime Lebanon: Decline of a State and Rise of a Nation* (London: The Center for Lebanese Studies in association with I. B. Tauris, 1993), p. 608.

guns on Maronite rivals from schools, hospitals, and convents, killing more innocents than the enemy. In this sense, Geagea and the Lebanese Forces defeated themselves. Gathering behind his definition of the Christian role in Lebanon, Aoun survived. But not for long. An exasperated Syria had decided to stop the fighting.

On October 12, 1990, Damascus sent in elite troops to take up positions on the borders of Aoun's enclave. At seven o'clock the next morning, the Syrian Air Force swooped down on the presidential palace while Syrian tanks, accompanied by Lebanese tanks from the part of the army opposed to Aoun, advanced on east Beirut. Two and a half hours after the attack started, the self-declared president who had vowed to fight to the death fled to the French embassy, where he was granted political asylum. The long war was truly over.

AS AN UNEASY peace settled over Lebanon, revenge stalked the streets. Sunni politicians hid acts of vengeance under their urban façade. The Druze extracted retribution from a range of old and new enemies. Shia militiamen from Hezbollah, the "Party of God," roamed the Christian areas, abducting Christians to exchange for Shia Muslims held by the defeated Aoun. On October 21, a purely political vendetta was delivered on Dany Chamoun, the son of Camille. Gunmen posing as army soldiers burst into Chamoun's fifth-floor Beirut apartment at 7:10 a.m. to riddle him with bullets. Replaying the vengeance once wreaked on Tony Franjieh, the son of another Maronite chieftain, the unknown assailants also turned their silencer-equipped machine guns on Chamoun's wife and their two sons—Tarek, five, and Jerome, seven. Only eleven-month-old Tamara survived. The question that remained was, Did Dany Chamoun die at the hands of Syria because he had stood with Michel Aoun? Or was he just another victim of the Lebanese' own tribal vendettas? Prime Minister Selim Hoss, surveying the carnage, issued his own verdict: "[This is] a brutal crime committed by an enemy with evil intentions against the march of reconciliation and legitimacy."*

Despite the lingering aftershocks of war, battle-scarred Lebanon began to resurrect. Bulldozers clattered into central Beirut's streets, where ghostly superstructures of once-elegant apartment houses gave silent testimony to the violence. Blackened signs over deserted store-fronts marked long-gone coffee shops, flower venders, and booksell-ers. Martyrs' Square, once the proud symbol of Lebanon, was piled high with debris from a hundred battles. At its center, the statue of the martyrs, whose flaming torch had beckoned those from the sea into the harbor of Beirut, was riddled with bullets. It was in the shadow of these ruins that bulldozers, grinding out noise and belching black smoke, began to push away the barricades that divided east and west Beirut. The bulwarks between the Lebanese people would not be so easily removed.

THE LEBANESE CIVIL war had proved neither heroic nor redemptive. Nor had the terrible bloodshed enabled the Lebanese state to establish its integrity. Nor had it advanced the process of transforming a fragile state into an authentic nation. If it had, then perhaps those fifteen years of carnage might have been memorialized as a "glorious" national event that stood proud in the country's collective memory. But the war, along with its origins and consequences, defined by those who lived through it as "the events," was anchored in no coherent set of ideas and ended with no resolution of the issues that had ignited it. In this sense, the war was simply an occurrence for which no one would bear moral or legal responsibility. This was its tragedy. The Lebanese civil war, in its most poignant terms, had been destructive and futile, ugly and unfinished. It ended only because the Lebanese became numb to each other and

* Quoted in the *New York Times*, September 22, 1990.

the armed presence of Syria. In place of the artificial Lebanon of the golden age, the Lebanese faced the reality of a Lebanon now portrayed by destroyed cities and villages, financial collapse and hyperinflation, poverty and social decay, displacement and emigration.

Out of a population of 3 million, more than 143,000 died. Perhaps only five to ten percent of these victims belonged to one of the dueling militias. The rest were civilian bystanders, 40,000 of them children under the age of fifteen. Another estimated 500,000 people permanently left the country, taking with them their skills and resources. Among those who stayed, more than forty percent were displaced from their homes or communities. This was the awful human toll.

In terms of sheer physical damage, the cost of the war could be seen in deteriorated residential buildings and collapsed infrastructure. With no governmental authority capable of standing guard over Lebanon's natural beauty during the war years, greedy developers and desperate refugees had eaten up pristine coastline and littered it with kitschy resorts and private marinas, shoddy tenements and sprawling shanty-towns. The same forces defoliated the greenbelts, public parks, and terraced orchards. As a result, beautiful Beirut came out of the war with one of the lowest proportions of open space per capita in the world.

Economic devastation went hand in hand with physical destruction. During the first two years of the war, booty looted from public and private assets precipitated what some claim to be the greatest redistribution of wealth in modern Lebanon's history. In the rearranged economic order, a new class composed of war profiteers, contraband traders, and large-scale thieves flaunted its new wealth and privilege. But by war's end they, along with everyone else, felt the effects of a shrinking economy. By 1989, Beirut, the once-bustling business center of the Middle East, had permanently lost its place to Dubai, Abu Dhabi, and other sheikhdoms on the Persian Gulf. Lebanon was left with rampant inflation that shrunk incomes to sixty percent of the level Lebanon had achieved in 1974. Those most hurt were the middle class.

In a replay of Weimar Germany after World War I, small-business owners, salaried employees, and professionals found themselves carrying large bags stuffed with devalued Lebanese pounds to the markets to buy nothing beyond the essentials of life.

As important as the economic ramifications of civil war had been, it was the massive social upheavals between 1975 and 1990 that offered up the Lebanese state to the altar of communalism. The war sharpened communal identities in a population now huddled in exclusive, cloistered communities where political attitudes passed through the filters of the communities' own myths. If one of these communities had emerged victorious during the war, that group's military and political dominance would have, in all probability, deadened Lebanon's communal contract politics. Instead the verdict of the war was "no victor, no vanquished." Therefore, maintaining peace remained a matter of "maintaining a balance—of sharing power—and of preserving the rights of communities that view themselves as the bedrock on which the Lebanese state is constructed."* Such lack of a clear victor all but ensured that the centuries-old clannish arrangements under which the *zaim* system functioned would continue. It was only the actors who changed.

The first two years of the war eroded the authority of the traditional leaders. In a pattern being repeated across the Arab world, they were replaced by less well-known leaders, usually of a lesser social class or a more recent background. Only among the Druze and the northern Maronites could the genealogies of traditional leadership be found in the younger Jumblatts, Franjiehs, and Gemayels. If the reform movement of 1958–1970 had succeeded in replacing feudal families with national leaders, Lebanon might have made the critical transition from a collection of fiefdoms to an authentic republic. Instead the civil war

---

* Joseph Maila, "The Taif Accord: An Evaluation," in *Peace for Lebanon? From War to Reconstruction*, Deirdre Collings, editor (Boulder, Colo.: Lynne Rienner, 1994), pp. 31–32.

broke apart many traditional patron-client relations and in their place rose the warlords controlling patronage from inside territories built and defended on the basis of confession.

As the war ground on, more and more Lebanese brandished their own confession as both emblem and armor—emblem because confessional identity furnished the most viable medium for securing vital needs and benefits, and armor because confession supplied the shield against real or imagined threats. The more vulnerable the emblem, the thicker the armor. Conversely, the thicker the armor, the more vulnerable and paranoid the community. It was in the restriking of the same link between threatened communities and the urge to seek shelter in cloistered worlds that chained postwar Lebanon to the past.

And so the cycle was complete. Protracted and diffused hostility rendered territorial identities sharper. The more defined and concentrated communities became, the more tribalism embedded itself as each communal group vowed to liberate society from the despicable evil inherent in the other. Thus "the community, locality, neighborhood, or quarter was no longer simply a space to occupy or a place to live in and identify with. It became an ideology—an orientation or frame of reference through which groups interact and perceive others."*

PRESIDENT ELIAS HRAWI, with the support of Damascus, acted with remarkable energy and speed to implement the Taif Accord of October 1989. Perhaps because the cabinet and parliament brought together the old and the new power blocs in the Lebanese political system, the principles and reforms agreed to at Taif began to be codified. How the population reacted depended on the communal group. The Maronites simmered with resentment and the Sunnis expressed great satisfaction.

* Samir Khalaf, *Civil and Uncivil Violence in Lebanon: A History of Internationalization of Communal Conflict* (New York: Columbia University Press, 2002), p. 265.

The Shia grumbled and the Druze went along because there seemed no alternative for those who had reluctantly agreed to the accord.

The cabinet that took office in 1990 was the largest in Lebanese history. Instead of a group sharing a common ideology and committed to implementing similar policies aimed at the common good, it was a shaky coalition of thirty ministers representing all political parties and leanings except the Shia of Hezbollah, the Christian supporters of Michel Aoun, and the nonsectarian Communists. The majority came from the old political families who quickly moved to reestablish the patronage networks linking them to their clients. The president led the way by appointing his son-in-law and two prominent business associates as ministers. But the warlords were at the table also. Among the ministers of state without portfolio sat no less than seven of the militia leaders who had prosecuted the war.

A similar pattern emerged in the new, enlarged parliament equally distributed between Christians and Muslims. Although many of those seats went to real and not-so-real political parties, all the old political families occupied the seats they had always occupied.* Some fourteen of the deputies were the sons or close relatives of deceased deputies from the prewar period. Perhaps nothing better illustrated the hard truth that Taif had failed to affect the attitudes, behavior, and perceptions of the prewar political system. Whereas the pre-1975 elite was made up of landowners, notables, and professionals, the postwar elite consisted of the warlords and rich entrepreneurs, including the old *zuama*, a scattering of military figures, and the clients of Syria. Collectively it paralleled the prewar elite in its determination to block any reform that might result in a diminution of the privileges of those within the charmed circle of power. Thus this new elite nurtured the same seeds of destruction planted by the old elite between 1943 and 1975. So it was that postwar Lebanon moved on.

---

* The two exceptions were the parties founded by Pierre Gemayel and Camille Chamoun, two *zuama* dealt out by the Lebanese Forces.

———

ON MARCH 20, 1991, the government moved boldly to reestablish the power and authority of the state by ordering all militias to surrender their arms or face the might of "the brotherly Syrian army." The exception was Hezbollah, which both Damascus and the Muslim politicians in the majority allowed to keep its militia engaged against Israel in Tel Aviv's self-declared southern security zone.* Taking the Syrian threat seriously, the other private armies, Christians and Muslims, loaded up their rockets, artillery shells, mines, and ton upon ton of ammunition. Trucks carrying the explosive cargoes were joined by tanks and personnel carriers rumbling north, east, and south into the strongholds of the respective militias to await shipment abroad. The heavy weaponry seized by the Lebanese Forces during the fighting went back into the arsenal of the Lebanese army. Only light arms escaped collection. There were just too many for the government to round up. Nevertheless by May 1, 1991, the rule of the large militias had ended. That left the Palestinians to be brought under the control of Beirut.

THE TAIF ACCORD did not explicitly mention the Palestinians. But the issues of the Palestinians' sense of national identity and their armed presence in Lebanon were crucial if the authority of the Lebanese state was to be established. The armed manpower and rich treasury of the PLO had made the Palestinians one of the most powerful actors in the country after 1969. The situation changed only after the Israeli invasion of 1982 destroyed much of the PLO's organizational and military infrastructure and sent thousands of Palestinians into deeper exile. The PLO had made an attempt to return to Lebanon in 1985 but failed. In the "War of the Camps" that spanned 1985 to 1987, the Shia Amal launched a series of assaults against the Palestinians inside the barricades of their

* See chapter 6.

camps, killing perhaps three thousand people and destroying tens of thousands of humble homes. Nevertheless, after the Lebanese civil war the Palestinians once again demanded from Lebanon what they had won in 1969—a state within a state—commanding the right to make war on Israel from Lebanese territory. This time the Lebanese refused to comply.

In mid-May 1991, the Palestinians in southern Lebanon were ordered to surrender their weapons to the Lebanese army. The PLO refused, arguing that its armed force did not constitute a militia but an army engaged in the liberation of Palestine. As such, its mandate and manpower lay outside the authority of the Lebanese state. From across almost all segments of the political spectrum, from the Maronite Phalange to the Shia Amal, the Lebanese replied in unison. Sharing a rare opinion that overrode communal interests, most Lebanese fervently believed that the whole Lebanese tragedy had begun with the Cairo Agreement of 1969. Comprising a problem that could be resolved only in a larger regional context, the Palestinians had become an intolerable burden for Lebanon. As a result, on July 1, 1991, Christian and Muslim soldiers of the Lebanese army sent artillery shells and rockets crashing into Palestinian positions in southern Lebanon. Claiming a sweeping victory three days later, the army of postwar Lebanon began to collect all of the Palestinian heavy- and medium-caliber weapons stowed outside the camps. By the end of the year, Yasser Arafat and his Fatah faction—the largest group in the PLO—had no other choice but to order the demobilization of all of its regular military forces in Lebanon. All that remained of what had once been a powerful Palestinian armed presence on Lebanese soil were the lightly armed militias locked inside the refugee camps.

Once contained, the Palestinians fell prey to the merciless revenge of Lebanese of all persuasions. Unlike the situation in some other Arab countries, the Palestinians of Lebanon were forbidden to work outside the camps except as common laborers in construction and agriculture.

For the most part, they were denied the right to own property and their children were barred from the public schools. The omnipresent Palestinians of the early 1970s had been reduced to living in Lebanon as a faceless, stateless people confined inside walled camps guarded by the reconstituted Lebanese army.

On an emotional level, the emasculated Palestinians served as an important symbol of the reunification of Lebanon and the core of the Lebanese people's emerging historical memory. By providing the scapegoat upon which most of the responsibility for the war could be loaded, the Palestinians absolved the Lebanese of their own culpabilities in the war, allowing them to jettison the baggage of their previous and murderous domestic conflicts. The unity of action against the aliens constituted, in the eyes of the Lebanese, a celebrated milestone in the reconstruction of the state and the generation of a specific Lebanese identity.

BY MID-1991, most Lebanese began to glimpse rays of hope rising out of their perceptions of the future. In that extraordinary summer, capital flowed in and thousands of Lebanese returning from safe havens abroad overbooked Middle East Airlines so completely that even *wasta* (connections) could not secure a seat into Beirut. However, the visitors proved to be only voyeurs, returning to reconnect with family, assess the damage to ancestral homes, bask in the warm summer sun, and sip a little arak. Perhaps they declined to stay to rebuild their country because the characteristics that had defined Lebanon for so long were still there: family and communal rivalries, haunting fears and festering grievances of one community against another, unbalanced economic growth, and foreign interference. As important as the Taif Accord had been, its concentration on limited political reform and administrative reorganization had done little beyond applying a thin coat of plaster to the economic, social, cultural, and psychological cracks that had been exacerbated by the war.

Just as before the war, the interests of the political and economic elite took precedence over the interests of a nation. Sectarianism remained firmly entrenched, protected from challenge, modification, or abolition by an elite composed of the surviving *zuama*, the new warlords, and the clients of Syria determined to preserve their power. The hallowed tradition of laissez-faire also remained largely untouched. Agriculture continued to be starved of capital; the promotion of shipping, reexport, and transit still ranked above the creation of goods; and businesses remained family oriented, closing off outside investment or expansion to nonrelatives.

Institutionally the Lebanese civil service remained a product of Levantine culture. From the rungs of the ladder of social status, the public continued to look down on government jobs and pitied those employed as civil servants. With no social or economic incentive to serve the citizens of Lebanon, government departments and agencies were plagued by absenteeism and the Ottoman legacy of corruption and nepotism. Across society, *baksheesh*, or the tip, continued to be accepted as the key to government services. As it had always been, a few bills attached to an application produced a driver's permit, import or export license, water or electrical service, an official school transcript, or a forged university degree. Although common cocktail conversation among the upper and middle classes produced grave pronouncements on the importance of a system of law applicable to everyone regardless of class or stature, someone invariably stuck out an arm encircled with an expensive gold watch to brag about the "small fee" paid to a government official to escape the customs tax. These infractions of the law were not always minor. Importers regularly shipped in all manner of luxury goods in boxes marked "canned tuna" or "medical supplies," thus depriving the state of desperately needed revenues. This atmosphere of permissiveness was not much different from that in 1969 when several ministers and military officers purloined such a high percentage of the funds appropriated to buy French Crotal missiles that little was left for the missiles themselves.

Attitudes toward work also stayed the same. Status in status-obsessed Lebanon demanded an occupation that did not require any element of manual labor. The more education a person possessed, the more distance he or she put between an occupation or duty that required "dirtying of the hands." On the domestic scene, a maid was essential to a functioning household. Since Lebanese women, regardless of how poor they were, refused employment sweeping floors and making beds, the market for women from Syria, Asia, and Africa boomed even though the Lebanese themselves suffered from a high rate of unemployment.

But of all Lebanon's endemic problems, it was those tied to the economy that most propulsively drove the Lebanese on toward the next opportunity for reconciliation and recovery: the 1992 election.

DURING THE FIRST six months of 1992, the Lebanese pound depreciated 60.4 percent against the dollar. At the same time, the price of basic commodities rose by 68.8 percent. Because most commodities were imported, they were priced in dollars while most Lebanese were paid in pounds at an exchange rate of 2,000 to the dollar.* In protest against the rapidly worsening economic situation, a general strike called for May 6 paralyzed the country. Public wrath crossed the communal lines to destroy the office of the prime minister, the home of the finance minister, a hotel owned by the speaker of the parliament, and a string of gasoline stations belonging to the president's son. Unable to save itself, the government called new elections.

The Lebanese who had struck the deal at Taif always regarded elections as a key component in salving the wounds of war and restoring the state. International observers, cognizant of the fact that Lebanon possessed more experience in democracy than any other country in the Arab world, also embraced elections as a catalyst for reconciliation.

* On the eve of the war in 1975, the Lebanese pound traded at three to the dollar.

Instead, the elections of 1992 would accentuate, even widen, some of the country's deep fissures. It should have served as fair warning to those in the West who so fervently believed in 2003 that democracy can simply be imposed on cultures embedded in their own traditions.

Before an election for parliament could be held, forty new members were needed—thirty-one to fill vacant seats resulting from death and resignation and an additional nine others to achieve the Muslim-Christian parity agreed on at Taif. In an attempt to decrease confessional voting, the electoral law established a list system. Under it, the voter cast his or her ballot for multiple candidates. For example, five seats were allotted to the constituency of Aley—two for the Maronites, one for the Greek Orthodox, and two for Druze. Therefore, the voter cast a total of five votes, allocated respectively among the Maronite, Orthodox, and Druze candidates. In theory, this meant that in order to win, a candidate had to appeal across confessional lines. But the construction of the lists—the key phase of the election—took place weeks or months before election day in back rooms with no outside windows where communal leaders secured the interests of their communities in private deals. Thus another chance to institute policies and programs that could merge the Lebanese into a common citizenship was lost.

It was only the beginning of a corrupt process. The regional weight of the seats added to achieve Muslim-Christian parity was grossly uneven, designating one representative for 16,000 voters in the Bekaa compared with a countrywide average of one for 18,500. In another example, an estimated one-third of all voters dislocated by the war were unable to vote in their home constituencies and fared differently according to group. Druze from the Chouf could vote more easily than those from the Christian north and the Shia south. The only constant was the purpose of the many electoral manipulations: to ensure that the predominately Sunni and Druze champions of the Second Republic and candidates favorable to Syria won and their opponents lost.

Before the vote, angered Christians called for a boycott of the election to deny legitimacy to the new parliament. Yet the Maronites only managed to keep a sizeable portion of the electorate from the polls, guaranteeing that those who called the boycott would be underrepresented. And there were more ordinary factors that called the vote into question.

Even though Lebanon, like other countries practicing various forms of democracy, hides a soiled history of corrupt voting tactics, minimum standards had been respected.* Election campaigns had been conducted without restraint; the ballot, secret; poll officials, civil servants; and results, published promptly and in detail. But not in 1992.

In Jubayl district, conflict at a polling station kept election officials from entering the premises to conduct the vote. In other places confronting the same challenge, resourceful officials circumvented the blockades by setting up polling stations in tents and car trunks. But this diversionary tactic failed elsewhere because of the absence of ballots and ballot boxes. In an enormously tainted procedure, only twenty percent of the population elected Lebanon's first postwar government. The final insult to the whole process was the failure to post the official results by the close of 1992.

In the end, the election only rattled the unsteady postwar equilibrium that ended the civil war. Although the power configuration had shifted from Maronite Christians to Sunni Muslims and their Druze allies and the political base had broadened, confessional groups and family loyalties still reigned supreme in the realm of Lebanese identity. Neither bloodshed nor negotiations had been able to dislodge most Lebanese from their communal identities reinforced by centuries of tradition. This was the most deplorable shortcoming of the whole Taif process—the failure to put Lebanon on the road to national unity. Thus Lebanon remained shattered, its government discredited, its people denied genuine partici-

* The exception was the 1974 election, the last one before the eruption of the civil war.

pation in decisions affecting their own destiny, let alone their country's sovereignty and territorial integrity. What was left of the Lebanese state lay at the feet of the past, two powerful neighbors—Israel and Syria—and militant elements of the Shia who brought with them their own definition of a Lebanese state.

Chapter 6

The Rise of the Shia

They took my gown and turban from me,
and they kept me thirsty.

—Shia lament

We are Hosain's men, and this is our epoch . . .
Our name is "zealot" and our title "martyr."

—Shah Ismail, fifteenth century

An island nation of only 277 square miles, Bahrain lies in the Persian Gulf at the end of a causeway anchored on the eastern shore of Saudi Arabia. Its sandy soil is so devoid of color that it is almost white, enveloping the landscape in a ghostly aura. For generations, Bahrainis lived off the proceeds from fishing and selling low-grade pearls gathered by divers from the floor of the shallow inlets. Then came the oil boom. The capital of Manama exploded with high-rise buildings, wide thoroughfares, showy shopping malls, and fast-food restaurants.

Even now, glimpses of the impoverished past are visible in the old part of the city, where the inglorious palace once occupied by the ruling family is tucked into the narrow streets. Before the age of air-conditioning, a tall, square wind tower ingeniously designed to catch the sea breezes and direct them downward and the thick mud walls from which hung carved doors of weathered wood were the only means of mitigating the torrid summer heat of the Persian Gulf. Sizeable wooden chests embellished with ornate brass plates held in place by hundreds of studs and the distinctive Arabic coffee pots sitting on now cold embers are outward symbols of Bahrain's culture. But what says the most about Bahrain is the view from a large window on the second floor that frames the elongated dome of a Shia mosque, flanked by standards on which black flags of mourning fly for forty days following Ashura, the annual observance of the martyrdom of the Imam Hussein.

The Shia, who comprise over sixty-five percent of the population, render Bahrain different from the other countries that line the western coast of the Persian Gulf. Although all host significant Shia populations, only those of Bahrain live as a majority under the authoritarian hand of the Sunni sheikh Hamad bin Isa al Khalifa.

The sheikh, who declared himself king in 2002, reigns from a grand palace set on a low hill outside Manama. It is approached by a four-lane road lined with thick, immaculately trimmed grass, blooming flowers, and stately trees under which strutting peacocks proclaim a royal residence. Halfway between the main highway and the palace itself, the parkway is bisected by a high gate constructed of heavy iron that shuts the king off from his subjects. Bahrain's ordinary citizens are also shut out of the "royal city," a multiple-square-mile area spreading out in all directions from the palace that is reserved for the king's Sunni relatives and his high-ranking Sunni allies to whom belong the power and the money. Outside its perimeters, the Shia, who have been agitating against the status quo since the early 1980s, await the opportunity to seize it all.

Northward and slightly westward of Bahrain, the Shia of Iraq—some sixty percent of the population—have already staked their claim to the post–Saddam Hussein state. In the Shia holy cities of Najaf and Karbala, the southern port of Basra, and the crowded slums of Baghdad, where men and women lived for generations under the boot of the Sunni minority, Shia now strut their militias, claim most of the major positions in a struggling government, and largely man the army and the police. Too often those who were once oppressed now act as the oppressor. In throwing off the yoke of second-class citizenship, the Shia are also reordering the social, cultural, spiritual, political, and economic patterns put in place in the seventh century AD by Islam's conquering army.

The Islamic state Muhammad established at Medina gathered believers into a community ruled by the commands of God as communicated to the Prophet. With his death, family interests, personal ambitions, and differing theological viewpoints tore at Islam's unity. In 680, at Karbala, Islam experienced the seminal event that would divide the faith into orthodox Sunnis and dissenting Shia. Through history, theology, law, and culture, each developed a different approach to the faith.

Within the Arab world, the Shia remained a small minority. Although the non-Arab Persians in the sixteenth century embraced Shiism as the official faith of what is now Iran, the Shia of the Arab world continued to live in societies and political systems dominated by Sunnis. For centuries, Sunnis protected their cultural template and held power within a region ruled by the Umayyads and Abbasids of the Islamic Empire and the Turks of the Ottoman Empire. The overwhelming majority on the Sunni side of Islam branded the Shia *rafida*, "rejecters of Islam," and reviled them as "heretics." With the acquiescence and backing of colonial masters—both Ottoman and Western—society remained divided between the Sunni haves and the Shia have-nots.

As the Arab colonial possessions transformed into independent states, the Shia remained at the bottom of the social and political order. Even during the oil boom of the 1970s, the Shia of Saudi Arabia, who cluster in the Eastern Province and provide labor for the country's major oil fields, lived like stepchildren in a house of plenty. To the north in oil-rich Iraq, the Shia remained trapped in poverty-ridden villages scattered over the treeless wastes of the south, hid in the vast marshes, or squatted in the squalid slums of Baghdad. Long disadvantaged by the oldest and most profound division among Arabs, the Shia began their current and crucial rise to prominence and political power in Lebanon. Today the Shia from Lebanon to Iraq are reordering the Arab world.

JEBEL AMAL IS composed of a chain of rocky hills and shallow valleys that track southward from Sidon and eastward to the border of Syria. Beyond the coastal road that links Sidon with Tyre, fields of rich soil have been cut and cleared of rocks by generations of Lebanese farmers. Although the region has long claimed a significant Maronite population, Jebel Amal is for the Shia a revered piece of geography where they have lived out the real and theological legacy of Shiism, characterized by persecution, suffering, impotence, insecurity, and martyrdom.

The Shia have inhabited southern Lebanon for centuries.* Throughout the period of the Ottomans, they lived on the fringe of a society dominated by Christians and Sunni Muslims who labeled them as "dirty," "ignorant," "vulgar," "tasteless," and "sexually insatiable." These descriptions were augmented by a whole body of "Abu Ali" jokes that portrayed the followers of Islam's dissenting sect as thieves. Exiled to the periphery of the political and economic system, the Shia sat passively and nursed the deep and abiding sense of injustice that dwells at the core of their psyche.

In 1919, armed clashes between the Shia and the Maronites handed France the opportunity to break Jebel Amal off from Syria and wedge it into Greater Lebanon. At the time, the Shia comprised only seventeen percent of the total population of the new state. Their numbers were enough to guarantee them a role in the political system but not enough to secure them a slice of real power. Tied to the land by tradition and economics, the Shia lacked an educated elite or business class able to offer effective representation in the urbane capital of Beirut. Instead, a collection of Shia clan chieftains and large landowners were allowed to feed with the establishment at the trough of the Lebanese state in return for keeping their community docile.

When Lebanon gained its independence in 1946, the Shia remained

---

* As early as the sixteenth century, Shia clerics from Jebel Amal traveled to Safavid Iran to build Shia centers of learning.

the despised in a state governed by a Maronite-Sunni alliance. Within the confessional system, the reigning power brokers grudgingly granted the Shia a mere 3.2 percent of the higher posts in the civil service. In every other aspect of political and economic life, the proportions allotted to the Shia fell far short of fair representation for their growing numbers within the population. With the Shia essentially frozen out, leadership of the government remained in the clutches of a Christian-Sunni elite, and Shia leadership stayed with traditional sheikhs more interested in the perks of privilege than in the upward mobility of their clients. Typical of these Shia leaders was Ahmed Assad, a Shia deputy in parliament who responded to a man's request for help in sending his gifted son to high school in Beirut, "Why do you want me to do that? Is it not enough for you that I am sending my son Kamel to school?"* It was a sentiment that brazenly illustrated the widening gap between the aspirations and realities of the Shia of Lebanon.

Under the reformist presidency of Fuad Shihab (1958–1964) a precious few government scholarships to Lebanese universities began to trickle down to the Shia. Education, in turn, offered the chance to compete for better-paying jobs abroad. Carried by their precious educations, hundreds of Shia escaped the grueling toil of the land and the grinding poverty of southern Lebanon to enter commerce in West Africa and the automotive factories of Detroit. The remittances they sent home provided a future for the next generation.

During the 1950s, the educated Shia of what had become a slowly expanding middle class gravitated to the socialist or communist parties on the political left. But these political ideologies, rooted in the inequalities of class, failed to address the Shia's particular situation or rub the touchstones of Shia identity. Instead of Marxism, the religious rituals associated with Ali and Hussein began politically to awaken the uneducated. In the uniquely Shia ceremonies of Ashura, simple men saw

* Quoted in Dib, *Warlords and Merchants*, p. 251.

in the practice of self-flagellation the prerequisite to revolution. Theology also produced the cleric who would lead the Lebanese Shia out of the political wilderness.

Old and sturdy cords bind the Shia communities of Lebanon to the religious establishment of Shia Iran. They are spun out of religious faith, kinship, and fraternity among clerics who trained at the same Shia seminaries. In 1957, a young Iranian cleric of great intellect and promise was called to Lebanon to take up a position as the religious leader of the southern city of Tyre. He brought with him a reformist theology concocted from equal parts traditional values and political action.

Musa al Sadr was born in 1928 in Qom, the major Shia theological center in Iran. A *sayyid*, or one who claims descent from the Prophet Muhammad, Sadr was an Arab by descent although he was Iranian by language and culture. In Shia culture, where personal charisma is a fundamental requirement for leadership, he possessed the looks and aura of a cult figure. Six feet, six inches tall, intense eyes blazing out of a strong face fringed with a lush, precisely trimmed beard, Sadr captivated his new followers. Yet it was the magnetism of his personality and the grandeur of his oratory that mobilized the disinherited Shia.

Throwing aside the practice of writing exhaustive treatises on obscure points of Islamic law, the highly educated and worldly Sadr seized on the great moments in the history of Shiism, infused them with political meaning, and lifted them up like torches before the eyes of the Lebanese Shia. In the martyrdom of Hussein at Karbala, Sadr held up before his followers political courage in pursuit of Shiism's central theme: justice within an equitable society. By similarly painting other religious traditions with contemporary imagery, he summoned the Shia into the political arena.

In the first phase of his master plan to empower the Shia, Sadr sought out young men who possessed the money, education, and will to elbow their way into Lebanon's rigid confessional hierarchy. Then he awakened the slum dwellers of Beirut, the peasants of the south, and the sometimes wild clansmen of the Bekaa. To them he issued his battle cry: "O rising generations, if our demands [for political and economic equality] are not met, we will set about taking them by force: if this country is not given, it must be taken."* But before Lebanon could give or the Shia could take, the country and its rebellious minority became trapped between the aims of the Palestinians and the resolve of the Israelis.

In 1968 when Palestinian commandoes began running raids into Israel from bases in southern Lebanon, Israel's low-flying planes struck back. Yet the bombs they delivered hit more Shia than Palestinians. As the war of wills continued to send Palestinian guerrillas into Israel and Israeli planes over Lebanon, terrified Shia farmers and shop owners piled family members onto the beds of pickup trucks or cardboard luggage on the roofs of battered Mercedes taxis for the desperate flight to Beirut. There, in the squalor of the city's southern quadrant, thousands of proud men—the custodians of family life in a powerfully patriarchal society—found themselves stripped of their honor. And thousands of women—the providers of the family's physical needs—faced the daunting task of putting together makeshift homes among strangers. Uprooted from their ancestral villages first by the economics of the 1940s and 1950s and later by the fear of the late 1960s, the Shia floundered. In the confusion and misery, what little authority had been retained by traditional political bosses shifted toward Musa al Sadr.

Benefiting from the personal devotion and obeisance to religious leaders that is one of the hallmarks of Shia theology, Sadr rallied his followers against a government both unable and unwilling to protect the south against the Palestinian commandoes and the increasingly bloody reprisals of Israel. In challenging the government, he also challenged the basic, if imprecise, Christian-Muslim and right-left divi-

---

* Quoted in Rabinovich, *War for Lebanon, 1970–1985*, p. 39.

sions of Lebanon. Rejecting labels in the name of his followers, Sadr proclaimed, "We are neither of the right nor of the left but we follow the path of the just."*

Sadr ranked as a Lebanese nationalist if for no other reason than he regarded Lebanon as *al watan nihai*, the final homeland of the Arab Shia. Although Shia economic interests lay with the left of the political spectrum, Sadr saw in the ideology of the Arab left the strong current of Arab nationalism, which in the twentieth century particularly had played its part in the Shia's historic subjugation to the Sunnis. Sadr also resisted the demand of the leftist bloc for subservience to the Palestinian movement, which was inflicting its own misery on the Lebanese Shia.

This combination of the demand for equality in the political system for a community that now constituted almost thirty percent of the population, and outrage at the government's failure to protect the Shia from clashes along Lebanon's southern border, led Sadr to launch the Shia's own political movement: Harakat al-Mahrumin, the "Movement of the Deprived."

BY THE EARLY 1970s, Sadr's followers had bestowed on him the title of imam, a distinction that he never accepted or rejected. Its significance resided in the symbolism of Sadr's status among his followers. Shiism recognizes only twelve Imams. The first eleven succumbed to battle, poison, or prison at the hands of what the Shia regard as unjust Sunni usurpers of religious authority. According to Shia theology, the Twelfth Imam vanished to live in concealment until he returns as the *mahdi*, or savior. Drawing from the Hadith, Shia tradition frames the promise of the Hidden Imam in these words: "He will fill the earth with equity and justice as it was filled with oppression and tyranny."

Among the Lebanese Shia, the last years of Lebanon's golden age

---

* Quoted in Norton, *Amal and the Shi'a*, p. 42.

belonged to Musa al Sadr. He was the beacon of the "Shia awakening and the stand bearer of [the] Shia challenge to both the gauzy fiction of pan-Arab unity and the cement hard-reality of Sunni hegemony."* In March 1974, seventy-five thousand people gathered in Baalbek to hear the "imam." In his sermon, Sadr struck a recurrent theme. Thrusting the Shia economic reality into the face of those in power, he cried, "Let us look at the ghettoes of Beirut: Oh men in power, do you not feel ashamed that a few kilometers away from your homes are houses that are not fit for human habitation?"† And he castigated those who wreaked havoc on the Shia south: "The PLO is a factor of anarchy in the south . . . We have had enough!"‡ That same year, demonstrators from remote Shia villages marched on the parliament building in Beirut carrying placards that read, "We are part of Lebanon, Mr. President."

These consistent calls for empowerment of the Shia were seen by the Sunni establishment and the Palestinians as a betrayal of Arabism. In a sense, that was Sadr's goal—the development of a political identity among the Shia distinct from the Sunni identity wrapped in Arab nationalism. Yet when the civil war came in 1975, Musa al Sadr reluctantly followed the leftist National Movement in which the Sunnis and Arab nationalism dominated. In the first phase of the war (1975–1976), roughly one-half of the thirty thousand to forty thousand Muslims killed were Shia. Assessing the carnage, Sadr secretly began to expand his own Shia militia, which he called Amal, or "hope."§ But the new arena of war

---

* Vali Nasr, *The Shia Revival: How Conflicts within Islam Will Shape the Future* (New York: W. W. Norton, 2006), p. 113.

† Quoted in Fouad Ajami, *The Vanished Imam: Musa al Sadr and the Shia of Lebanon* (Ithaca, N.Y.: Cornell University Press, 1986), p. 158.

‡ Quoted in Juan R. I. Cole and Nikki R. Keddie, *Shiism and Social Protest* (New Haven, Conn.: Yale University Press, 1986), p. 165.

§ Amal is the acronym for Afwaj al Muqawama al Lubnaniya, or Lebanese Resistance Battalions.

in which Lebanon's protagonists were playing out their rivalries no longer included the field of moral persuasion in which Sadr so excelled.

Despite strong opposition from Maronites, Sunnis, Druze, and Palestinians, Sadr continued his frenetic travels on behalf of the Shia cause.* But the awakening of the Shia by the voice of Sadr had become for some Sunnis an intolerable threat to pan-Arabism throughout the Arab world. On August 25, 1978, Sadr arrived in the Libyan capital of Tripoli accompanied by one of his clerical assistants and a journalist. Six days later, a group of Lebanese acquaintances observed him leaving his hotel to attend a meeting with Muammar Qaddafi. No one ever saw Musa al Sadr again. That night his luggage arrived in Rome on Alitalia flight number 881 and was checked into the Holiday Inn by two Libyans. The imam had vanished.†

Sadr's disappearance restored any of the mystique he had lost to his rivals and detractors. To the Shia of Lebanon, he became the vanished imam, the concealed one moving among them who would one day return to preside over a redeemed world. As extraordinarily important as he had been before vanishing, Sadr became even more significant afterward. Perhaps this was appropriate. The cleric had always dealt in symbols, and no symbol held more meaning for the Shia community than a leader—an imam to most—vanishing without a trace. What he left behind was the box of Shia grievances he had opened.

THE POLITICALIZATION OF Lebanon's Shia was already a reality when revolution rocked Shia Iran in 1979. Although it began as a

---

* Shia support for Sadr in Lebanon was not universal. Some were critical of the wedding of religion and politics, others were rivals for his power and prestige.

† Although his disappearance remains a mystery, suspicion focused on Muammar Qaddafi, who perhaps saw himself as the instrument through which the Sunnis would quell Sadr's appeal to the Shia throughout the region.

broad-based revolt by people of all social classes and religious persuasions against the monarchy of Muhammad Reza Shah, the movement
for political reform fell into the hands of Ayatollah Ruhollah Khomeini,
the steel-edged symbol of resistance to the shah. Within two years, he
would dismantle the secular republic created in the aftermath of the
shah and put in its place an Islamic republic ruled by clerics.

More than a rebel against the existing political order, Khomeini was
a theological revolutionary. In a series of nineteen lectures delivered
in 1963 in the seminary in Najaf, Khomeini shifted almost thirteen
hundred years of Shia theology in the framework of the *velayat-e faqih*,
the "Guardianship of the Jurist." Rejecting the "quietist" tradition of
Shiism that maintains a high, thick wall between the pious believer
and the "corrupting influences" of government of whatever form or
persuasion, Khomeini declared that religion is politics and politics is
religion. What followed was his argument for an Islamic state built on
a simple premise. Divine will established Muhammad's just and sacred
community on earth. On his death, the future of that divinely inspired
community fell to the Twelve Infallible Imams beginning with the just
and righteous Ali and ending with Muhammad al-Muntazar, who disappeared in 874. In the absence of the Twelfth, or Hidden Imam, divine
will permits neither injustice nor ungodly rule. Until the Twelfth Imam
physically reappears, it is the most just and the most knowledgeable
among the *mujtahids* who possess the religious and political authority
to direct the Muslim community.* All other authority including king-
ship is illegitimate.

But not all Shia agreed with Khomeini's revolutionary revision of
Shia theology. Other learned ayatollahs among the highest reaches of

---

* The *mujtahid* or "jurist" is a combination of theologian and judge. In Shia Islam,
the *mujtahids* gain their position through their followers. As representatives of not only
the Twelfth Imam but also of those who look to them as spiritual guides, theoretically
the "just jurists" make their decisions in the interests of the people.

the clerical hierarchy warned against the contaminating effects of a system of governance in which there is no division between the realm of God and the realm of the state. But after the Iranian revolution in 1979, mullahs seeking to become politicians imposed their views upon the dissenting clerics through public rebuke, ridicule, intimidation, censorship, and house arrest. Outside Iran, the Shia of the Arab world became bolder in seeking their rights and representation under the Khomeini model. Yet in Lebanon, Amal stayed on the path originally charted by the missing Musa al Sadr—Shia empowerment in the existing political order.

In 1980, Nabih Berri, a forty-one-year-old lawyer as bland as Musa al Sadr had been charismatic, took leadership of Amal. He possessed none of the customary credentials for political leadership in Lebanon. Born in Freetown, Sierrra Leone, he was the son of a Lebanese Shia who had emigrated to West Africa to become a successful businessman. He graduated from neither Université Saint-Joseph nor the American University of Beirut but from the heavily Muslim Beirut University College. He left Lebanon after graduation to live in the United States in the early 1960s and again briefly in the 1970s. And he represented the Shia middle class rather than a network of downtrodden peasants and urban poor. Lastly, he was incapable of fulfilling the role of successor to Musa al Sadr because he was a secularist who brought with him none of the religious credentials of Amal's founder.

When Berri took over Amal, the movement's actual membership relative to the number of its sympathizers was miniscule. In one major Shia village, only ninety men out of an active male population of fifteen hundred carried an Amal card. The rest who said they were with "Harakat Amal" were merely confirming their acceptance of Amal's message, not affiliation with its organization. At the time, they did not embrace the revolutionary theology of the Iranian revolution but shared Musa al Sadr's opinion of Khomeini as a rabble rouser spewing unorthodox views on religion and politics. But a new chapter in Shia politics was about to open, and again the first sentence would be written by another Israeli invasion of Lebanon.

ON MARCH 14, 1978, the Israelis unleashed their firepower in another attempt to cleanse south Lebanon of Palestinian commandoes. In the process, Israel killed two thousand Shia, destroyed twenty-five hundred Shia houses, and sent another wave of Shia refugees fleeing toward Beirut. Driving north of the Litani River east of Sidon, Israeli army units fanned out over the hills, rounding up Lebanese Shia along with Palestinians. The international community, interested in containing the violence in Lebanon, responded through United Nations Security Council Resolution 425. Passed on March 19, it ordered Israel out of Lebanon and put in place as peacekeepers the United Nations Interim Force in Lebanon (UNIFIL). Israel complied by moving back across the border, leaving behind a proxy militia.

Then came 1982. The Shia initially welcomed the Israelis as a force to liberate them from the Palestinian commandoes. Consequently, as tank-led columns rolled through villages, smiling Shia tossed flowers to Israeli soldiers and ran alongside the open personnel carriers, offering cold fruit juice while murmuring words of thanks for their deliverance. But the Israelis proved ignorant of the Shia and ignored the warning delivered by the Israeli Arabist Moshe Sharon prior to Tel Aviv's move into Lebanon: "Do not join those who murdered Husain, because if you bring the Shia to identify you with the history of [their] suffering, the enmity that will be directed at you will have no bounds and no limits. You will have created for yourselves a foe whose hostility will have a mystical nature and a momentum which you will be unable to arrest."*

Instead of partnering with the Shia against the PLO, Israel slammed down its iron fist, turning the Shia's liberation from the Palestinians

---

* Quoted in Norton, *Amal and the Shia*, p. 113

into occupation by the Israelis. In sweeps through villages, members of the Israeli Defense Forces (IDF) and its militia, manned by Maronites of the south and Shia mercenaries, gathered up Shia suspected of sympathies with the PLO. In violation of the Geneva Convention, some were marched across the border to detention in Israel. Back in their villages, frightened women clutching weeping children clustered together as they watched their houses systematically blown apart by demolition teams on the mere suspicion that their husbands or sons were PLO collaborators. In some cases, whole villages were reduced to pulverized concrete. To the north, the Shia of Beirut were living through the merciless Israeli siege of the city, which lasted from June to August. Across Lebanon, the words of Musa al Sadr came back to the Lebanese Shia: "Israel is the very embodiment of evil."* The irony of Israel's venture into Lebanon was the birth of Hezbollah, the Islamist wing of the Lebanese Shia inspired and encouraged by Ayatollah Ruhollah Khomeini.

During that dreadful summer of 1982, a segment of Amal began to split away from Berri and the policy of seeking equal rights in a secular Lebanon. Fed by the utter despair brought by the Israeli invasion, inspired by the success of the Iranian revolution, and confident of the charismatic Khomeini's support for their political activism, Amal's dissenters drove toward their goal of an Islamic state in Lebanon. In a compelling litany, militant Shia clerics cried that the Shia had suffered at the hands of the Ottoman Empire, the Western colonial powers, the Christian and Sunni Lebanese, the Palestinians, and now the Israelis. Hurling their fury at Arab countries that had failed to come to Lebanon's defense against Israel, they rejected the Arab nationalism of the Sunnis and the Marxism of the leftists. In the complexity and confusion of wartime Lebanon, the Shia militants offered a simple message: the future of the Shia lay within the distinctive culture of the followers of the martyred

* Quoted in Cole and Keddie, *Shiism and Social Protest*, p. 149.

Ali and Hussein. They would create a political world of their own in multireligious, multisectarian Lebanon.

Thus a number of the militant Shia clerics organized fledgling groups that shared the common goal of creating an Islamic state in Lebanon. Some of these groups coalesced into a fluid organization called Hezbollah, the Party of God. The name came from a verse in the Koran that reads, "Those who accept the mandate of God, his prophet and those who believe, Lo! The Party of God, they are victorious."* Although Hezbollah at the time was more an idea than an organization, its devotees looked to Sheikh Muhammad Hussein Fadlallah as the ideologue, face, and voice of that idea. Counter to Musa al Sadr's commitment to a common national identity for all Lebanese, Fadlallah stressed loyalty to the transnational ideology projected by Iran's Khomeini. Yet in an important sense, Shia militancy that boiled out of Hezbollah was the culmination of the process of politicalization initiated by Sadr.

While the Israelis were still pounding Beirut, Hezbollah began to add muscle to the bare bones of its organization when an estimated one thousand Revolutionary Guards dispatched by Iran arrived in the Bekaa Valley. Armed with Ayatollah Fadlallah's message of Islamic revolution and reenforced by Iranian manpower and money, Hezbollah drained support away from secular Amal. As early as 1982, the men of Hezbollah mobilized the mystique of martyrdom within Shiism to add another tactic to their strategy: political theater performed on the stage of terrorism.

It was not Hezbollah that introduced terrorism into the Lebanese civil war. Throughout the long years of the conflict, wanton acts of terror had been inflicted by faceless individuals and groups but elicited notice only if the victims were people of rank like the French ambassador or the Lebanese publisher of *Al-Hawadith*, a well-known newspaper. In 1982 the radicalized Shia changed that pattern. Dismissing anonym-

* Sura 5:56.

ity, they proudly lay claim to acts of terror perpetrated for political purpose. Their main target would prove to be the Western presence in Lebanon, particularly that of the United States. In a series of savage, spectacular attacks, the American embassy was hit by suicide bombers more than once, and in October 1983 a jerry-rigged barracks near the airport collapsed under the force of explosives delivered by a Mercedes truck. Two hundred and forty U.S. Marines died. By early February of 1984, the rest of the leathernecks in Lebanon boarded ships headed for home. Militant Islam had taken on the United States and won.*

Soon Westerners still hanging on in Beirut began to disappear off the streets. Although the hostage takers included radical Palestinians, a suspected Sunni Muslim group, and cells with unconfirmed origins and ties, in Western eyes it was those who shared the ideology of Hezbollah who became synonymous with the terrorism of captivity. Then on June 14, 1985, the men of Hezbollah upped the ante again when hijackers forced TWA flight number 847 from Athens to Rome to land in Beirut. For seventeen days, a negotiator from Amal shuttled back and forth between Hezbollah and those governments seeking the release of the hostages. The drama ended in a six-way deal among Amal, Hezbollah, the United States, Israel, Syria, and Iran. But as the hijacking of a plane faded from the headlines, the random kidnappings of Westerners ratcheted up again as the number of those who were or had been hostages surpassed seventy.

Hostage-taking had become a cheap expression of power, for "it is not in the existence of terrorism, but in the image of impotence and vacillation that terrorist attacks can create . . . [that shapes a perception] of growing and ever-more-militant dissent. "† In the scramble for power within Lebanon, little men who had spent their lives at the bottom of

---

* See chapter 7.

† Mazher A. Hameed, *Arabia Imperiled: The Security Imperatives of the Arab Gulf States* (Washington, D.C.: Middle East Assessment Group, 1986), p. 51.

Lebanon's social order soared in status as hostage takers of the previous giants of the West.

The expulsion of the PLO from Lebanon in 1982 had removed the Palestinian yoke from the neck of the Shia. Those drawn into the circle of militant Shia politics began to claim their place as the dominant Muslim force in Lebanese politics. In 1987, Hezbollah, supported by Iran, and Amal, backed by Syria, lined up against each other in a showdown to determine dominance within the Shia community of Lebanon. In urban warfare in May 1988, a curly haired, unshaven Amal militiaman carrying a grenade bag and an automatic rifle peered out from behind the corner of a west Beirut building plastered with pictures of Nabih Berri. Across a space littered with burned-out cars and a denuded tree, another militiaman wearing a full beard, a ragged shirt, and an elastic headband bearing the yellow-and-green logo of Hezbollah glimpsed his Amal adversary before empting his recoilless rifle in his direction. Civilians caught between Amal and Hezbollah retreated into basement bomb shelters and pockmarked stairwells to wait out the fighting, while the International Red Cross issued urgent appeals to the rival militias to allow rescue workers into cordoned-off streets to remove decaying bodies. Outside Beirut, picturesque towns in the south devolved into pits where the Shia inflicted suffering on their own people. As a measure of the contest, two thousand Shia died and six thousand others were wounded during the autumn and winter of 1987–1988 in the struggle for hegemony.

When the parties to the Lebanese civil war arrived in Taif in September 1988 to negotiate an end to the war, Hezbollah already overshadowed the more moderate Amal. Much of the reason lay in Hezbollah's armed resistance to the Israeli occupation of southern Lebanon dating back to the Litani operation of 1978. Holding high its shield as the vanguard against the Israeli presence in southern Lebanon, Hezbollah rejected the demand that all militias turn over their weapons to the Lebanese army, the reconstituted agent of central authority in Lebanon. In the end, the other parties hammering out the new order for Lebanon caved in to Hezbollah's demand for one reason: there was no other choice if the historic compromise necessary to reconstitute the Lebanese state was to succeed.

Hezbollah again demonstrated its power in 1990 when it concluded a truce with Amal. In the deal, the secularists of Amal disarmed their militia but the Islamists of Hezbollah continued their own guerrilla campaign to drive Israel out of southern Lebanon. Most Lebanese, including those in Amal, were willing to stand aside and let them try.

EVER SINCE THE PLO planted commando bases in southern Lebanon, Israel had employed military might, advanced technology, and tough diplomacy in an ongoing effort to secure its border with Lebanon. That is why Tel Aviv sent its troops across that border in March 1978 and why Israel continued to hold sway over a strip of land in the south one hundred kilometers (60 miles) long and eight to twenty kilometers (4.8 to 12 miles) wide, which was essentially a buffer zone between the Israeli border and the rest of Lebanon. It was patrolled by a two-thousand-man militia that Israel trained and supplied with uniforms, weapons, ammunition, provisions, and paychecks. Manpower was drawn from the local population that had long been thirty-five percent Christian and sixty percent Shia. The Christians joined for the cause of Christian Lebanon. The Shia hired themselves out as mercenaries. Originally put in place after Israel bowed to the United Nations' demand that it withdraw from Lebanon, the militia's status and operations increased in May 1980, when it became the South Lebanon Army (SLA).

After the 1982 Israeli invasion of Lebanon failed to cleanse the south of Palestinian commandoes, the thin layer of insulation along Israel's northern territory rose to the level of strategic imperative in the eyes of those responsible for Israel's security. As a result, Tel Aviv inserted elements of the famed Israeli Defense Forces (IDF) into the "security zone."

But the combination of the SLA and the IDF failed to seal the border against threats coming from Lebanon. Consequently, Israel made two more major incursions into southern Lebanon: Operation Accountability in 1993 and Operation Grapes of Wrath in 1996. Both were aimed at Hezbollah, which by then had become a greater military challenge to Israel than the decimated Palestinian presence in Lebanon.

Operation Accountability, designed to eliminate Shia guerrillas and punish those responsible for attacks against Israeli civilian and military targets, began on July 25, 1993. It confirmed the warning to the Islamic militants issued by Prime Minister Yitzhak Rabin: "If there is no peace and quiet for our settlements, there will be no peace and quiet for those who attack them."* For a week, artillery, attack helicopters, jet fighters, and naval warships punished an arc from the Mediterranean coast to the slopes of Mount Hermon. Defiant Hezbollah fighters hit back firing Katyusha rockets into northern Israel, forcing thousands of Israelis to take refuge in bomb shelters. But it was the Shia of southern Lebanon who suffered the most.

The destruction wrought by the Israeli onslaught was staggering. In towns and villages, small merchants and weathered farmers stood speechless outside devastated shops and dwellings. Others sat in ruins, sobbing and cursing Israel for the attack, Hezbollah guerrillas for provoking it, and the Lebanese government for failing to provide protection. Still others fled. Upwards of three hundred thousand people, out of a total population of eight hundred thousand, bundled children into trunks of cars with missing lids, and tied mattresses, cooking pots, and bundles of clothes on roofs punctured with shrapnel, to join the caravan heading north to Beirut. Along the jammed coastal road and in the narrow streets of Beirut's southern suburbs, young men of Hezbollah collected donations for the new refugees now piling into temporary shelters provided by schools and mosques.

* Quoted in *Macleans*, August 9, 1993, p. 26.

Yet Operation Accountability failed to contain Hezbollah militarily. Israeli soldiers in the security zone continued to fall victim to guerrilla attacks. Pressure exerted on the militant organization by Syria and Iran went unrewarded. And the Lebanese government reconstituted at Taif found itself powerless to stop Hezbollah from firing rockets into northern Israel. If the Lebanese government deployed the army of the state to contain Hezbollah, the public reaction threatened to set the country on fire from the northern border of the security zone to the southern suburbs of Beirut. No one understood this better than Rafik Hariri, the Sunni prime minister, who publicly acknowledged that "nobody can put the resistance in jail . . . It would spark a new civil war."*

A feeble attempt to give a measure of authenticity to Beirut's claim of control over southern Lebanon was made by establishing a checkpoint near the security zone manned by members of the Lebanese army. But when Israeli missiles began to fall, the soldiers of the national army fled, leaving the bearded fighters of Hezbollah to stand against the armed power of the Israelis.

Hezbollah survived in the field of the security zone because it enjoyed the same advantageous conditions shared by all guerrilla organizations: a geographic base, local support, a decentralized military structure, mobility, and tactics that included ambushes and hit-and-run attacks. But Hezbollah possessed something more: moral certitude. While Amal had evolved into a traditional political party with its leader, Nabih Berri, presiding as the speaker of the Chamber of Deputies, Hezbollah remained a creature of the *velayat-e faqih* conceived by Iran's Ayatollah Ruhollah Khomeini. Functioning under a theology that combines politics and religion, its clerical leadership controlled membership as well as policy. New recruits passed through rigorous indoctrination into Hezbollah's ideology and culture, acceptance of the dictates of the party's leadership, and the importance of martyrdom as a dimension

* Quoted in the *Independent* (London), August 7, 1993.

of politics and faith. More than military training, the Hezbollah recruit underwent a spiritual transformation. At the end, he was emotionally and psychologically committed to armed *jihad* even at the cost of his own life. Imbued with the sense of martyrdom that is so central to Shia Islam, the Hezbollah fighter lined up for guerrilla operations.

From what were little more than toeholds of territory, Hezbollah militiamen ran attacks against a far-superior armed force. And as expected, martyrdom was often the result. But by 1995, the ratio of Hezbollah casualties to those of the IDF were no longer heavily skewed in favor of the Israelis. Heavier armaments provided largely by Iran, plus experience and improved tactics, had steadily dropped the casualty rate to less than two militiamen to one Israeli. Feeling the pressure from this declining ratio, Israel once again attacked southern Lebanon on April 11, 1996, in Operation Grapes of Wrath.

Withering firepower from the Israeli arsenal shattered houses and shops, tore down power lines, ruptured reservoirs, smashed roads and bridges, and slaughtered livestock. On day eight of the onslaught, perhaps as many as thirty-six 155-millimeter howitzer shells crashed into the UN post at Qana, where six hundred Lebanese refugees had spent a week hanging out their laundry on the fences and tethering their livestock in adjacent fields under the protection of UN peacekeepers. When the shelling ceased, 102 people had been literally blown to pieces.* The shaken commander of the post reported, "There were babies without heads. There were people without arms and legs."†

Operation Grapes of Wrath, which caused an estimated $200 million in damage, resulted in a rare moment in Lebanon—Muslims and Christians united in anger and mourning. This solidarity, not seen

---

* The attack is still controversial, as is the actual number of people killed. Israel claimed the camp was not targeted. According to Tel Aviv, the bloodshed came as a result of misguided fire aimed at Hezbollah military positions.

† Quoted in *Time*, April 29, 1996, p. 52.

since before the war, was symbolized by black ribbons tied on car antennas, candles burning on balconies in both east and west Beirut, mosques packed to capacity with men bowed in prayer, and church bells tolling in remembrance of the dead. On April 30, Shia and Sunni Muslims, Druze, and Christians gathered at Qana to remember those killed. Behind a mass grave, photographs of the victims hung from a concrete-block wall. Black banners draped around them decried Israel's "terrorism" and "barbarity." To the side, the Shia had planted a sign characteristic of them alone. It read, "Qana is the Karbala of the twentieth century."

Despite its ability to inflict terrible pain on southern Lebanon, Israel suffered its own pain at the hands of Hezbollah. Over the duration of Operation Grapes of Wrath, Hezbollah fired six hundred of its own rockets into the northern Galilee, sending twenty-five thousand Israelis into bomb shelters. On the Lebanese side of the border, Israeli soldiers remained prey to the increasingly effective and disciplined Hezbollah resistance. The ongoing attacks by committed guerrillas carrying the image of Ali constituted more than military operations. They were also psychological strikes on Israeli soldiers burrowed in defensive positions who, in spite of their tanks and sophisticated weapons, felt increasingly isolated in a foreign land. Hezbollah's television station kept up the pressure with its infamous "Who's Next" campaign. A constantly updated collection of pictures of Israeli casualities ended with a blank space filled with a large question mark. By 1997, IDF soldiers were paying a steep price for Tel Aviv's occupation of the security zone.

In February, seventy-three Israeli soldiers died when two helicopters collided en route to Israeli-occupied southern Lebanon. In late August, five more burned to death in a brushfire started by Israeli shelling. On September 4, eleven elite commandoes making a coastal landing at night north of the security zone ran into an ambush. In a mortar attack on the rescue team sent in to recover the bodies of the commandoes, a military doctor died.* Twenty-two other Israelis died in various attacks over the course of 1997. In all, it was a bleak year for the IDF, leading Hezbollah to boast, "The resistance has made a mockery of the Israeli war machine."†

Hezbollah fielded only an estimated five to six hundred hard-core fighters. It could draw on a further one thousand men who, when called, dropped their tools of trade to reenforce the regulars. No longer a ragtag force, Hezbollah soldiers were equipped with M16 or AK47 assault rifles, radios, night-vision goggles, flak jackets, and helmets. Special units owned and used 81- and 120-millimeter mortars, the Sagger wire-guided missile, and the Spigot antitank weapon capable of knocking out Israel's state-of-the-art Merkava tanks. But the roadside bomb remained the cheapest, most effective weapon in Hezbollah's arsenal.

Across the border, the longer Israel's citizen-soldiers operated in Lebanon, the more morale in the whole IDF declined and the more collective fatigue weighed on the Israeli public. Finally, in January 1999 the Israeli defense minister issued a sudden and startling announcement: his government was ready to comply with United Nations Security Council Resolution 425, which in 1978 called for the Jewish state to withdraw from southern Lebanon.

In the run-up to Israel's December elections of that year, Ehud Barak, the Labor Party's candidate for prime minister, answered growing Israeli opposition to occupation of the security zone by promising to "bring the boys home" from southern Lebanon by July 2000. There was one caveat verbalized by the deputy defense minister: "It is absolutely clear that any agreement with Lebanon has to include [the condition] that Hizbollah will not exist, at least in south Lebanon . . . or there will be no with-

* This encounter represented one of the unusual joint operations of Hezbollah, Amal, and the Lebanese army.

† Sheikh Nabil Qaouk, quoted in Nicholas Blanford, "A Testing Time," *Middle East* (London), December 1997, p. 9.

drawal."* Hezbollah refused to respond and Israeli casualities continued to mount.

In the end, unarmed Lebanese civilians precipitated the occupation's collapse. On May 21, 2000, a crowd of Shia protesters reclaimed the village of Qantara located on the fringes of the occupied zone. The Israeli army had withdrawn from its defense perimeter a week before, leaving the SLA to cover its retreat. But when the demonstrators arrived, the militiamen simply dropped their guns and gave themselves up. The emboldened protesters pressed on, walking unopposed into seven more villages, effectively cutting the occupation zone in half.

For two more days, the Israeli army and that part of the SLA that had not defected to the Lebanese army or joined the resistance tried to hold back the surge.† But the Israelis had left too few troops in the enclave to bolster its faltering militia. With the remaining Israeli troops exposed, Ehud Barak had no choice but to order the IDF—the pride of Israel—to immediately pull out of Lebanon.

An orderly withdrawal originally planned for July 7 degenerated into a messy and haphazard retreat. A thousand refugees created by the unraveling of the SLA fled into Israel. Israeli soldiers still in Lebanon abandoned their heavy weapons, including some tanks, in the rush to get over their own border. That left Israeli planes to fly north, swoop low over the Lebanese landscape, and blow up as much of the abandoned equipment as possible.

On the ground, joyful Lebanese teenagers swarmed over armored vehicles that had escaped destruction. Moving them with grinding gears and jerking motion, they careened along the roads ahead of processions of Shia celebrating victory. At village after village, people poured out of their houses and into the streets, where women threw rose petals and

---

* Ephraim Sneh, quoted in *The Times* (London), December 27, 1999.

† Almost all those who continued to fight were Maronite Christians. Almost all those who defected were Shia mercenaries.

men raised green banners that gave thanks to Hezbollah for the Shia's deliverance from occupation.

Exhibiting its best behavior, the Party of God posted guards against the rowdy revelers outside Christian villages allied for twenty years with the SLA. Then delegations of turbaned clerics entered the villages, one at a time, to kiss the local priests. To these leaders as well as their followers, the bearded emissaries of Hezbollah mumbled phrases about security and national unity.

Having sacrificed 1,375 "martyrs" in the fight against Israel, Hezbollah relished its image as liberator. Ignoring the supporting role played by Amal and the Lebanese army, most segments within Lebanese society hailed the militia for accomplishing what the Egyptians, Jordanians, Syrians, and Palestinians had never been able to do—achieve a forceful evacuation of Israel from Arab land. In commemoration, the postal service issued stamps in honor of the "jihad," which most Lebanese saw as the restoration of Lebanese territory rather than the threat of an Islamic state in multiconfessional Lebanon. Even armed clashes in June and July resulting from Amal's attempt to claim some of the credit for the Israeli withdrawal did little to diminish Hezbollah as the military and moral defender of Lebanese sovereignty. By forcing Israel out of Lebanon in 2000, Hezbollah laid before the Lebanese and all Arabs the reality of Shia power in a largely Sunni world. The centuries-old tensions pitting the orthodox against the dissenters of Islam took on new potency. And Shia Iran joined Sunni Syria, Jewish Israel, and the Christian West in competition for Lebanon and for influence and power in the larger Arab world beyond.

Chapter 7

A Tale of Four Countries

My friends, because my horse is stolen, you have
hastened one and all to tell me my faults and shortcomings.
But strange, not one word of reproach have you
uttered about the man who stole my horse.

—Khalil Gibran,
The Forerunner (1920)

Al Hamidiya, the covered souk at the center of Damascus, was notable before the time of the apostle Paul. It remains a dark crowded maze much like the old souks of Cairo, and those of Riyadh before the capital of Saudi Arabia was transformed by petro dollars. Here traditional wares—copper and brass plates, vessels, and utensils; wooden boxes inlaid with hundreds of bits of mother of pearl; silver worked into intricate patterns of filigree; and silk brocades once woven on hand looms—are laid out before the small shops that line the narrow passageways. Few items have changed in style, only declined in quality and desirability.

In the new sections of timeworn Damascus, electronic stores, cell phone kiosks, and Internet cafes exist. But the stores selling radios, televisions, audio equipment, computers, and wireless communications offer only a restricted inventory displayed in dim light above dusty showcases. The small Internet cafes tucked away on side streets lack both the customers and the conviviality common to the twenty-first century's rendition of the old Arab coffeehouses. Syria's oppressive melancholia is produced by the country's moribund economic system and the obsessive fears of its leadership, which rise out of the internal and external vulnerabilities of the Syrian state.

Like all countries of the Arab Middle East, Syria is sheathed in a particular character spun from its own geography, history, and culture. Geographically the Syrian state occupies the near center of the Fertile Crescent. Its ancient city of Damascus is famed as one of the crown jewels of the Roman Empire, the capital of the early Islamic Empire, and the center point on the axle of Arab nationalism that defined the Arab world in the last half of the twentieth century. Its scholars, poets, and artisans linked the name "Damascus" with Arab intellectualism for centuries. But no longer. Today Damascus is stalled between its illustrious past and its uncertain future.

Syria, like Iraq, is a collection of hostile quarrelling communities enclosed by boundaries drawn by others. Within these contrived borders, city stands against countryside; sect divides from sect; ethnic group resents ethnic group; and parochial interests war against the national interest. From independence in 1946 until 1970, the name "Syria" was synonymous with political chaos. During that period so many coups and countercoups followed one after the other that the Egyptian newspaper *al Ahram* described Syria as an insane asylum rather than a state. But Syria is a state that harbors its own ambitions and anxieties.

Strategically situated on the route from the Nile to the Euphrates, Syria has always invited invasion. Through the centuries, its cities felt the heel of the Egyptians, Hittites, Assyrians, Babylonians, Persians, Macedonians, Romans, and Byzantines. Then the Arabs and Islam came to conquer. Under the Umayyads, Damascus secured prestige as Islam's capital from 661 to 750. When the Islamic Empire weakened in the eleventh century, Syria was overrun by the Seljuq Turks. It was grazed by the Crusaders in the twelfth, raped by the Mongols in the thirteenth, and finally incorporated into the Ottoman Empire in the sixteenth century. In the early twentieth century, the French came to claim possession.

This pummeling from east and west came in large part because Syria
lacks natural defenses. To the east of Damascus, the sparsely populated
desert that borders Iraq summons intrusion. In the north, the high
ground belongs to Turkey. Even the heavily populated southern region,
bisected by the main road running toward the border with Jordan, seems
naked and vulnerable. Only when Damascus is approached through the
mountains of Lebanon does Syria throw up any natural defense. In the
twentieth century, a succession of governments sought protection by
grabbing hold of the ideology of Arab nationalism and wrapping Syria
in the bonds of Arab brotherhood. In doing so, it, like other Arab countries, became entangled in the conundrum of Arab unity.

Those who identify themselves as Arab place themselves in a mystical whole composed of time, religion, language, culture, and tradition.
In this sense, the Arab world reflects a mighty nation aligned against all
who would seek to humble it. But this same world resonates with its
own rivalrous discord as Arab states duel with each other over national
interests; leaders compete for the right to exercise their own power
within the region; and their people vie with each other over differing
visions of the Arab world and their identity within it. The Arabs are
trapped between their intense sense of unity as a people and tangible
conflicts arising from competing parochial and national interests. This
duality has rendered the Arab world treacherous territory for outsiders.
The Ottomans could not contain Arab nationalism. Britain and France
met frustration and failure when they tried to press the Arabs into a
Western colonial structure. The Soviet Union came up empty when it
attempted to gain power and influence in a region distrustful of both
Marxism and Westernization. Israel has spent its whole history as a state
attempting to untangle the Arab countries aligned against it. And the
United States, in trying to mold Iraq into a unified, democratic state
linked to the West, found itself in a quagmire created when perceptions
were disconnected from realities.

The escalating tensions that threaten to engulf both the Arabs and the West erupted first out of the fissure between the mythology of Arab unity and the reality of competing interests. Second, they arose from the actions of outsiders, including the West. In an era in which the West's stake in the Arab world is enormous both economically and strategically, small Lebanon provides a large stage on which to see a complex play starring this cast of emotionalism attached to Arab unity, the realpolitik of parochial interests, and the blind interference of Arab and non-Arab nations pursing their own national agendas. Its long run continues because multifaceted Lebanon is a geographic prize and an irresistible site for competitions and proxy wars waged by others.

In the early years of the civil war, the Lebanese chose to judge the chaos consuming their lives as "the war of others on Lebanese land." There was a certain truth to the claim.

The intensity, if not the cause, of the war in Lebanon never resided with the Lebanese. It came from the Palestinians and Israelis fighting each other over possession of historic Palestine; from Syria's attempt to establish hegemony over Lebanon as Damascus's first line of defense of its own territory and the lever to be applied against Israel; from the United States' dual role as the protector of Israel and the guard against the Soviet Union's advance into the region; and from Iran's ambition to export the power of the Islamic revolution. Lebanon provided a convenient location for them all to pursue their own interests at the expense of a weak state. And they continue to use Lebanon to chase their own aspirations and strategies in the larger world of the Arabs. Together they are imperiling the increasingly fragile stability of the Arab world from Beirut to Baghdad.

ISRAEL'S DEEP AND complex involvement in Lebanon began with the collapse of the Ottoman Empire, which hastened the germination of the seeds of Zionism shipped from the West. When the Levant fell to Allied Forces in 1918, the French general Henri Honore Gouraud hailed the

West's most penetrating entry into the Arab world since the Crusades by standing at the tomb of the man who broke the back of the Christian armies in 1190. To the crowd assembled in Damascus, Gouraud boasted, "We came back, Saladin!" Thirty years later, the war for Palestine thrust the new state of Israel into the affairs of every country in the Arab world. To the Arabs it was Israel, not France, that reigned as the new Crusader state, the new shield of Western imperialism. It is in that context within Arab perceptions that the Arabs have faced Israel for the last six-plus decades.

The specific connection between Israel and Lebanon was forged before 1948. The Zionists, led by the wiry-haired David Ben-Gurion, regarded Lebanon, with its powerful contingent of Maronites, as the weakest link in the chain of Arab states that surrounded Palestine. After 1948, Tel Aviv set out to manipulate the divisions within Lebanese society for its own ends. Targeting the Maronites, Israel assiduously courted the Roman Catholic Francophiles as allies against the Palestinians. After 1967, when the Palestinians took charge of their own affairs following the defeat of Gamal Abdul Nasser's own version of Arab nationalism, Israel focused on a single goal in Lebanon: control of the Palestinian threat gathering within its territory. As 1975 approached, the expanding power of the PLO and its alliance with the Lebanese Sunnis pushed the Maronites toward the protective arms of Israel. When war broke, the arms and ammunition Tel Aviv dispatched to the imperiled Maronites were nothing less than the hardware of Israeli policy written by the founders of the Jewish state.

While Israel sought the consolidation and security of its state between 1948 and 1975, Syria was mired in the bog of its own internal squabbles. The one theme that unified its families, tribes, religions, and sects was an intense, burning grudge born of the dismemberment of what the Syrians regard as Greater Syria. Under the Ottomans, Syrian territory encompassed what is now the state of Syria as well as Palestine, Jordan, Lebanon, and part of western Turkey. At the end of World War

I, Greater Syria lost everything except a truncated core that included the ports and mountains of Lebanon. Those were lost in 1920 when Lebanon was carved off by France. Still another territorial loss came in 1967 when Israeli forces climbed the Golan Heights, sacked the city of Quneitra, cleared its surrounding villages, and stripped Syria of an additional 454 square miles of its territory. Dividing Syria from Israel, the Golan became the shameful badge of Syria's defeat, the searing emblem of Syrian hatred of Israel, and the all-consuming obsession of Hafiz Assad.

Assad was the Syrian defense minister during the 1967 war. The broad-browed, ramrod-straight Assad emerged from the short conflict convinced that Israel was, by its nature, an expansionist power that could be contained only through immense Arab effort. Carrying this judgment like a sword, Hafiz Assad led a military coup in 1970 that took charge of chaotic Syria. Presiding over a secretive, autocratic regime where power concentrated in the hands of the president, Assad pursued Syria's lost territory on the Golan, cultivated the image of Syria as the "beating heart of Arabism," and locked Lebanon and the approaches to Damascus in the stable of Syrian interests.* Until he died in 2000, he would reign as the enigmatic "lion of Damascus" and a central figure in the Arab political arena.

THE UNITED STATES, the third in the quartet of countries that have intervened in Lebanon over the last several decades, was all but absent from the Middle East until after World War II. To Washington, the world of the Arabs belonged in the sphere of Britain and France. Beginning in 1948, America actively engaged with Arab countries for two overarch-

---

* As a member of Syria's Alawite community, theologically a segment of Shiism, Hafiz Assad championed secularism and broadly defined Arab nationalism to protect his regime against Syria's Sunni majority.

ing reasons: to protect the oil fields of Saudi Arabia snagged in 1938 by Standard Oil Company of California and to ensure the security of Israel. The tempo of American involvement escalated during the mid-1950s when Egypt's Gamal Abdul Nasser mobilized the Arabs against the West and opened the gates of the Middle East's most populous country to Soviet arms and military advisors. From then until 1989, the United States would act to keep its Cold War adversary out of the Middle East.

Having sent troops into Lebanon in 1958 to contain the threat of Nasser, the United States acted more subtly in the 1960s and 1970s. Washington stood aside in 1967 as Israel, armed with American money and weapons, destroyed what many Arabs regarded as the messiah of Arab nationalism. In the summer of 1970, as tensions between Jordan's King Hussein and the Palestinians edged toward Black September, President Richard Nixon discreetly strengthened the hand of Hussein. By the time the king went to war against the PLO, the American president had quietly amassed enough military, political, and economic clout in the region to all but assure Hussein's victory. It was the events of 1973 that demanded a more visible role for the United States in the world of the Arabs.

When Anwar Sadat sent Egyptian forces across the Suez Canal to break the post-1967 stalemate in the Arabs' contest with Israel, an Arab alliance constructed of manpower, arms, money, and an oil embargo threw the Jewish state on the defensive for two weeks. In the third week, the tide turned decisively against the Arabs when American transport planes, landing directly behind the Sinai front, delivered tanks and sophisticated weapons to beleaguered Israel. With their devastating losses of equipment replaced from the stores of American combat troops, the Israelis drove two hundred Arab tanks and fifteen thousand troops back across the canal, wiped out Egypt's Soviet-supplied surface-to-air missile batteries, and forced the Syrians on the eastern front to fall back to a point only twenty miles from Damascus. Washington seemed triumphant when an American proposal calling for an immediate cease-fire and negotiations for peace between Israel and the Arab states became United Nations Security Council Resolution 338, the framework for peace between Israel and the Arabs. As 1975 approached, the United States saw Lebanon as little more than another component in its complex effort to keep Persian Gulf oil flowing into the American market, protect Israel, and hold closed the door that shut the Soviet Union out of the Middle East.

Of the big four that would so complicate the Lebanese civil war, only Iran was essentially absent from the Arab arena in 1975. The ambitions of Muhammad Reza Shah, the "king of kings," centered in the Persian Gulf, not the Levant. For that reason, when economically stressed Britain announced in 1970 that it would pull back all of its military forces "east of Suez," the shah stepped up to assume the role of policeman of the Gulf. Blessed by the United States, armed with American weapons, and, after 1973, drenched in oil money, the man who regarded himself as the modern manifestation of the ancient Persian kings was content to remain in the Gulf. From his perspective, Persian Iran was outside the Arabs' disputes among themselves and with Israel.

Thus, as 1975 dawned in Lebanon, an alarmed Tel Aviv looked across its northern border at Palestinians positioned to launch a full-scale guerrilla war against Israel; a frightened Damascus saw Syria's whole western flank imperiled; anxious Washington worried that the tenuous stability of the Middle East was in danger of crumbling to the detriment of American interests; and dispassionate Tehran sensed the possibility of a conflict that would play to Iran's benefit by diverting Arab attention and resources away from the Persian Gulf. One by one each of these foreign powers would intervene at some point in the coming Lebanese conflict in pursuit of its own particular agenda. Although not the source of the civil war, the foreigners would multiply its complexity and intensity. And the Lebanese—having recruited those foreign powers to serve the narrow interests of competing factions—would pay the terrible price.

BY THE TIME the Lebanese civil war exploded, Israel was already moving in and out of Lebanon to check the Palestinians, and Hafiz Assad had set Lebanon at the center of his strategy to protect his borders and limit Israeli power. Yet as the Maronites, the Sunnis, and the Palestinians, along with their assorted allies, opened fire on each other, Assad chose to wait out the unfolding events. What he specifically watched for was the development of a political vacuum that would suck into Lebanon any of Syria's rivals. In the spring of 1976, the man often referred to as the "sphinx" could wait no longer. The Lebanese revolutionaries and the Palestinians were gaining ascendancy over the militias of the Maronites, and the Israelis were sitting on the southern border of Lebanon ready to intervene in order to contain the Palestinians. Suddenly the Lebanese war confronted Hafiz Assad with the prospect of a regional conflict that carried immense consequences for Syria. In June 1976, Assad sacrificed the myth of Arab unity to Syrian national interests by sending forty thousand Syrian troops into the whirlpool of Lebanon in order to save the Maronites.

Denounced across the Arab world for siding with anti-Muslim forces, Assad calmly claimed that he had acted to preserve Lebanon's unity, pluralistic community, and national independence. Further justifying his action, Assad argued that left alone, the Maronites would seek a formal alliance with Israel, thereby creating a "Christian Zion" in the Arab heartland. Most of the Arab states, no more amenable than Syria to the carnage in Lebanon, accepted his rationale. Hailed by a few, grudgingly accepted by most, bitterly condemned by a minority, the Syrian presence in Lebanon confirmed for Syria and Hafiz Assad centrality in the Arab world.*

But in 1977, Syria shifted away from the Maronites toward the Muslims when the Lebanese Forces appeared to be gaining the upper

---

* It was from this position that Hafiz Assad was able to lead the Arab rejection front to the 1978 Camp David Accords, which made peace between Egypt and Israel.

hand. This time the public rationale of Damascus was that Syria was acting to preserve the Arab character of Lebanon. This intervention on the side of the Christians in 1976 and intercession on the side of the Muslims in 1977 set the pattern of Syrian military and political intrusion in embattled Lebanon. Throughout the war, Hafiz Assad constantly maneuvered to block any Lebanese faction from gaining dominance over its rivals. To Assad's credit, the Syrian presence on the ground did initially succeed in restoring some order. And until 1982, Assad succeeded in keeping Israel out of Syria's front yard by dancing a mutually beneficial minuet with Tel Aviv. According to its precise steps, neither partner crossed the Litani River, which divided Lebanon into two spheres of influence labeled "Syria" and "Israel." Israel tolerated the Syrian presence in Lebanon as long as it was directed against the Palestinians and their Lebanese allies. And Syria allowed Israel to operate in Lebanon as long as its military action fell on the Palestinians and Lebanese, not on the Syrians. Neither sought military confrontation with each other until the music stopped when Israel invaded in 1982.

THE IMPETUS FOR ending Tel Aviv's somewhat comfortable strategic understanding with Damascus came from the victory of the Likud Party in Israel's 1981 election. Emerging as the defense minister of the new government, the burly hawk Ariel Sharon brought with him a "grand design" for the Middle East that encompassed relations with Egypt, Syria, and Jordan; further integration of the conquered territories of 1967 into Israel; and the destruction of the Palestinian's military and political structure in Lebanon.* Anticipating George W. Bush's strategy for Iraq two decades later, Sharon intended to do nothing less than reshape the Arab world to the requirements of Israel.

---

* Israel annexed the Golan Heights to Israel proper in December 1981.

Operation Big Pines, launched on April 6, 1982, marked the first step on the road to the new Middle East. The second was to disassociate Lebanon from Syrian control by placing in power a Christian-dominated regime willing to ally itself with Israel. But like the American adventure in Iraq in 2003, the invasion proved far more complicated and difficult than Sharon and his supporters envisaged. Phase one—the military operation to cleanse southern Lebanon of Palestinian commandoes—unfolded with few complications. But phase two—obliteration of the PLO's institutional structure and the installation of a Lebanese government allied with Israel—became mired in unintended consequences. As the Israeli army paused south of Beirut, the only salvation from dreaded street-to-street combat in densely populated urban areas rested with its own high-performance and heavily armed aircraft plus the military, economic, and diplomatic power of the United States. From 1982 to 1984, both Israel and the United States would be seared by Lebanon.

IN THE SUMMER of 1982 when Israel and the PLO appeared willing to duel to the death in Beirut, the attention of the United States swung from the Middle East peace process launched by the 1978 Camp David Accords to the slaughter in Lebanon. Beginning in 1958, the United States had shown a propensity for risking blood and resources in conflicts in the Middle East without comprehending the complexities of communal schisms in the Arab world. Washington's 1982–1984 adventure in Lebanon would follow the same path. The United States entered Lebanon as it entered Iraq two decades later—unprepared for the realities that awaited.

For seventy days, Israel pounded Beirut with bombs and mortar rounds that revived memories of wasted Dresden in World War II. Shelling came from the coastal plain, from the hills, and from the sea. Terrified people poured into basements as flashes of orange and yellow announced the destruction of ammunition dumps and neighborhoods.

From bunkers buried within the heart of the city, PLO leader Yasser Arafat described Beirut as the "Stalingrad of the Arabs," where anything Israel delivered from the air would be resisted by the Palestinians. In the ensuing weeks, guerrillas hung on in ravaged buildings while Palestinian poets penned the Palestinian message on placards hung around the smoking city that read, "Tell your children what Israel has done." With Beirut consumed by fury, Arafat and his PLO eventually faced no other choice but to leave in order to save the Lebanese and themselves. Their safe exit would be guaranteed by the United States.

To everyone except the Phalangists and some of their Christian supporters, the inferno created with the help of American shells and American money was as much the fault of the United States as Israel. But rather than promoting U.S. interests by engaging as a genuine broker for peace, the Reagan administration decided to intervene in Lebanon to pull Israel's chestnuts out of the fire of the Beirut siege. The decision came from those in the administration who zealously believed Israel constituted the anchor of U.S. strategic interests in the Middle East. To Secretary of State Alexander Haig particularly, Israel was the counterweight to the Palestinians, Syria, and, by projection, Soviet power in the area. Understanding the complexities of Lebanon even less than the Israelis, the Reagan administration undertook America's disastrous and amateurish venture in Lebanon.

It began on August 8, 1982, when Washington agreed to contribute a thousand U.S. Marines to the Multi-National Force (MNF) being sent into Lebanon to help maintain order and provide protection for PLO guerrillas boarding ships, planes, and vehicles for the exodus from Lebanon. Like all plans devised in haste and desperation, there were traps laying all over the scheme. First there were the political risks to the United States' already problematic Middle East policy. Second was the certainty of unintended consequences. And third were the physical risks to the Marines. One Reagan administration aide perhaps said it best: "You're putting kids in combat and asking them to be policemen. They don't know what the hell to do. Can you imagine figuring out the differences between Druze, Muslims, Maronites, and Israelis?"* Nevertheless, at precisely five o'clock on a clear morning in late August, a landing craft pulled into the port of Beirut and the 32nd Marine Amphibious Unit stepped ashore. For the second time in twenty-four years, U.S. Marines had landed in Lebanon, this time to evacuate the PLO and end the Israeli siege of Beirut.

Over the next twelve days, the Lebanon-based PLO went into exile; the Israeli bombardment of Beirut ceased; and the depleted 1972 Lebanese parliament elected as president Bashir Gemayel, the fiery leader of the Maronites' Lebanese Forces. Believing that Lebanese affairs were at last on track, the American government withdrew its troops on September 10 along with those sent by other governments of the MNF.

But Lebanon was not on track. Bashir Gemayel was assassinated on September 14. Between September 16 and 18, the Phalange, with the complicity of Israel, massacred hundreds of Palestinians in Sabra and Shatila.† In the wake of the atrocity, President Reagan, on September 20, ordered U.S. Marines back into Beirut.

Like Israel, the United States had painted its own grand design for Lebanon. Washington would employ its undeniably close relationship with Israel to secure an agreement with the Maronite-dominated government under which Tel Aviv would withdraw its forces from Lebanon. Once this was achieved, the Lebanese government, given backbone by American support, would pressure the Syrians to withdraw. Then Amin Gemayel, elected as president to fulfill the term of his assassinated brother, would build on these successes to broaden his political base by drawing into his government some of the leaders of

---

* Quoted in *Newsweek*, July 19, 1982, p. 17.

† In 1983, a commission appointed by the Knesset confirmed that Israel had indeed played a part in the Palestinian deaths.

the Muslim communities. With these diplomatic initiatives underway, the United States would use American troops and arms to strengthen the Lebanese army so that Gemayel could confront the various militias, including the Lebanese Forces. Finally, Lebanon would move into the Middle East peace process by formally recognizing the state of Israel. The elementary flaw in this whole elaborate policy was that the rivals of the Maronites saw collusion with Israel as an odious scheme to ensure continued Maronite control of Lebanon. Ignoring the Arab obsession with conspiracy theory, Washington stumbled toward its next mistake, which came in 1983.

To convey the message that American troops in exposed positions around the Beirut airport would protect themselves against mortar fire from the Chouf Mountains, the Pentagon ordered the cruiser *Virginia*, the destroyer *John Rogers*, and the battleship *New Jersey* to fire a combined total of six hundred rounds of heavy shells into the tiny town of Souk al Gharb. Although the attack was directed more at the Druze than the Shia of the area, the firepower of mighty battleships forcefully played into the Shia's image of their centuries-old struggle against their enemies. One Shia articulated the emotions of a growing cadre committed to Shiism's radical side: "If America kills my people, then my people must kill Americans."*

For this and other reasons, Lebanon became the first location in which the United States experienced the wrath of militant Islam. "Warriors of God" had already struck on April 18, 1983, when a large van loaded with the firepower of five hundred pounds of TNT raced up the circular driveway of the American embassy in Ain al Meisse and exploded, killing fifty-eight people, seventeen of them Americans.

By October, the Marines deployed as peacekeepers around the Beirut airport were burrowed behind ten vertical feet of sandbags, watch-

---

* Quoted in Robin Wright, *Sacred Rage: The Wrath of Militant Islam* (New York: Simon and Schuster, 1985), p. 83.

ing sniper bullets kick up dirt.* The hostile fire came from the Shia
slums around the airport. On October 23, snipers became suicide
bombers when at 6:20 a.m. a Mercedes truck carrying two thousand
pounds of explosives turned toward the parking lot of a jerry-rigged
barracks in Beirut airport's aviation safety building. When he reached
the gate that guarded it, the driver hit the accelerator. The truck sped
toward the entrance of the four-story building, vaulted a wall of sandbags, lurched into the lobby, and exploded in a deafening roar. The roof
momentarily lifted off the "Beirut Hilton" and then collapsed.† In those
moments, the United States lost 241 Marines, the worst disaster for
the American military since the Vietnam War. The wound inflicted on
American power by the militant Shia heralded a new kind of fighter,
one who drove to his death repeating the words of the Koran: "Who
fighteth in the way of God be he slain or be he victorious, on him we
shall bestow a vast reward."

In the days following the attack, "consistency" and "stay the course"
constituted the keywords of the U.S. State Department's press briefings.
After all, President Reagan had declared that stability in Lebanon was
central to American credibility on a global scale. Three months later, on
February 3, 1984, Ronald Reagan, insisting that the United States was
not prepared to "surrender" in Lebanon, warned, "If Lebanon ends up
under the tyranny of forces hostile to the West, not only will our stra-

---

* Marine frustrations were summed up in a cartoon by Dwayne Powell of the
Raleigh News Observer in which a lieutenant stands before a map of Lebanon with a
pointer in his hand. He is telling his helmeted squad, "OK, Marines—We're faced
with Druze and Shia Moslems being backed by the Syrians against the Christian Phalangists. The Druze and Shias are divided among themselves, as are the Christians.
The Israeli pullout is leaving a gap that the 'Lebanese army' probably can't fill and the
PLO is creeping back in . . . Nobody likes us, and it's all preceded by 2,000 years of
bloodshed. Any questions?"

† Minutes later, a building in the seafront neighborhood of Bir Hasan, where the
French contingent of the MNF was housed, erupted in a similar explosion.

tegic position in the eastern Mediterranean be threatened, but also the stability of the entire Middle East, including the vast resource areas of the Arabian peninsula."*

Nevertheless, a year later when Ras Beirut, the heart of Western life in prewar Lebanon, fell to Hezbollah, Amal, the Druze, and assorted leftist factions, the last shreds of U.S. policy in Lebanon disintegrated. America's grand strategy was proving too expensive. Consequently, on February 7, 1984, President Reagan abruptly announced that the U.S. Marines in Lebanon would be "redeployed" to ships off the coast. A little less than two and a half years after they had arrived to move the PLO out of Beirut and turn Lebanon into an island of stability in the turbulent Middle East, the Marines struck the battalion flag. The French who came in 1920, left in 1946, and returned in 1982 had already departed. In the wake of the West, another foreign power pursued its own agenda in Lebanon.

EVER SINCE THE Islamic Empire had begun to disintegrate in the tenth century, Persian Iran involved itself little in the Arab world. But after the 1979 Iranian revolution, Ayatollah Ruhollah Khomeini and his lieutenants vowed to spread revolutionary Islam beyond the borders of Iran. Although the clarion call to Muslims made no theological or ideological differentiation between Shia and Sunnis, Iran's revolutionary leaders first targeted the Shia populations of Arab countries adjacent to Iran or across the Persian Gulf—Iraq, Kuwait, Saudi Arabia, and Bahrain. Nevertheless, it was the more distant Lebanese Shia who proved to be the most receptive to Khomeini's appeal to turn the secular Lebanese state into a theocracy modeled on the *velayat-e faqih,* the "Guardianship of the Jurist."

The Iranian revolution's successful courting of the Shia population of

* Quoted in the *Economist,* February 24, 1996, p. L6.

Lebanon was not totally the result of revisionist theology or government policy. Khomeini's message of politicized Islam passed across personal ties between the Shia clerics of Iran and the Shia clerics of Lebanon. For generations before the Iranian revolution, the circles of learning in Najaf and Qom drew Shia clerics from Lebanon, many of whom came to share similar, although not identical, theological views. They also became part of the tight network of personal friendship and clerical kinship that bound them together even after they left the seminaries. When Iraqi troops on the orders of Saddam Hussein poured over the border of Iran in September 1980 without protest from the United States, and the Israeli invasion of Lebanon in April 1982 thrust U.S. military power into the Levant, the anti-American clerics of Tehran countered by sending Iranian men and money into the Lebanese civil war. Both came through Damascus with Syria's blessing.

Bowed by the Israeli juggernaut of 1982 that all but neutralized the Syrian military presence in Lebanon, the secularist Hafiz Assad proved willing to accept help from theocratic Iran in his quest to dislodge Israel and the United States from Syria's front yard. When the Shia political organization Amal split between those whose goal was to secure Shia political rights within a secular Lebanon and those who sought to turn Lebanon into a Khomeini-style theocracy, Syria embraced Hezbollah. It was Hezbollah, sponsored by Iranian revolutionaries, that would help redress the balance in Lebanon that Hafiz Assad regarded as crucial to Syria's security.

For Iran, Lebanon offered the Islamic regime its first direct point of contact with a major Shia community in the Arab world. This in turn provided Tehran not only a base from which to project its influence into the Arab heartland but also a regional role it had never before possessed. Benefiting from conditions in Lebanon, Tehran galvanized a range of disaffected Shia Muslim groups in Lebanon for whom Amal did not speak, clerics who had studied with Khomeini in Najaf in the 1970s, willing foot soldiers from the southern Bekaa, and ordinary Shia of southern Lebanon and the slums of Beirut. They all signed on to the Iranian agenda.

Tilling this fertile ground, Iran financed new mosques for the clerics, built militia bases in the Bekaa, staffed them with Revolutionary Guards charged with training armed fighters, and bankrolled social services in and around Beirut. Initially much of the money came directly from the Iranian government. Through Hezbollah, Iran positioned itself to play the same destabilizing role that populist and revolutionary Arab regimes had played in the Arab world during the 1950s and 1960s. In a replay of the Palestinian guerrilla movement of the 1960s and 1970s, it was now the armed Islamic militants sponsored by Iran who threatened to create a state within a state in Lebanon.

Hezbollah's ties to Iran and its goal of installing an Islamic order in Lebanon stood in direct opposition to Syria's goal of securing its own strategic interests there. Hafiz Assad proved willing to tolerate Hezbollah's agenda and its Iranian sponsor only because he held the trump card. Simple geography gave Syria, not Iran, direct access to Lebanon and to Hezbollah. Fully understanding this reality, Tehran and its Lebanese client accepted the Taif Accord that underwrote the continued Syrian presence in Lebanon.

THE LEVEL AND nature of foreign interference in Lebanon differed after the 1989 agreement reached at Taif, which effectively ended the Lebanese civil war. In the pre-Taif era, foreign powers, through their shifting patronage to different factions, were major contributors to the madness. Not only did they feed weapons to their allies and put their armies on the ground, but they often functioned as the principal architects of agreements that attempted to reward their clients or control the violence. Without exception, they violated these agreements either unilaterally or through their local or regional allies. How any foreign power acted at any particular time depended on regional and international conditions that impacted on the specific national interests of each. By 1989, the foreigners were living in an environment in which the war in Lebanon no longer served their needs. Following the collapse of the Soviet Union, the United States could dispense with the Lebanese conflict as part of the West's confrontation with Marxism and Soviet power. Consequently Washington was less forgiving of Israel's sledgehammer tactics delivered across its northern border and more willing to accept Syria's dominant role in Lebanon. Israel itself no longer regarded Lebanon as the critical front line of its defense. Although it still faced Hezbollah in southern Lebanon, the dreaded Palestinians were contained. Iran, almost bled dry by the Iran-Iraq War, was, in 1989, more interested in rebuilding the Iranian nation than spreading Islamic revolution. At the moment of Taif, the Americans, the Israelis, and the Iranians seemed willing to leave the Lebanese alone to either resolve their internal conflicts or suffer the consequences. Yet none of the foreign powers was willing to give Lebanon a seat at the table where all parties to the conflict negotiated a regional settlement. As a result, the Lebanese achieved an end of the war but only at the cost of their independence. It was as if the pessimistic prediction made five years before had become a reality. "The new Lebanon will not be independent, will not be unified; will not be democratic . . . [Instead] Syria will dominate Lebanon."*

As the other foreign interlopers backed off, Syria dug in its heels. In a blunt statement on Damascus's position, the foreign minister declared, "The Syrian army will remain in Lebanon to continue its national mission and to defend the honor and dignity of the Lebanese people."† But just as it appeared that Syria, with the acquiescence of the other foreign players, would reign as the single, overarching "patron" of Lebanon, one more national actor thrust its hand into Lebanon, extending the war for another act.

---

* Paul A. Jureidine and R. D. McLaurin, quoted in Hanf, *Coexistence in Wartime Lebanon*, p. 567.

† Quoted in Hanf, *Coexistence in Wartime Lebanon*, p. 580.

Michel Aoun, the disputed president of Lebanon, had been able to hole up in Baabda palace and duel with the Lebanese Forces in 1989 because Iraq supplied him with weapons to wage Baghdad's proxy war against Syrian control of Lebanon. But on August 2, 1990, Saddam Hussein defeated himself when he sent his army over the border of Kuwait to claim the sheikhdom as the nineteenth province of Iraq. With the crucial oil supplies of the Persian Gulf threatened by Iraqi aggression, American president George H. W. Bush called the international community to oust Iraq from the territory of its small Arab neighbor. To the astonishment of the Arab world, Hafiz Assad stepped forward and took his place at the side of his longtime American adversary. On one level, he acted because the Syrian Baath Party and the Iraqi Baath Party had been bitter rivals since the 1960s. On another, Hafiz Assad and Saddam Hussein personally hated each other. On a third, the lion of Damascus astutely judged that by aligning himself with the United States against Saddam Hussein's blatant aggression, he would gain status in American eyes. He was right.

In combat lasting a hundred hours, Saddam Hussein suffered a humiliating defeat in a war in which the coalition allied against him pursued a precisely defined objective with overwhelming force. Having boxed up the butcher of Baghdad within his own borders using UN sanctions, the United States, the leader of the wartime coalition, engaged in a full-court press to achieve a comprehensive peace settlement that would end six decades of conflict between Zionism and the Arabs. For Washington, it was crucial that Syria, sitting at the geographic center of the Arab Middle East and embedded in both the Palestinian question and Lebanon, be included.* In pursuit of this goal, Washington moderated its scrutiny of Syria's Lebanon policy.

---

* The United States was also desirous of Syria's help in freeing its citizens held hostage in Lebanon.

HAFIZ ASSAD PROCEEDED to implement the provisions of the Taif Accord to suit his own purposes. On May 22, 1991, Damascus demanded from Lebanon the so-called Treaty of Brotherhood, Cooperation and Coordination, to be followed by the Pact of Defense Security the next September. The newly chosen parliament played the central role of cementing the Lebanon-Syrian alliance at the center of the Taif Accord. With both the new prime minister and president personally in favor of close collaboration with Syria, the Lebanese experienced a level of stability unknown in years.

In this atmosphere, the Lebanese government wisely refused to make a single important decision without first securing the Syrian government's stamp of approval. Accepting the nature of the relationship, the Lebanese code-named the Syrians "the Swiss" and the Beirut-Damascus highway over which Lebanese politicians trekked to the Syrian capital "the bourse."

The extreme imbalance of power enforced by Syria's right to station troops on Lebanese territory turned Lebanon into a vassal state for which the Roman god Janus could have served as a symbol. One face represented the restoration of the Lebanese state, the other face portrayed restrictions on Lebanese sovereignty. This reality of the so-called Second Republic was something most Lebanese were willing to live with for a time. There was no other way to disarm the militias. But soon the price of Taif became apparent. The pro-Syrian majority in the Chamber of Deputies squeezed Lebanon's frail democratic tradition, sucked the blood from the country's fragile rule of law, and drained the independence and spirit from the Lebanese press. In the 1992 election meant to celebrate the rebirth of the Lebanese state, the real winner was Syria.

WHILE SYRIA REIGNED supreme in most of Lebanon, Israel continued not only to hold its southern security zone but also to take a certain satisfaction in it. For Tel Aviv, the presence of the Israeli Defense Forces coupled with the Palestinian denouement of 1982 kept Syria from encroaching too close to the Israeli border. From this point of view, the security zone in southern Lebanon was an achievement pulled out of the disaster of the 1982 invasion. But Israel's relatively comfortable position in Lebanon deteriorated in the 1990s when southern Lebanon became an open field on which Israel, Syria, and Iran played out their rivalries.

Israel's incursion into southern Lebanon in 1993 had as much to do with the power equation between Israel and Syria as with disabling Hezbollah's guerrillas. Three years later when Israeli F-16 fighters struck power plants east of Beirut, the purpose was to compel Syria to pressure Iran into controlling Hezbollah. But for Hafiz Assad, Hezbollah was proving to be a useful pawn in the chess game to force Israel to make concessions on the future of the Golan Heights. This, not stability in southern Lebanon, was Assad's real priority, leaving Hezbollah free to pursue its increasingly effective guerrilla war against Israel.

By 1999, a majority of the Israeli public was convinced that the strategic game Tel Aviv was playing in southern Lebanon was eating the soul out of the IDF. Many worried that the Zionist commando who gave birth to the Israeli state with little more than a rifle and an ammunition belt had gone soft. In the 1990s, a soldier of the IDF serving in Lebanon was supplied not only with the firepower of sophisticated weapons but also battery-heated sleeping bags and self-inflating mattresses designed to make the time spent waiting to intercept Hezbollah guerrillas as comfortable as possible. Zeev Schiff, the longtime military analyst at *Haaretz* newspaper, gave his own assessment: "It's a reflection of a different society—of a society that has gained a lot of weight."*

There were other reasons why the Israeli military and the Israeli public seemed to no longer feel fire in the belly. First, the ordinary Israeli,

---

* Quoted in *Newsweek*, April 13, 1998, p. 19.

for the first time in Israel's short history, failed to see the occupation of Lebanon as necessary for the very survival of the nation. Second, for a country used to short wars and big victories, fifteen years in the quagmire of Lebanon was enough. Finally, both Lebanon and the ongoing uprising of the Palestinians in the occupied territories confronted the Israelis with the changing environment of the Arab world. Israel, to its profound discomfort, was discovering that it could no longer dominate either its neighbors or the Palestinians with military power alone.

Israel's relationship with Lebanon had begun with such high hopes. The Zionist vision of Lebanon in the years that preceded Israel's statehood was one of an Arab society willing to live with the Jewish state. After all, the Yishuv and Lebanese Christians shared a wide range of economic and political interests, and leading Zionists and Maronites, drawn together by similar positions as minorities within the Arab world, shared warm personal relationships. Menachem Begin took those same ideas and that same logic into Lebanon in 1982, where history dealt them a devastating blow, for Lebanon was no longer the Lebanon of 1948. The exploding Shia population had overwhelmed the Maronites. It was not just numbers but attitudes that had shredded the Shia's centuries-old tradition of quietism. As the Zionists had once glowed with ideological passion, it was now the Shia who were enflamed with meaning and purpose. And it was Syria, not the French or the United States, who was the major power broker on Israel's northern border. Eitan Haber, a former aide to Prime Minister Yitzhak Rabin, expressed the Israelis' growing sense of powerlessness: "We whose arsenal is full of atom bombs, who extricated the hostages at Entebbe [airport], who snatched radar systems from under the noses of drowsy Egyptians, who killed terrorist chiefs in their beds [in Beirut] with soldiers dressed as women, and we have no solution?"*

---

* Quoted in the *Financial Times* (London), March 2, 1999.

By 2000, there was no choice for Israel but to withdraw from southern Lebanon. Perhaps appropriately, a twenty-one-year-old sergeant from Jerusalem delivered the final line of the Israeli occupation of Lebanon: "I closed the [border] gate for the last time and it felt bad. Such a waste of lives."* Little Lebanon had eaten another foreign occupier. Two of the outside powers that had directly intervened in the Lebanese civil war were gone—the United States and Israel. Two were left—Syria and Iran.

OVER THE YEARS of the Syrian presence in Lebanon, Damascus had dropped its ground force from the forty thousand that arrived in Lebanon in 1976 to roughly twenty thousand by 2002. But even as the numbers dwindled, the Syrian presence remained strong, visibly manifested at strategic locations and significant checkpoints manned by soldiers in Syrian fatigues. The Lebanese felt a more intrusive Syrian presence in the unknown number of shadowy figures that served Hafiz Assad's security services—the real power of Syria in Lebanon. In their plain clothes, they tapped telephones; spied on political figures; arranged the disappearance of business rivals of themselves and their Lebanese allies; and arrested, tortured, and sometimes killed those deemed a threat to Syrian hegemony over Lebanon. This combination of Syria's army, security services, Lebanese allies, and political control further undercut the institutions of the Lebanese state that the Lebanese themselves had assaulted in 1975. By 2000, the Lebanese government had operated for almost a quarter of a century under the direction of Damascus. By now, for many Lebanese, Syria was no longer a stern nanny holding Lebanon's factions in check but an unyielding stepmother gripping a rebellious child.

Syria had stayed in Lebanon both to secure its western front and to

* Quoted in *Newsweek*, June 5, 2000, p. 20.

bolster its own moribund economy. Since the collapse of the Soviet Union in 1989 had taken with it Moscow's aid to Damascus, Lebanon ranked as Syria's principal economic partner. Despite the damage sustained in the war, Lebanon provided employment for perhaps 1.4 million Syrian laborers, who in turn fed foreign exchange into Syria's needy economy. Lebanon's banks provided Syrian businessmen with capital, and Syrian officials in the upper echelons of government raked in fortunes by smuggling goods into Syria via Lebanon.* But as France, the United States, and Israel had been unable to mold Lebanon to their national agendas, neither could Syria.

Rafik Hariri, a billionaire businessman backed with money and influence from Saudi Arabia, had begun rotating in and out of the Lebanese premiership in 1992. In office or out, the highly popular Hariri consistently pressured Syria in the name of Lebanese sovereignty.† But Hafiz Assad held firm, refusing to loosen his grip on Lebanon. Then on June 10, 2002, Hafiz Assad, the cunning brain of Arab politics and the architect of Syria's presence in Lebanon, died of heart disease. His thirty-seven-year-old son, Bashir, took over his father's regime. Groomed to the position only after his brother, Basil, died in an automobile accident in 1994, Bashir came into the presidency as a Western-trained ophthalmologist. Young, inexperienced, and lacking the keen political intelligence of Hafiz, he was ill equipped to deal with the complexities of Syria or the larger Arab world. He neither possessed the influence nor commanded the clout to stand astride Syria's domestic politics, dominate his father's inner circle, or enforce his will over the multiple communal factions of Lebanon. Yet Syria's denouement in Lebanon had begun before the death of Bashir's maneuvering father.

In 1998, Hafiz Assad had handpicked as president Emile Lahoud,

---

* Rifat Assad, Hafiz Assad's corrupt brother, is rumored to have benefited from deals of this nature that amounted to billions of Syrian pounds.

† See chapter 8.

a Maronite with close ties to Syria whose style of governance is best described as sitting by a swimming pool holding a tanning mirror while waiting for instructions from Damascus. Concerned that Prime Minister Hariri was undercutting Syrian support among the Sunnis, Damascus sent orders to Beirut that the president assume absolute control over Lebanon's military and security apparatus and appoint his allies to all key cabinet positions. Although unhappy at his diminished power, Hariri stayed in the government as prime minister. Despite his consistent stand against Syria's presence in Lebanon, Hariri was reluctant to openly confront Damascus, which was seen by his Sunni Muslim constituency as Lebanon's portal to the geographic heart of the Arab world. Ignoring the balancing act Hariri maintained between Lebanese interests and Syrian demands, Lahoud challenged the prime minister and torpedoed reforms aimed at strengthening the Lebanese government.

In 2004 when Lahoud's term was due to expire, Bashir Assad demanded that the Lebanese constitution be amended to allow Syria's compliant puppet to extend his term by three years. This was the final straw for Hariri, the face and voice of Lebanese independence. He resigned as prime minister, stepped up his criticism of the Syrian occupation, and rounded up international support against Syria's continued presence in Lebanon. On September 9, 2004, the United States led the United Nations Security Council into Resolution 1559, calling for noninterference by all parties in Lebanese affairs, disarmament of Hezbollah's militia, and withdrawal of all foreign forces from Lebanon.

To test the strength of the popularity of his movement, simply called Future, Rafik Hariri invited visitors to his Beirut mansion on January 10, 2005, the day of the Muslim feast of al Adha, which marks the end of the annual haj. Syria and its Lebanese allies shuddered when twenty thousand people appeared to hail the symbol of Lebanese sovereignty.

A little over a month later, Rafik Hariri's motorcade passed the restored Phoenicia Hotel in the broad daylight of a Beirut lunchtime and swung around the elegant old Hotel Saint Georges. As the former prime minister's limousine passed a car parked just beyond the hotel's marina, thirty kilograms of explosives packed inside blew up with a deafening roar followed by a ball of fire. Hariri was dead on arrival at American University Hospital. As the other dead and wounded from the explosion continued to arrive, the floors of the emergency room pooled with blood. In the mayhem, the director of nursing who had worked at the hospital during most of the civil war lamented, "All the past came back."[*] At the scene of the assassination, dazed and bloodied victims stumbled over broken glass and twisted rebar while firemen poured water on two-dozen blazing cars. Although an unknown group identifying itself as Support and Jihad in Syria and Lebanon claimed responsibility, it was the crowd in front of Hariri's house whose chant spoke for the majority of Lebanese: "Rafik Hariri is the martyr of Lebanon. Syria out, Syria out."

Renewed calls to enforce UN Security Council Resolution 1559 sounded from the international community. But the real pressure against Syria came from the streets of Beirut. On the night of Hariri's death, thousands of Lebanese marched into Martyrs' Square to turn the historic center of the city into a sea of red, green, and white Lebanese flags. Those who stayed on to camp out in the historic center of Beirut day after day were largely the young, many dressed in fashionable jeans, designer T-shirts, and wraparound sunglasses. Nevertheless they spoke for a broad range of Christians, Druze, and Sunni Muslims who embraced Rafik Hariri as the martyred symbol of Lebanon's long servitude under Syrian control. By February 28, public protests forced Damascus's handpicked prime minister, Omar Karami, to resign.[†] But President Emile Lahoud held on as Syria calculated its response.

In the second week of March, Hezbollah turned out perhaps half

---

[*] Quoted in the *Chronicle of Higher Education*, June 10, 2005, p. 3. In all, twenty people, including six of Hariri's bodyguards, were killed by the bomb.

[†] Karami was reappointed ten days later.

a million people, mainly Shia, in support of Syria. Nevertheless on March 14, the one-month anniversary of Hariri's death, close to a million Lebanese gathered at his tomb to chant anti-Syrian slogans. Wind-swept Martyrs' Square overflowed, pushing the crowd into side streets where college students wearing Che Guevara T-shirts stood next to mature women carrying Louis Vuitton handbags and men dressed in pin-striped suits.

Even before the demonstrators lit their candles of protest, Bashir Assad was signaling the United Nations that Syria would pull out of Lebanon. During the preceding week, Syrian weapons and personnel had been moving toward the Bekaa Valley, where convoys were waiting to take them across the border. They were followed by an unknown number of Syrian intelligence agents who had emptied their offices and folded away the giant portrait of Syria's president that hung on Beirut's seafront cornice. By the end of May, they were gone. But the Lebanese in their euphoria needed to remember the old Arab proverb, "When a cow dies, the number of butchers always increases."

WHEN SYRIAN TROOPS exited Lebanon in 2005, a wave of patriotism swept across the country. Many Lebanese believed their small, wounded country at last stood on the threshold of independence and sovereignty. But the lifting of the Syrian occupation came at a time when the United States had 140,000 troops on the ground in Iraq and Iran had elected a government committed to the preservation of the Islamic Republic envisioned by Ayatollah Ruhollah Khomeini in 1979. Returning the promotion of revolutionary Islam to the forefront of Iran's foreign policy, President Mahmoud Ahmadinejad openly challenged the security of Israel and the predominance of the United States in the Middle East. Playing to a strong hand dealt by the United States' problems in pacifying Iraq, the diminutive Iranian president laid the card of Lebanon on the table. There Hezbollah had put Iran in the heart of the Levant and on the border of Israel. Working in tandem, the Shia of Tehran and the Shia of Lebanon picked up the challenge to Israel and the West that had been dropped over the years by Gamal Abdul Nasser, the Palestinian Liberation Organization, and Arab governments from Cairo to Riyadh. In the summer of 2006, the presence of militant Shiism mouthing support for Shia Iran put Lebanon in the crosshairs of the Arab world. For it is here that a deadly convergence of the interests of Iran, Syria, Israel, and the United States met. These same foreign powers had contested control of Lebanon during the war years. Now they faced each other again. Behind them stood militant Islam in both its Sunni and Shia forms.

Chapter 8

ISLAM AS POLITICS

But fear God . . . and follow not the bidding of those
who are extravagant, who make mischief in the land,
and mend not their ways.

—SURA 36:150–152

G aza is a fetid strip of land where 1.4 million people squeeze
into 140 square miles. Its towns are little more than collections of improvised housing often perched around the edges
of huge, smoldering, malodorous garbage dumps. Most streets are
unpaved alleyways separating substandard housing. This is where children play games of revolt with guns assembled from scraps of wood.
They, along with their parents, grandparents, aunts, uncles, and cousins, live day by day trapped in a cage of hopelessness from which there
is little chance of escape. In the abject poverty in which roughly sixty
percent of the population survives, the militant Islamic group Hamas
plasters the walls of decrepit buildings with posters printed on cheap
paper. In colorful imagery, they promise economic justice and societal
redemption in a political system built on Islamic law.

West across the Sinai, three men in the long loose garments of the
poor known as *galabias* stand on the shoulder of a busy Cairo intersec-
tion tending a few sheep and goats matted with urban filth. For them,
the street is a marketplace where they sell the few animals that provide
their sparse livelihood. Behind them is Mashiet Nasser, a vast collec-

tion of shoddily built, poorly maintained apartment buildings fronted by hills of garbage that no municipal department deigns to pick up. As undesirable as it is, Mashiet Nasser is better than some of the many areas of Cairo where families driven from even greater poverty in the countryside have resettled over several decades. In a city of 15 million, they survive by their wits in a system where there are no laws designed to better their lives, no government services to mitigate their insecurities, and no prospects for a future in a country governed by an elite that has been embedded in power for decades. In this malaise, Cairo's masses stir to the message of the Muslim Brotherhood: "Islam is a religion of construction. Islam is a religion of investment. Islam is a religion of development. In an Islamic government, no one will be hungry."

The poor of Egypt and Gaza are not unique. In much of the Arab world, the nonelites are mobilizing around the issue of inequality, lining up behind demands for reform, and embracing an ideology that speaks in terms of their own cultural identity. Left behind are illusions of the postindependence era that invested the Arab's future in Western models of politics and economics. Left behind is the ideology of Marxism that marginalized, neutralized, or even suppressed religious institutions and practices. In the absence of any secular ideology that charts a course to empowerment of nonelites, many Arabs are finding their political voice in Islam. Islam speaks not only to the poor but also to elements of the middle class and the nonreligious who have long found the doors to political and economic equality closed to them. But it is not only the theology of Islam that draws them to the mosque. They also come in the interest of practical politics. Islam provides a shield behind which the nonelites can attack governments in command of armed might capable of storming any building in which dissidents meet. Moreover, thanks to the powerful constraints of Islamic culture, these same governments cannot violate the mosque with impunity. Thus, as in Iran in the 1970s, even secularists are joining the local mosque where politicized Muslims rail against their weakness within exclusive political systems.

The allure of militant Islam to so many comes not solely from politics and economics. It is also about culture and identity in a world where the relentless march of globalization is battering the weathered walls surrounding the traditional societies of the Arab world. No longer can governments, sometimes in league with the clerical establishment, protect the psychological comfort of the past by controlling the content of what people see on their large television screens and hear on their small radios. Nor are those who exercise power immune from the enticements of personal economic opportunities created by merging markets marching to the beat of the West. There is no more potent example of these two realities than ultraconservative Saudi Arabia, which is ruled by the House of Saud.

During the early 1920s, Abdul Aziz al Saud hammered out his kingdom on the anvil of Wahabbism, Islam's most unadorned and rigid sect. Over eight decades and six kings, the House of Saud bolted its legitimacy to Wahabbism. In the most outwardly religious and socially conservative country in the Arab Middle East, the Committee for the Protection of Virtue and the Prevention of Vice has patrolled the streets armed with camel whips to enforce the strict Wahabbi social code with the blessing of the House of Saud. This same House of Saud, the self-declared guardians of Islam's two most holy sites, has allowed construction of the soaring, multistoried Abraj al Bait mall across the street from the Grand Mosque of Mecca. For fourteen centuries, the minarets that surround the Kaaba, the point to which all Muslims pray five times a day, stood in unspoiled splendor against an empty blue sky. Now the backdrop of this sacred structure is large-scale monitors projecting ads for Starbucks, Kentucky Fried Chicken, Gucci, Cartier, Tiffany, H&M, and Topshop. For most Saudis, these ubiquitous advertisements of Western commerce represent nothing less than an assault on Islamic culture.

Any observer of the Arab world today sees societies lacerated by conflict. The ties of culture strengthened in the twentieth century by mass communications and easy movement across national boundaries never proved strong enough to produce the political union projected by the ideology of Arab nationalism. Instead wealth, unevenly distributed between states and within states, has led the masses to question the justice of the social order and the legitimacy of their governments. The regimes of Jordan, Saudi Arabia, Syria, and Egypt, along with most of the sheikhdoms of the Persian Gulf, still claim a degree of stability, achieved by successfully linking the interests of those who rule to other powerful elements in society. It has been enough to win the support of a sufficient number of people willing, at least up to a point, to help maintain the regime in power.

At the same time, there has existed since the late nineteenth century a deep and troubling feeling among most Arabs that Arab society suffers from a lack of direction, mission, and accomplishment. Once, most of those seeking release from their discontent looked to Arab nationalism, which featured a strong component of socialism. In the late 1980s, the collapse of the Soviet Union and Marxist economics stripped that ideology bare. Now many see the answer to the malaise of the Arab world in Islam, wherein resides a mystical, utopian alternative to the often-wretched reality in which so many in the Arab world live. In this sense, Islamist groups and movements are ascending out of multiple and protracted crises in the Arab world that are political, economic, social, cultural, and spiritual.

Islam as a political ideology is hardly new. There has always dwelled among Arab Muslims a sense of common destiny for those who have inherited the religion of Muhammad. In the twentieth century, Islam as politics became more defined. In Egypt in 1928, a group known as the Muslim Brotherhood organized around the tenet that modern society, like traditional society, should be structured on the doctrines and laws of Islam. It was an idea that drew followers among the urban populations of poor laborers and not-so-poor craftsmen and tradesmen, as well as professionals outside the charmed circle of the dominant elite.

During the 1940s and 1950s, some leaders of the nationalist movements against the Western colonial powers, who were themselves members of the elite, also employed the words and images associated with Islam. But the Islam of these modernizers was not the Islam of the Muslim Brotherhood. Nor was its aim theocratic government. Rather, those among the elite who spoke of Islam aimed to reformulate the faith to enable society to meet the challenges of modernization.

Even through the years in which Gamal Abdul Nasser strode across the landscape of the Arab world waving the banner of secular Arab nationalism, a certain Islamic element remained important in that combination of ideas that made up the political thought of the era. When the crushing defeat of the 1967 war came, many Arabs asked whether political salvation and societal redemption might be found in the religious cultural traditions that had once given order and meaning to Arab life.

The oil boom of the 1970s only intensified the ideological contest between the present and the past. As Baathists among others pointed to Islam as the malefactor of Arab backwardness, the opposition discussed Islam as a system of religious belief encased in a body of inherited culture. To them what the Arabs needed was a genuine historical understanding of the Islamic past coupled with a willingness to transcend that past by selecting elements of Islamic culture, language, and tradition to mold into a new future. Finally, there were the Islamists who held that Islam was more than a culture. For them, Islam was not only a faith, but also a system of politics and economics.

By the end of the 1970s, Islam within the Arab world seemed to shift backward from reform to tradition, tainted with modernity, as the less educated wrenched the question of faith and politics from the intellectuals. In the Arab world with its Sunni majority, Islamic militancy played against the background of bulging cities constantly fed by rural immigrants escaping the overpopulated countryside. Inspired by the example of the Islamic revolution in Iran, they moved Islam as politics from discourse to action.

Finding jobs as manual laborers, watchmen, or peddlers, the new arrivals, even more than their predecessors, lived in a society in which they were largely observers and victims rather than participants and beneficiaries. Like those in the mass migrations of the 1950s and the 1960s, these refugees from rural poverty became urbanized to a degree, but they remained creatures of the countryside and tradition. Cut off from the ties of kinship and neighbors that held the society of the villages together, rural refugees counterbalanced their deep sense of alienation from the political and economic system under which the cities were governed with the assurance that they belonged to a universal community of Islam. Within that community, there were values and rules expressed in a language that they not only understood but one in which they could express their own grievances and aspirations. Those who wished to mobilize these urban masses for political action used the same language. Thus Islam became a force of opposition to Western power; to those accused of being subservient to Western influence; to governments regarded as corrupt, ineffective, and immoral; and to societies that seemed to have lost their way.

Despite repression by some regimes and bribery by others, politicized Islam began to send its power against those branded "oppressor." In November 1979 Sunni militants seized the Grand Mosque of Mecca in a dramatic statement of opposition to the House of Saud. The Muslim Brotherhood assassinated Egyptian president Anwar Sadat in 1981 and attempted to topple Syria's Hafiz Assad in 1982. In 1983 Hezbollah, militants from within Islam's Shia sect, delivered bombs by truck to the American embassy and an American military barracks in Lebanon.

Through the 1990s and into the new century, Islam as politics marched on. In the presence of grinding poverty and the absence of an agreement with Israel on a Palestinian state, Hamas, Islamic Jihad, and other Islamic groups among the Palestinians drained power away from Yasser Arafat and the PLO. Elsewhere, imams in the mosques of Egypt preached religious revolution. And in Saudi Arabia, the House of Saud, built as it is on the foundations of the ultraconservative Wahhabi sect of Islam, faced the wrathful ideology of Osama bin Laden. Scion of one of the kingdom's leading families, he held the ruling family responsible for the corruption of the faith that underpinned their legitimacy. From his base in Afghanistan, he indoctrinated and trained a transnational army of terror known as al Qaeda.

On September 11, 2001, the stealth power of militant Islam in its most contorted form struck New York's World Trade Center as well as the Pentagon in Washington. The perpetrators and their supporters had sent a murderous message of anger against Western cultural intrusion, repressive governments undergirded by American support, and the failings of their own societies. In the most inhumane of acts, carried out under the most perverted theology, the merciless hijackers of four airliners demanded change in their world.

In 2003, radical change did come in one Arab country: Iraq. There an American invasion was launched to remove the secular regime of Saddam Hussein and put in place a democracy that would serve as a model for the rest of the region. Instead Islamic politics within this tormented country put a new face on the conflicts of the Arab world.

Just what the ideal of Islamic justice is and how to achieve it encompasses a spectrum of views. For the true believer among the Islamists, every aspect of life is wrapped in Islam. To others, the Islamic ideal means a society derived from the cumulative tradition of Islam, carefully and reasonably applied by lay politicians to contemporary conditions. For still others, the government belongs to the *ulama*, the learned clerics of Islam who as men of peace or men of *jihad* direct their followers

Regardless of how the Islamic ideal is expressed, Islamists comprise only one side of the intense debate among Arabs on the nature of society and governance. The other side is largely populated by a generation that has grown up since the oil boom, many of whom have been educated in Western schools and universities. In their perception, the enemy is no longer colonialism, Israel, or dominance by the West. Rather it is the cancerous growth of Islamic extremism operating on the fringes of the political system. Fueled by dogmatic clerics and legions of nonelites, Islamic militancy threatens the realization of political and economic power for the secular middle class.

The rise of militant Islam in all its forms results from a protracted crisis in Arab society that encompasses religion, culture, politics, and economics. There are causes and reactions that are common to all Arab countries, and microcatalysts that differ from state to state. What is transpiring across the Arab world represents three deeply rooted and interlocking conflicts: the struggle between tradition and moderniza- tion; the confrontation between Islam and the West, which dates back to the Crusades according to Islamic radicals; and the contest within Islam between the orthodox Sunnis and the deviating Shia. From a Western perspective, the most poisonous and the least understood of the three is the clash between the Sunnis and the Shia for the right to define the world of the Arabs.

On a global basis, neither the Sunnis nor the Shia are monolithic communities. Within the Arab world specifically, adherents of each sect divide by location and class. They disagree about theology and politics. They split between the pious, not so pious, and the outright secular. Yet they coalesce under sectarian labels because there is deep, bitter, and abiding hostility between Islam's two main branches that extends back to the faith's early decades. This fourteen-hundred-year-old enmity rises out of different perceptions of Islam, different theological approaches, different views of authority, and different societal models. And it bur- rows in profound, longstanding inequalities in politics and economics. These differences express themselves in the suspicion and abhorrence with which the orthodox regard the dissenters and the dissenters view the orthodox.

In essence, the Sunni-Shia conflict in the Arab world is a battle for the soul of Islam conducted by foot soldiers carrying different identities. "It is not just a hoary religious dispute, a fossilized set piece from the early years of Islam's unfolding, but a contemporary clash of identities. Theological and historical disagreements fuel it, but so do today's concerns with power, subjugation, freedom and equality."*

THERE ARE DIFFERENCES in how militant Islam expresses itself among the Sunnis and Shia. The weight that each sect exerts within a society and political system differs from country to country. Yet politicized Islam within both sects is reverberating through the whole region—even in Lebanon, where militancy in its Sunni form is all but absent, and Jordan, where there are essentially no Shia—impacting on the Arabs, western Asia, and the West.

When one looks at general patterns within the highly complex subject of militant Islam, the Islamists among the Sunnis fall into three categories sorted by ideology and history: the practioners of Islam as a political ideology; the followers of the ultraconservative theology of the Wahhabis; and the angry, anti-Western salafis who share the Wahhabis' dogmatic attitude that decrees religion the absolute focus of private life and society. Although there are precise lines between these groups, there are also crosscurrents of faith, goals, and motivation.

Islamists who are on the attack against sitting governments in the Arab world are largely the disenfranchised of existing political systems as well as those who reject the hybrid culture of the Westernized elites who rule them. They carry banners imprinted with various versions of an early slogan of the Muslim Brotherhood: "The Koran is our constitution." The dozens of groups seeking political and economic reform within a specific environment are essentially organisms within a political sphere rather than advocates of a universal Islamic order. Although the Muslim Brotherhood as the earliest proponent of politicized Islam provides an ideology that resonates with many of the dispossessed,

* Nasr, *Shia Revival*, p. 20.

the goals of most of these groups reflect their own particular environment. Thus Hamas and Islamic Jihad in the Palestinian territories war against Israel as well as their own elite. The moderates among the Muslim Brothers in Jordan demand an authentic voice in electoral politics within the restricted democracy presided over by the Hashemites. The more restrained of the Islamists of Saudi Arabia denounce not only the House of Saud but also leading figures of the ulama accused of selling their religious authority to the regime.

Those who pursue Islamic politics in any specific environment are not of one mind either ideologically or operationally. Even individuals collected under the same name often pursue different goals using different tactics. At one end of the spectrum, there are those who seek redress of genuine grievances within reformed governments that reflect broad Islamic values. At the other end, there are those who demand nothing less than Islamic government in all its political and social dimensions. Those who see in militant Islam salvation for themselves and their societies are often the ones who practice acts of terror against their foes. Yet all these groups are motivated by politics, economics, and cultural preservation rather than a particular school of theology.

In contrast, the Wahhabis carry a specific theology and a long history in which religion and politics are linked. What is known as Wahhabism dates to 1745 when Muhammad ibn Abd al Wahhab, a fire-breathing reformer dressed in a loose, ankle-length garment and crude sandals, appeared at Diriyah, an oasis settlement near the present city of Riyadh. There he railed against the scholarly ulama of Islam who held a monopoly on religious authority. Denouncing them as "defilers of Islam's original purity," he stripped the religion revealed to Muhammad down to its basic tenets as al Wahhab saw them. It was a theology that appealed to the Bedouin and therefore fit the political ambitions of the tribal sheikh Muhammad ibn Saud.

More than two hundred years later—in the early 1920s—Abdul Aziz al Saud, a descendant of the eighteenth-century Sheikh Muhammad, put together the Kingdom of Saudi Arabia by presenting himself to the Bedouin tribes of the Arabian Peninsula as the defender of the Wahhabi version of Islam. It was under the flag of Islam in its most "Puritan" form that the Bedouin tribes provided Abdul Aziz his army. And it is Wahhabism to which the Sauds still tie their legitimacy and promote the interests of Saudi Arabia as the self-declared defenders of the mosques at Mecca and Medina. After the 1979 Iranian revolution and the seizure of the Grand Mosque by some of its own angry Wahhabis, the House of Saud began to pour copious amounts of money into Islamic causes in the Arab world, Africa, and Asia. Constituting political defense rather than genuine piety, their money continues to build seminaries, mosques, and educational institutions to train preachers, academics, political activists, writers, and journalists to articulate the Wahhabi message. Yet the politics of religion has bought the House of Saud only influence, not security against politicized Islam's extremists.

The salafis became infamous because of September 11 and the insurgency aimed at the American occupation of Iraq.*Theologically, the salafis are brothers of the Wahhabis. But they combine the literal interpretation of sacred texts, which jettisons fourteen hundred years of legal theory and precedent, with an absolute commitment to *jihad*, or "holy war," against the United States, whom they judge as Islam's greatest threat.

The roots of today's jihadist movement can be traced to Afghanistan of the 1980s, where Islamic militants gathered to fight the Soviet occupation with Saudi money and American technology. In their successful campaign against one of the two superpowers of the time, the jihadists developed their own leadership and their own power independent from the government of any state.

---

* The salafis represent only one small element in the Iraqi insurgency. Others include the Baathist supporters of Saddam Hussein's regime, the dictator's tribal allies, the militia of the cleric Muqtada al Sadr, and ordinary criminals taking advantage of inadequate policing power in the hands of the central government in Baghdad.

After the Soviets deserted the battlefield of Afghanistan, those Muslims who judged the Arab world to be usurped by the "ungodly" were called to a new type of holy war, one fought to defend Islamic identity against Western encroachment. The level of the call escalated in the late summer of 1990 when the United States, as part of the military campaign to oust Saddam Hussein from Kuwait, put troops into Saudi Arabia. When the Gulf War ended in 1991, a remnant of those troops stayed on in the cradle of Islam to protect the House of Saud and its oil against its foreign enemies. The most ardent objector of "infidels in the land of Muhammad" was Osama bin Laden, a Saudi who had begun an organization of jihadists in Afghanistan in 1986.

Through al Qaeda, bin Laden spoke to the devout middle class rather than the poor of the lower classes. This is where he found the 9/11 hijackers whose spectacular act of terrorism was designed to transform extremists into champions of the cause of Islam. These are the true radicals of Islam. Their agenda goes beyond addressing political and economic grievances, leveling the social hierarchy, or stripping Islam of ideas that came after the Prophet. The jihadists of the salafi movement want nothing less than to drive the West out of the Islamic world, purge and cleanse existing Islamic states with the blood of their martyrs, re-create Muhammad's original community, and place themselves in position to govern the entire Islamic world.

Unable to sustain a tight organizational structure after the United States and a number of its allies disrupted its base of operation in Afghanistan, al Qaeda is now more of an ideology than the central force of salafist theology and anti-Western hatreds. In its place are dozens, perhaps hundreds, of cell-like groups organized around a leader who might or might not command resources capable of inflicting damage and disruption on Western targets. Al Qaeda's weakness as the master tactician of a lethal network is evident in its inability to maintain the unity of Islam against the West. Some of those who follow al Qaeda's ideology are proving to despise their co-religionists, the Shia, more than the West. In a letter to bin Laden, written in February 2004, Abu Musab al Zarqawi, the murderous leader of al Qaeda in Mesopotamia, poured out his hatred of the Shia. He described them as "the insurmountable obstacle, the lurking snake, the crafty and malicious scorpion, the spying enemy." He concluded, "The danger from the Shia . . . is greater . . . than the Americans."*

This long-hidden enmity between the Sunnis and the Shia is the new reality in the Arab Middle East. In Iraq, the two main sects of Islam have engaged in civil war. In Saudi Arabia, Jordan, and Egypt, governments backed by their Sunni populations are issuing dire warnings of an ascendancy of Shia power. In Lebanon, the lines manned by the Sunnis and Shia run through the political arena and extend out to foreign powers ready to turn the tiny country into a battleground on which to fight for the future of the Arab Middle East.

THE PALESTINIAN LEADER Yassir Arafat once compared the forces at work in the Arab world as sand dunes that constantly form, alter, merge, and blur without respect to borders. Since the midpoint of the twentieth century, several of these metaphorical "dunes" have drifted into each other in Lebanon. The most current mountain of sand threatening both the country and the region is militant Islam.

Lebanon is not a perfect microcosm of the Arab world. Lebanese society is more culturally diverse than any other in its region, except Iraq. Like Iraq, Lebanese Muslims are split between Sunnis and Shia, each of which holds a large bloc of the population. But contrary to Iraq, where tribal identities and rural values are strong, the Lebanese, through their geographic location, urban traditions, and long association with Christians, have developed patterns of behavior different from

* Quoted in Fareed Zakaria, "The Road to Reformation," *Newsweek*, February 12, 2007, p. 39.

Muslims in other Arab countries. As a result, the Lebanese, regardless of religion or sect, boast that they are the most "liberal," "modernized," and "Westernized" of the Arabs. Perhaps this is why Sunni militants exist only in scattered pockets in Lebanon. It is the Shia who brandish the sword of politicized Islam in a society built on confession and sect.

THE LEBANESE LIMPED out of the 1975–1990 civil war clutching a battered cultural unity set on the precarious foundation of communalism. Although the National Pact of 1943, which enshrined the confessional system, always stood as the great obstacle to social integration and national unity, confessionalism survived the war. Despite what the Lebanese suffered collectively, the feet of the individual citizen were still set in the hard concrete of sect. The war had only hardened the cement by validating in the mind of the individual the fears and biases of his or her group. Thus political life remained a zero-sum game in which the gain of one sect meant a loss for the others. And the state, rather than representing the collective will of a nation, survived as a fragile shell within which the sects could conduct combat. All that the war had changed were relative strengths within the communal configuration.

The prewar posture of the Christian community, which had managed to project the image of a vital majority, had shrunk to that of a dwindling minority. With even greater intensity than before the war, they feared the Muslim threat to their Christian identity, status in society, and standing in the political system. They had reason to be anxious.

Maronites, the most numerous and organized of Lebanon's Christians, now made up perhaps as little as twenty percent of the population. Compounding the problem of numbers was the absence of any leader of stature. Michel Aoun, the discredited former president, lived in exile in Paris; Samir Geagea, the leader of the Lebanese Forces, had so offended his community with the brutality of the inter-Maronite war of 1990 that he would go to prison in 1994 for allegedly ordering the assassination of Dany Chamoun; the toothless Gemayels had only Amin, a former president who was suspected of being more Lebanese than Maronite; and the pro-Syrian Franjiehs were out of favor with the anti-Syrian majority. Yet the Maronites, along with the old families who survived the war and the new deal makers created by the war, still held an important place within the elite.

The Muslim community, having achieved a numerical edge during the war, failed to maximize its majority. The Druze, always meager in numbers compared to the Sunnis and Shia, were further weakened when they lost their foreign patronage in the collapse of the Soviet Union. The Sunnis, the nobility among the Muslims before the war, split between those who supported the Syrian presence in Lebanon and those who opposed it. Yet the greatest challenge to Muslim unity came from the Shia. Their ascendancy during the war years was propelled not only by demographics but also by those who spoke for them. Gone were the feckless traditional notables of the prewar period. In their place stood the political descendants of Musa al Sadr. But they too were divided.

Sadr's movement for Shia rights, birthed in the 1960s, split during the civil war. One side of the Shia divide was inhabited by Sadr's Amal. Under the leadership of Nabih Berri, Amal claimed to promote Shia rights and privileges in secular Lebanon. The other side was held by Hezbollah. Unlike the urbanites of Amal, its recruits came from the sector of Shia society most wedded to Shia tradition. They were found among the peasants of the Bekaa and the south and the urban poor of Beirut who were joined by businessmen running small enterprises, shopkeepers, landowners of insignificant tracts, some professionals, teachers, and clerks. They all resented the dilution of the Islamic ethos in Lebanese society. In their eyes, decades of Westernization had undercut their religious and cultural identity as well as their economic interests. Although a crop of radical Shia Islamist groups called Islamic Amal, Islamic Jihad Organization, and the Organization of the Wretched of the Earth had sprouted under the same conditions and motivations, Hezbollah proved itself the most effective in terms of theology, organization, and recruitment.

Amal as an organization representing Shia interests and social values was in decline largely because it had assumed the role of a conventional political party in the polluted Lebanese political system. As speaker of the parliament, Nabih Berri gathered the perks of power that placed him alongside the clique of the old *zuama* and the new warlords. In the perception of many Shia, Amal had become too subservient to Lebanon's Byzantine politics to fulfill its original role as promoter and defender of the downtrodden Shia. In contrast, Hezbollah pronounced a theology that combines politics and religion in the name of social justice and presented a leadership unique for its incorruptibility. But that leadership also restricted membership in the party and tightly controlled its policy. New recruits passed through a rigorous indoctrination that drilled into them Hezbollah's tenets and culture, acceptance of the dictates of the party's leadership, and the importance of martyrdom as a dimension of the faith.

Expounding a commitment to the downtrodden, Hezbollah stretched its tentacles far beyond the ideologues at its core. Particularly during the later years of the war, the Party of God, drawing on contributions from its followers and funds from Iran, had provided an array of services to people who received little or nothing from the Lebanese government. In the worst slums and poorest villages, Hezbollah built schools, opened clinics, extended emergency financial aid to those caught in the cross fire between Israel and the Shia militia, and gave comfort to those in crisis. Although the equality of believers is a central tenet of the Islamic faith, the concept of social justice is most powerful in Shiism. Ignoring the Islamist groups advocating a return to the time of Muhammad, Hezbollah invited Lebanon's lower classes into an Islamic revival. And it was Hezbollah, not Amal or the Sunnis, that vowed to send its soldiers of social justice against Lebanon's elite.

Demonstrating the same lack of responsibility that characterized prewar Lebanon, the postwar Lebanese elite ignored the profound issues that continued to bedevil Lebanon. Consequently, the political system stayed intact because every communal leader dug in to defend the narrow interests of his followers. The missing seventeen thousand Lebanese were forgotten. The displaced remained separated from their former homes. The poor were brushed aside. And the rule of law stayed hostage to the confessional system, which fed the interests of the elite. In the entrepreneurial culture of Lebanon, those at the top of the political order seemed to respond to the needs of the state only in the presence of an economic crisis.

The vultures of the war years were already circling over the Lebanese economy in February 1992, when fighting in southern Lebanon between Hezbollah guerrillas and Israel sent the value of the Lebanese pound plummeting to 1,400 to the dollar. It stabilized in March at 1,150 before economic stagnation and inflationary pressures sent it back into free fall. By May, the Beirut currency market was trading the pound at a staggering 2,600 to the dollar. That sent hundreds of thousands of people storming into the streets to protest against a government paralyzed by economic catastrophe. The angry demonstrators attacked banks and businesses, blockaded highways with burning tires, and demanded that Prime Minister Omar Karami resign. Karami responded by doubling government salaries, which further inflated the economy. This escalating economic crisis produced in the elections of 1992 a hero figure among the politicians, and Hezbollah as a player in the politics of Lebanon.

Since the end of the civil war, Hezbollah's legitimacy had grown under the twin flags of social service and military resistance against the Israeli occupation of southern Lebanon. After an intense debate within the leadership, Hezbollah abandoned its chosen position of radical outsider to enter the upcoming elections. Presenting itself as a political party, Hezbollah accommodated itself to the country's agreed-upon formula of communal coexistence accepted at Taif. At the same time, Hezbollah challenged the country's elite in the name of the have-nots, most of whom were Shia. When the election results were announced, Hezbollah, with the blessing of Syria bestowed by Damascus's alliance of convenience with the Islamic Republic of Iran, won eight seats in parliament. But the major story of the election was the rise of a new, charismatic leader for Lebanon: the billionaire Rafik Hariri.

The sleepy-eyed Hariri epitomized the entrepreneurial spirit of Lebanon. The son of a poor Sunni Muslim citrus farmer from the small southern town of Saida, he picked fruit to finance his education. Needing to support his young family, he dropped out of Arab University of Lebanon in 1965, packed his bags, and headed for the Persian Gulf. In talent-hungry Saudi Arabia, Hariri quickly moved upward from teacher to accountant to owner of his own construction company. In 1977, at the age of thirty-three, he ingratiated himself with the House of Saud by building the $150 million Intercontinental Hotel in Taif within the eight-month deadline. Raking in hefty profits from the avalanche of government contracts that followed, Hariri acquired Oger, the French building giant, as the linchpin of an international empire built on construction, real estate, banking, and telecommunications that put him on *Forbes* magazine's list of the world's billionaires.

Although his meteoric rise to prominence secured the rare privilege of Saudi citizenship, Hariri remained Lebanese at heart. Over the years, his native country benefited from his public largess, his diplomatic skills, and his deft political game played among the ruling elite. When the old guard needed to go to Taif to end the war in 1989, Hariri's private jet flew them there. And when top government officials in the postwar government needed housing, they moved into Hariri-owned apartments on an elegant old street, now named Boulevard Rafik Hariri. It was from this base of money, influence, and favors that Hariri ascended to the job of prime minister.

The Lebanese greeted Hariri's appointment to head the government as the equivalent of winning the lottery. The general expectation, bordering on allegory, put the new prime minister in a plane flying over

Beirut tossing bundles of pounds into Lebanon's postwar economy. The illusion was not all fantasy. Hariri's wealth constituted the great gift for Lebanon that he brought to his position. He was an enormously wealthy businessman who operated in the world of international finance. He possessed the name and the connections to deliver foreign investment to his war-shredded country.

In October 1992, Hariri swung into action by filling his cabinet with financiers, businessmen, and some of his closest aides and advisors, who effectively stabilized the exchange markets for the next decade. Before them remained the daunting challenges of rebuilding Beirut's business core, restoring Lebanon's infrastructure, returning the thousands of displaced Lebanese to their villages and homes, reviving the educational system, reforming the civil service, and strengthening the Lebanese state. Despite the fine goals and personal glitter of the prime minister, neither he nor the rest of the Lebanese leadership committed themselves to leveling the social playing field. Avoiding debate over the essential question of whether Lebanon's future resided in stones or humans, the prime minister, the recycled *zuama*, the warlords, and the much-heralded advisors proceeded to rebuild Lebanon physically while ignoring both the deep needs of Lebanese society and the calamitous flaws in the Lebanese political system. In essence, the Sunni prime minister, the Shia speaker of the parliament, and the Maronite president functioned as a troika that divided wealth and power among themselves. And while the government plowed away the debris of broken concrete and ruptured pipes to lay the new foundations of Lebanon's postwar infrastructure, ministers and parliamentarians sank in the mire of charges and countercharges of corruption, favoritism, and mismanagement of resources.

Hezbollah watched as the notables of prewar Lebanon locked the state in the restraints of their own interests. Purposefully staying outside the councils of power, the Party of God tended its eight newly won seats in parliament, protected its independence by refusing to join the cabinet, operated its social service network, and pursued its guerrilla war against Israel inside the southern security zone. As the election of 1996 approached, alarm bells, triggered by Hezbollah, were sounding within the elite. Hariri complained of the militant Shia's defiance of the state through retention of its militia while people close to the prime minister whispered the slogan, "What Hezbollah won in aggression, they must lose in the elections." Hariri's followers were not alone. Murmurs spreading through the body politic were symptomatic of the growing unease among both non-Shia Lebanese and the Shia Amal over Hezbollah's Iranian-backed militia operating inside the territory of the Second Republic; its ideology, which promoted values and goals alien to Lebanese political culture; and access to Iranian funding, which underwrote its social program.

Since the muscular hand of Syria still gripped the Lebanese political process, the parliamentary elections of 1996 more or less affirmed the status quo. Although its representation in parliament dropped from eight seats to seven, Hezbollah remained part of the Lebanese political configuration in the role of outsider. This raised the central question that surrounds all Islamist political organizations, whether Sunni or Shia: What is the ultimate goal of politicized Islam? Depending on the organization, the location, and the political environment in which its operates, every Islamist group will give one of two sweeping answers. One states that politicized Islam is the only effective route by which to bring the numbers and demands of the nonelites into the political process of a secular state. The second declares the broader goal of turning a secular state into a theocracy. For Hezbollah in Lebanon in 1996, the short-term answer was delivered by the reality of demographics. Any party or movement controlling far less that fifty-one percent of the electorate had no choice but to bargain if it were to remain politically relevant.

Hezbollah not only bargained within the existing Lebanese system but did so with a level of success. According to the Islamists' colleagues in parliament, including senior Maronites, a former Sunni prime minister, and several highly respected Armenian representatives, the deputies of

Hezbollah between 1992 and 1996 built political alliances on pragmatic grounds. Far from fixating on the primacy of Islamic law, Hezbollah's representatives behaved like conventional politicians. They won funding for projects that benefited their constituents and built a credible reputation by leading journalists around Beirut to point out potholes the Ministry of Public Works had failed to fix. To many inside and outside Lebanon, the Islamic militants of Hezbollah appeared to have come to terms with the hard truth that it was impossible to establish a system of Islamic rule in a multiconfessional society except through armed force.

But there was an opposite view. According to its proponents, Hezbollah's acceptance and cooperation within the existing political system was nothing more than an instrument of expediency in the grand design to achieve a theocracy. This suspicion of subterfuge hid in Shia history and attitudes.

Having spent centuries as a minority in the Islamic world, the Shia had survived by becoming accomplished practitioners of *taqiyeh*. This unique concept among the Shia calls for "dissimulation of the truth" in order to protect the faith against its religious and secular enemies. *Taqiyeh* could include everything from publicly converting to another sect or religion to participating in secular government. Thus the question remained as to whether Hezbollah was becoming a genuine practitioner of politics or a hidden force of Islamic revolution in support of the theological concept that originated with Iran's Ayatollah Ruhollah Khomeini.

In a revolutionary theology constructed within the parameters of Shiism, Khomeini turned the core Shia value of social justice into a theological/political order that differs from the politicized Islam found among the Sunnis. According to its precepts that conform to traditional Shiism, obedience of the believer belongs first to God followed by the Prophet Muhammad, and the Twelve Imams. Until the Twelfth Imam reappears, the *mujtahids*, the most just and most knowledgeable among the clerics, direct the faithful. It is at this point that Khomeini broke with traditional Shia theology by bestowing on the *mujtahids* political as well as religious authority in an order called the *velayat-e faqih*. In a political system built on clerical leadership, one chosen from among the most respected of the clerics acts as the *faqih*, or the spiritual leader. It is he who exercises final authority in the direction of public policy and every specific act of government. After the Islamic Republic of Iran was established in 1981, Khomeini was the *faqih*. On his death in 1989, it fell to the *mujtahids* inside the political structure of the Islamic Republic of Iran to decide who should succeed to the position. Their choice changed the leadership and the future of Hezbollah in Lebanon.

Muhammad Hussein Fadlallah, Abbas al Musawi, and Hassan Nasrallah were among the clerics who led Hezbollah away from Amal in the early 1980s. All three were part of a circle of religious scholars studying in Najaf in Iraq and Qom in Iran during the 1960s and 1970s who were influenced by Khomeini's ideas of Islamic government. When theocracy became reality in Iran, these men set about applying Khomeini's model to Lebanon. As Hezbollah came out of the shadows during the 1982 Israeli invasion of Lebanon, Muhammad Hussein Fadlallah was its voice. In contrast to Musa al Sadr's commitment to a Lebanese identity, Fadlallah spoke of loyalty to the transnational ideology of Khomeni's *velayat-e faqih*. In 1984, the cleric declared, "Hizbollah was born in the atmosphere of the Islamic Revolution in Iran . . . It is an organization born from Islamic concepts that are trying to face political reality . . . The birth of Hizbollah in Lebanon is part of the overall Islamic challenge of the existing regimes and imperialism in its old and new forms."*

But Fadlallah never filled the role of master over an organization in which leadership was collective and, at times, contentious. When Khomeini died in 1989, the clerical leaders of Hezbollah were debating whether to pursue armed militancy or political pragmatism in the setting of Lebanon. The pragmatists won the argument. Yet this was a

* Quoted in Wright, *Sacred Rage*, p. 95.

debate in which Fadlallah was not a principle. His issue was different. Ali Khamenei, the chosen successor of Ayatollah Khomeini, proved a controversial choice as *faqih* both inside Iran and among non-Iranian devotees of the *velayat-e faqih*. Fadlallah, himself a highly respected authority within Shiism, refused to accept Khamenei. His objection lay in Khamenei's lack of the precise credentials of scholarship that for centuries have bestowed authority within Shiism. He shared with others the opinion that Khamenei had been chosen by Iran's revolutionary clerics solely on the basis of his political credentials. Thus the most public face of Hezbollah split from its other leaders—Abbas al Musawi and Hassan Nasrallah—who swore allegiance to the new *faqih* sitting in Tehran. In 1992 when al Musawi was assassinated by an Israeli gunship on a road southeast of Sidon, the charismatic Nasrallah became the secretary-general of Hezbollah. As the organization's face and brains, he made Hezbollah into the most effective political organization in Lebanon and installed Iran as a player in the Levant.

Part of Nasrallah's charisma among the Shia comes from his own story. Born in Beirut in 1960, he grew up in Karantina, an east Beirut neighborhood of impoverished Christians, Druze, Palestinians, and Shia. Unlike the sons of the elite, he attended public school until the age of fifteen. On the eve of the war, he left Lebanon for a Shia seminary in Najaf. There he lived in the shadow of the dome of Ali's shrine until Saddam Hussein began expelling Shia clergymen in 1978. Returning to Lebanon, Nasrallah, along with the rest of the Lebanese, lived out the war. In 1989, he traveled to Qom in the Islamic Republic of Iran to study with the disciples of Ayatollah Ruhollah Khomeini.

Taking over leadership of Hezbollah in 1992 at the age of thirty-two, Nasrallah pushed the guerrilla war against the Israeli occupation of southern Lebanon. It was to that cause that he sacrificed his son Hadi, who was killed in September 1997. This personal and profound loss added another layer to his mystique. In the Arab world, the children of leaders do not suffer for a cause pursued by the state and certainly not for one embraced by the masses. For the Shia, Nasrallah's sorrow joined his modest lifestyle and reputation for incorruptibility to further separate him from the Lebanese elite.

As a subscriber to the *velayat-e faqih*, Nasrallah's theology envisioned an Islamic order that would bestow the social justice that neither "Godless communism" nor Western-inspired ideas of political and economic development had delivered. Promising salvation to those sentenced by their sect to an inferior status, Nasrallah began to take charge of Hezbollah's operations and policies. His tactics would be both militancy and pragmatism. According to his critics, the more favorable the circumstances in the power equation, the more likely it was that Hezbollah would employ militancy and arms to pursue its goal of an Islamic state. The less favorable the environment, the more likely it was that Hezbollah would pursue politics as the slow path to the same goal.

As another round of elections approached in 1998, Hezbollah continued along the political path. Although in 1992 and 1996 Amal and Hezbollah had put candidates on joint lists that had been adopted to help mitigate strict communal voting, Hezbollah in 1998 chose to go head-to-head with its Shia rival. The motivation lay in the fact that these were municipal elections. The nature of municipal government—the provision of social services—played to Hezbollah's strength. When the votes were counted, the secularists of Amal had managed to retain Tyre but lost the densely populated southern suburbs of Beirut. But it was not only Amal that found itself on the defensive. Through its much-heralded social work, Hezbollah had lanced the patronage system of the *zuama* and the warlords who presided over the parasitic government. This was the elite that shopped in the fine stores and ate in the expensive restaurants while much of the rest of the population struggled to make a living. In south Beirut particularly, a million people were now jammed into the eleven-square-mile "belt of misery" slung across the south side of the city. Most of them were Shia who listened to Hezbollah's interpretation of Shia theology and its messages of justice, American "imperialism," and Israeli occupation.

In 2000, when Israel withdrew from the security zone in southern Lebanon under pressure, Hezbollah burst out of its lower-class Shia base. The broadly accepted notion that once Israel withdrew from southern Lebanon Hezbollah would fade into the rugged Lebanese political landscape quickly evaporated, for the leadership of Hezbollah never regarded southern Lebanon as its endgame. Rather, its rightful patrimony was the realm of Islam. Standing as a popular giant at the portal of the Arab Middle East, Hezbollah cast an even larger shadow when the United States' war against Saddam Hussein delivered Iraq to the ascendancy of Shiism in the Arab world.

THROUGHOUT THE HISTORY of Islam, Cairo, Damascus, and Baghdad had cradled the Sunni version of Islamic law and learning. These cities also anchored Arab nationalism, which was born in the mid- to late nineteenth century, flourished in the 1950s, 1960s, and 1970s, and survives in Arab imagination and dialogue. Among them, only Baghdad hosted a large Shia population. Like the Shia of Lebanon, they lived as the stepchildren of the Sunni establishment. But unlike Lebanon, Iraq's Shia constituted a majority in the population long before the turn of the millennium. It was a majority whom Saddam Hussein questioned as being loyal to either the Baathist regime or the Iraqi state. In 1980 when Ayatollah Khomeini called Iraq's Shia to join the Islamic revolution, the tyrant in Baghdad invaded Iran. When Iraq's Shia revolted in 1991 at the end of the Gulf War, he crushed them in the jaws of his Revolutionary Guards. But the Shia would not be the ones to eventually destroy Hussein's tyrannical regime. The United States would.

Ideologues in the Bush administration sold the idea to a compliant Congress, sleeping media, and naive population that the United States would eliminate Saddam Hussein as a threat to regional peace and lead the Iraqis into a brave new world of democracy. As an awesome American military machine parked on the Iraqi landscape and Washington spoke proudly of Iraqi freedom, the Shia gathered to challenge Sunni political power and Sunni religious orthodoxy. That first Ashura after Saddam Hussein fell, and for the first time since the observance was banned in Iraq during the Hussein era, a multitude of Shia flocked to Karbala to participate in Shiism's central ritual. Another two million gathered forty days later to observe Arbaeen, the end of the mourning period for the martyred Hussein. In the much-heralded elections of 2005, the Shia won control of Iraq's fledgling government. American-sponsored democracy was on the way to delivering Iraq to the Shia. As month followed month and one year gave way to another, Iraq took its place on the eastern point of the crescent of Shiism that arcs across the Arab Middle East. Its western point was Lebanon, where the bearded clerics of Hezbollah and their electoral network had become a major political force within Lebanon's precarious republic. At a time when Sunni militancy as expressed by the Wahhabis and salafis was also on the rise, the battle lines charting the future of the Arab world were drawn.

FIVE YEARS BEFORE Iraq began to descend into the hell of sectarian conflict, Rafik Hariri, the man so many had seen as the savior of Lebanon, left office under a cloud. During his 1992–1998 term, the national debt had risen from $2.6 billion to more than $18 billion. Reconstruction of the war-torn center of Beirut by Hariri's construction company, Solidere, had contributed perhaps the largest share to that debt. Growth in the gross domestic product (GDP), the key to managing the debt, had fallen from a high of eight percent to two percent. And sectarianism, the primary cause of Lebanon's weak central government, bloated civil service, and unbridled entrepreneurship remained endemic in Lebanese political culture. Yet Hariri's successor, Selim Hoss, did no better in either managing the bills or reforming the system. Together with the

Maronite president Emile Lahoud and the Shia speaker of the parliament, Nabih Berri, Hoss refused to attack sectarian patronage or adopt any reforms. Meanwhile the debt continued to climb toward $21 billion, 140 percent of GDP. Yet when the parliamentary elections rolled around in late August 2000, Hariri's star was once more in ascent. But the prime ministership was his only if Syria agreed. Agreement came from Damascus because Syria's continuing presence in Lebanon depended on its ability to maintain for the international community the illusion of a freely elected government in Beirut willing to live under Syrian tutelage.

When the ballots in the 2000 election were counted, Hariri had won control of nineteen seats in the Chamber of Deputies, the satisfaction of defeating the sitting pro-Syrian prime minister, and the right to once more join the elite in the councils of power. Passing judgment on the new government, one seasoned diplomat wryly commented, "There is change, but there is also status quo."*

Hariri's troubled second voyage as prime minister began with an attempt to rein in a debt approaching $32 billion with budget cuts and privatization. But every move the prime minister made in any area of governance was met by Lahoud and his pro-Syrian allies. Faced with Emile Lahoud ensconced in the presidential palace, Syria posted within Lebanon's borders, and the unmet demands of UN Resolution 1559, Rafik Hariri resigned as prime minister on October 21, 2004. Over the rest of the year and into 2005, the masonry under Syrian power in Lebanon continued to erode. Hariri and the formerly pro-Syrian Walid Jumblatt of the Druze became the most public faces of the opposition. But it was Hariri with his stature, enormous resources, and international prestige that most threatened Damascus. On February 14, 2005, he died in the force of a massive car bomb, presumably at the hands of Syria.

* Quoted in the *Washington Post*, September 5, 2000.

Rafik Hariri's body, accompanied by two hundred thousand weeping mourners, was buried next to the magnificent Muhammad al Amin mosque at Martyrs' Square. In the days following his death, suspicions of Damascus's hand in the assassination stoked the feeble sense of nationalism that hides in the souls of most Lebanese. Popular protests accompanied by music and theatrical performances that hailed Lebanon and denounced Syria brought the young of the left and the right, of Christianity and Islam into the streets.

Alarmed about what a Syrian withdrawal would mean for Hezbollah's future as a militia as well as its place in Lebanese politics, Hassan Nasrallah summoned his own crowd for a rally on March 8. Stepping out on a platform before hundreds of thousands of the faithful, the black-turbaned cleric raised his arms and spoke: "Lebanon is above humiliation, above being divided, above dying. Lebanon will not change its name, history, nor identity nor will we remove our skins and throw our hearts to the dogs . . . We want to keep our special relationship with Syria, we want the resistance, we want the return of the [Palestinian] refugees [to their former homes] and we reject [U.N Resolution] 1559."* The crowd roared but declined to raise the flag of Hezbollah. The party, operating in its political mode, had staged an event that was national in tone and purpose. Exceeding a shallow political tactic on the part of Hezbollah, the numbers and message constituted a defensive move employed against the growing possibility that Syria, unable to resist the heat of international pressure, would disengage from Lebanon, leaving Hezbollah to face more than one unsavory scenario. If it chose to adapt to the new reality of Syria's absence, the organization likely faced the excision of its beating heart—its militia. The dissolution of the militia risked reducing Hezbollah to just another party jostling for influence in the ruthless Lebanese political arena. Yet if Hezbollah continued to defend the Syrian presence, it could find itself on a collision course with

* Quoted in the *Christian Science Monitor*, March 9, 2005.

a future Lebanese government. What that government might look like materialized on March 14 when one million anti-Syrian demonstrators, almost a fourth of Lebanon's population, took over Martyrs' Square.

Christians, Druze, and Sunni Muslims created an encampment built of tents and sleeping bags interspersed with kerosene lamps and charcoal braziers. It seemed the Lebanese had begun the process of bridging their old divides and healing the bitter legacies of the civil war. For three months in early 2005, the Lebanese expressed themselves eloquently and peacefully in the streets of Beirut in what American president George W. Bush acclaimed the "Cedar Revolution." The Lebanese themselves labeled the outpouring of patriotism as the "independence uprising." This proved to be the more accurate term. The only question engaging the demonstrators was the expulsion of Syria, not the structure of the Lebanese political system or the terms on which the Lebanese were willing to commit themselves and their communities to a nation. Instead the citizens of Lebanon squared off in two groups—one that saw its interest in a Syrian withdrawal and the other that perceived its interests in a continuing Syrian presence. In the aftermath of the Hariri assassination, Michael Hudson, director of the Center of Contemporary Arab Studies at Georgetown, observed, "We're seeing the national unity movement with new vigor and pressing Syria to get out of the country, but at the same time we see a counter movement in the counterdemonstration Hizbollah is sponsoring. It raises the question of whether the future holds the kind of civil strife that has hit Lebanon before."*

The elements aligned against Syria won the first round of what developed into a contest between the secularists and the Shia Islamists for the right to determine Lebanon's future. The victory came when Damascus caved in to international pressure and began to withdraw its troops in April 2005 under the dictates of UN Resolution 1559. On April 15,

---

* Quoted in the *Christian Science Monitor*, March 8, 2005.

Omar Karami, Syria's puppet prime minister, resigned. Elections for the 128 seats in parliament, evenly divided between Christians and Muslims, were to begin August 17 using the gerrymandered districts drawn by the Syrians in 2000.

In these elections, old clan rivalries evaporated in the euphoria of a new national unity. Giant banners with the likenesses of Rafik Hariri and his son and heir, Saad, went up all over Beirut. Trucks and cars mounted with loudspeakers circulated through the streets blasting the recorded speeches of the martyred Rafik accompanied by chants of fidelity to his son. T-shirts emblazoned with a picture of the dead prime minister stamped with a simple phrase, "With You," turned up on the backs of thousands of Lebanese. But despite the politics of the street, the politics of communalism was in full swing. With little meaningful outreach made to the average voter, the most crucial decisions were being struck in backroom deals that threaded through the labyrinth of sectarian divisions and time-honored tradition. They would prove that Lebanon's first free election since 1974 would be as complex, convoluted, and contradictory as the country itself.

With emotions engendered by the assassination propelling a large turnout, the elections were expected to empower the "anti-Syrian" opposition at the expense of the "pro-Syrians" who dominated the sitting parliament. But divergent attitudes toward Syria were no longer the salient dividing line. It was *taifiyya*, the complicated and delicate system of power sharing among Lebanon's confessional communities. Tragically, fifteen years of war followed by fifteen years of Syrian occupation had not resolved or altered the basic conflicts the Lebanese had with each other. Essentially nothing of the fundamentals of Lebanese politics had changed. Instead Lebanon's confessional system produced another weak government committed to perpetuating sectarian identification at the cost of the Lebanese state. Thus Lebanon remained a country whose political system lacked formal definition, whose cosmopolitan politicians stayed rooted in a feudal era, and whose chronic internal imbalances fed the threats from external enemies.

The Hariri alliance took 72 of the 128 seats in parliament. Hezbollah won 14 and agreed to enter the government by accepting two ministries —Energy and Water. Emile Lahoud stayed on as president because the collective elite was not ready to rock the boat of the new government. Outside the election, the UN special investigator Detter Mehlis was scheduled to issue his report on the Hariri assassination in October. On the Sunday preceding its release, a miniscule congregation of Presbyterians meeting in the chapel of Beirut's Near East School of Theology listened to a sermon on the topic of courage. The message of the minister was as political as it was theological. "While we wait for the Mehlis report and the violence it may bring, Lebanon's politicians are in Paris. They are there for their personal safety. They are not here to take care of the needs of Lebanon or the needs of you."*

Tensions mounted as tanks rolled into the streets. Shops closed early. Traffic thinned out in west Beirut. In east Beirut, events were canceled in anticipation of disorder and violence. But the night the suspicious footprints of Syria on the body of Rafik Hariri had been exposed to the world, thousands flocked to Martyrs' Square for an orderly display of joy in the absence of their leaders, who remained in Paris.

In that fall of 2005, the Lebanese seemed ready to leave political discourse behind to pursue their favorite pastime—doing business. The jewel of urban design that Rafik Hariri had set in central Beirut evoked the sense of the lost golden age. Along the pedestrian mall that radiates out from the clock tower in front of the reconstructed parliament building, sidewalk cafes hosted the sophisticated elite of Lebanon who spent their afternoons under green umbrellas eating French cuisine and drawing on bubbling *naghiles*. Along the coast northward, a succession of beachfront resorts, condominiums, shopping areas, and even a few

* Reported by the author.

industrial sites heralded the return of cosmopolitan Lebanon. Even the new roads south that flowed into the sparkling corniche of Sidon swept inland to avoid once-pristine beachfront where wartime refugees still lived in cramped housing for the poor and avoided Bourj al Barajneh, the decades-old camp confining Palestinians. But prewar Lebanon had not been reincarnated no matter how much the Lebanese wished it. Hezbollah now ranked as the most powerful single group in Lebanon in terms of sheer numbers, organization, and arms. Their presence and force strutted at Baalbek.

For centuries, the magnificent Roman ruins of Baalbek, which rise out of the floor of the Bekaa, have stood as testament to Lebanon's place at the crossroads of civilizations. Over the centuries, the towering columns and graceful portals built in the second and third centuries AD have hosted everyone from metal- and leather-clad Roman legionaries sent by Julius Caesar to silk-draped Ella Fitzgerald, who came in the 1960s as the ambassador of American jazz. In 1974, the commanding presence of Musa al Sadr took the stage to proclaim the political demands of the Shia. In October 2005, Baalbek was again the stage set for the current drama of Lebanon written by Hezbollah.

In the city that rings the ancient walls, yellow banners hung from flagstaffs and fluttered on the antennas of cars. At the center of each, the green silhouette of a raised fist gripping an automatic rifle erupts out of Arabic script that proclaims the "Islamic Revolution of Lebanon." The walls of the buildings surrounding the ancient temple were papered with pictures of revered, turbaned clerics. The influence of these spiritual and political guides of Hezbollah manifested itself at midafternoon when the words "Allahu Akbar" sounded from the minarets of three mosques that sit on the doorstep of Baalbek's ruins. At the end of the ritual of prayer, the voices of the political clerics, preaching sermons punctuated with anger and defiance, poured forth from these same speakers. Each spoke to the Shia faithful who through the history of the Arab world and the Lebanese state remained chained to the bottom of the social and political order. Now Hezbollah was providing the vehicle of Shia cultural and political ambition. But Hezbollah's view of Lebanon was not a secular Lebanon nor did it see Lebanon as part of an Arab world defined by Arab nationalism. Rather its mission and leadership saw Lebanon as part of a transnational Islamic movement propelled by the Shia.

Hezbollah's leader, Hassan Nasrallah, had elevated himself to an icon. The party commanded two hundred thousand members personally committed to his leadership. He drew funding from Iran's government as well as foundations and charitable organizations under the control of the spiritual leader Ali Khamenei. To these, Hezbollah added contributions from its followers, frequently amounting to one-fifth the annual income of the donor. Other monies came from Shia-run companies and banks scattered in Africa, Latin America, Australia, Europe, Canada, and the United States. An institutional order unto itself, Hezbollah remained a major political force in Lebanon even after the Syrian withdrawal. From its headquarters on the south side of Beirut, Hezbollah surveyed Sidon, Tyre, and the villages of the south and the Bekaa to the east—a whole region in which Shia Islam constitutes the basic culture. Beyond Lebanon's southern border stood Jerusalem, which Nasrallah proclaims is "the land of Allah; it constitutes an Islamic cultural dimension not subject to negotiation or compromise."* Those who heard this message included Hamas, the militant Sunni group promoting politicized Islam in the promised Palestine.

Over almost sixty years, Israel has been the symbol of the Arabs' humiliating relationship with the West and the Palestinians have served as the poster children of Arab disgrace. As 2005 closed, Hezbollah was employing both images to challenge Israel, the Sunnis of Lebanon, and the United States in the name of Islam. In the process, the organiza-

* Quoted in Ahmad Nizar Hamzeh, *In the Path of Hizbullah* (Syracuse, N.Y.: Syracuse University Press, 2004), p. 39.

tion would convert Lebanon from the site on which foreigners fought their proxy wars to an actor in its own right in the conflicts of the Arab world. All the elements were in place for an upcoming conflagration involving the interests of Iran, Syria, Israel, and the United States as well as those of Lebanon and Islam within the Arab world.

EARLY SUMMER OF 2006 graced Lebanon. Symbolic of the revived tourist industry, the hotels along the Mediterranean poured guests onto the beaches while Beirut throbbed as only Beirut can. The city was plastered with what has come to substitute for public art—billboards advertising liquor, lingerie, cigarettes, and cell phones. A host of television stations broadcast the American-produced *Law & Order*, *The Tonight Show with Jay Leno*, and *The Simpsons*; French-language channels carried couture fashion shows from Paris; and Arabic channels provided readings from the Koran and soap operas from Egypt. Among the Lebanese, there was a reluctance to even talk about the terrible civil war or the possibility that armed conflict could again descend on Lebanon. The best and the brightest of the rising generation seemed more interested in spending their time playing cards in front of the student affairs building at the American University of Beirut than in contemplating the challenges of Lebanon. The more religious, less privileged students at Lebanese University had seemingly entered a pact with each other that forbade words that might recall the terror of the war.

The most haunting portrayal of the civil war remained the burned-out shell of the old Holiday Inn that had fallen victim to the "War of the Hotels" in 1975. But war has a way of resurfacing. Lebanon had failed to construct the institutions of government, to drain away the power and privileges of the elite, to define a nation rather than a confederation of competing identities. Therefore the façade of Lebanon in the summer of 2006 was a mirage. Before the summer ended, the mirage evaporated into another war that joined the sectarian conflict in Iraq to radically alter the landscape of the Arab world.

Shebaa farms is composed of fourteen plots of land spread out over a ten-square-mile patch of the Golan Heights. As a result of the Israeli annexation of the heights in 1982, it is claimed by Israel. To the Lebanese, it is part of Lebanon.[*] To Hezbollah, Shebaa farms is the last piece of Lebanese territory occupied by Israel. On July 12, 2006, Hezbollah—in its self-defined role as the sword against Israel—crossed into the area, snatched two Israeli soldiers, and took them back across the border.[†] The action ignited a war with Israel that all but destroyed Lebanon's expensive postwar infrastructure and drove an estimated seven hundred thousand Lebanese from their homes. Yet by simply surviving, Hezbollah, the perpetrator of the conflict, emerged from the rubble as a hero to Lebanon's Shia and a shining emblem of resistance to Israel to the Sunnis of the Arab Middle East.

Since 2000, there had been a series of minor encounters in Shebaa farms between Hezbollah militiamen and the Israeli army. But by 2006 conditions had changed for both protagonists. With the withdrawal of Syria from Lebanon, Hezbollah faced the dreaded possibility of interruption in the overland shipping route for its Iranian-supplied arms. That left one pillar of its power in Lebanon potentially weakened—the resistance to Israel. The other pillar was political clout within Lebanese politics. In all probability, the incursion into Shebaa farms to take hostages to exchange for Hezbollah fighters imprisoned by Tel Aviv was conceived as a low-risk venture to shore up Hezbollah's position in Lebanese politics. For its part, Israel had been waiting for an opportunity to destroy its Lebanese adversary. Replaying its earlier strategy against the Palestinians, Israel intended to pulverize and humiliate the Hezbollah presence on its border. In this sense, the Arab world had

---

* Syria also has legal claim to the area although it has ceded the issue to Lebanon.

† In subsequent clashes, eight soldiers died.

come full circle. Hezbollah was employing Israel and the Palestinians to pursue its own agenda just as Nasser had once used them to push the interests of Egypt. And Israel, abandoning the path of negotiation begun with the 1993 Oslo Accords, returned to a policy of brute force employed for decades against the enemies of the Jewish state.

With few warnings of the consequences to Lebanon of Hezbollah's failure to release the Israeli soldiers, Tel Aviv launched a massive bombardment of its northern neighbor that took on the character of cold-blooded revenge for more than two decades of humiliation at the hands of its Shia adversaries in Lebanon. The onslaught of explosives delivered from the air turned south Beirut, where Hezbollah headquartered its political infrastructure, into an inferno; knocked out the control tower and runways of Beirut airport; and put craters in the highways that ring the southern suburbs. For days, black smoke rose from rubble where only tattered pieces of black-streaked clothing hanging from twisted balconies hinted that these ruins once housed people. Similar destruction rained down on southern Lebanon, where villages, roads, bridges, and hospitals exploded under the unrelenting Israeli assault—which its arms supplier, the United States, declined to end. In the shifting dynamics of power energized by the American invasion of Iraq, Washington shared Tel Aviv's interest in destroying Hezbollah, the client of Iran. Lebanon was left standing alone, a victim of its own inherent weaknesses and international exploitation.

Condemnation descended on Hezbollah from inside and outside Lebanon. The fragile Lebanese government elected in 2005 blamed Hezbollah for the destruction. The Sunni governments of Saudi Arabia, Jordan, and Egypt nervously clucked about Hezbollah instigating a war that could destabilize the whole region. But as the enormity of the Israeli assault moved north of Beirut, the amount of destruction escalated, the number of refugees multiplied, and the movement of relief supplies stalled, blame slid off the shoulders of Hezbollah. Instead a

wide spectrum of Lebanese remembered 1996 when Israel had punished Lebanon in the operation called Grapes of Wrath.

But unlike ten years before, Hezbollah fighters burrowed inside
the crowded neighborhoods stood their ground against the Israeli
onslaught. And in contrast to 1996, Katyusha rockets and Farj 5 missiles stored in bunkers, tunnels, and apartment buildings began to hit
Haifa and other Israeli towns. On the Arab street, Hezbollah rapidly
ascended as a new phenomenon in the Arab world—a guerrilla army
in possession of sophisticated weapons and remarkable discipline in
battle. Gone were the empty threats of Gamal Abdul Nasser. Gone was
Saddam Hussein's hollow vow to "burn half of Israel." Gone was Yasser
Arafat's promise to lead the Palestinians back to Jerusalem. In their
place was Hassan Nasrallah, who combined the leadership of a cleric
with the resolve of a general.

When the air war failed to bow the head of Hezbollah, Israel launched
a ground offensive. But by the thirty-third day of the conflict, the Israeli
Defense Forces held only seven kilometers of Lebanese territory. Nevertheless Hezbollah as well as Israel was wounded; the United States
had abandoned its position to provide American weapons and American
assent to Israel's assault on Lebanon; and the United Nations had been
summoned to hammer out a cease-fire. When the fighting ended on the
thirty-fourth day, exhausted and hungry Hezbollah fighters emerged
from the debris of southern Lebanon to announce, "We are still here."

Hezbollah's ability to stand up to Israeli armed might accomplished
for the second time in six years an Israeli evacuation of Arab territory.
Defiant and unbowed by the savage ordeal, Hassan Nasrallah sent in
Hezbollah's postconflict troops. With perhaps a hundred million dollars
of Iranian money and millions more from its own supporters, Hezbollah
swung into action as the agent of reconstruction. As bulldozers cut lanes
through giant piles of rubble, representatives of Hezbollah followed.
Equipped with clipboards and a promise of twelve thousand dollars for
rent, "decent and suitable" furniture, and food for every family that had

lost a home, they fanned out to villages and neighborhoods. Once again Hezbollah was filling the vacuum left by the Lebanese state. According to Amal Saad-Ghorayeh, a professor at the American University of Beirut, Hezbollah had become not a state within a state but rather "a state within a non-state."* It was the moment to assert the Shia militants' new level of power.

On September 22, Hezbollah brought hundreds of thousands of people to a thirty-seven-acre rectangle in south Beirut that had been cleared of buildings by Israeli bombs. Called to witness Sheikh Nasrallah's first public appearance since the war, the crowd turned the desolated area into a parade ground filled with bright yellow Hezbollah flags proclaiming the power of Hezbollah and the Shia. In mesmerizing rhetoric, the black-turbaned Nasrallah gave voice to Shia anger fueled by the Shia's historic sense of victimization. And he harshly criticized the American-backed government of Prime Minister Fouad Siniora.

By November, six Hezbollah cabinet members in that government had resigned and Hezbollah's leader was demanding a national unity government in which Hezbollah would claim eleven of thirty cabinet seats. Rather than forging unity following the Israeli onslaught, Nasrallah further destroyed the euphoria that had come in the heady days of the so-called Cedar Revolution. With politics once more in the street, two contending sides took a name from the dueling demonstrations of March 2005: the March 8 movement of Hezbollah and the allies of Syria, and the March 14 opposition of Sunnis, Druze, and most Christians under the leadership of Fouad Siniora.† The confrontation over power in the Lebanese government escalated on December 1, 2006, when Nasrallah called the devotees of the March 8 movement to the center of

---

* Quoted in the *New York Times*, August 16, 2006.

† The ever-mercurial Michel Aoun, the anti-Syrian, Maronite president who prompted the last act of the civil war, was now allied with Hezbollah and its Syrian sponsor.

Beirut. They spread out their tents and sleeping bags to block roads, interrupt business, and paralyze government. In January 2007, Fouad Siniora went on the offensive by traveling to Paris to an international donors conference called to address the reconstruction of Lebanon's destroyed infrastructure. There those interested in preserving the anti-Syrian, anti-Iranian government pledged $7.6 billion. The most generous of the contributors was Wahhabi Saudi Arabia, pressed into its own offensive game by the rising power of Shia Iran.

By March, the Chamber of Deputies could not meet because Nabih Berri, the leader of Amal and the speaker of the parliament, refused to call the body into session. The losses sustained by the tourist industry sucked foreign exchange out of the economy. Workers lost jobs in the paralysis of business. And government remained crippled in an atmosphere in which the competing parties refused to embark on the path of dialogue and compromise that promised the only salvation for Lebanon and its people.

In a few short months, Lebanon had joined Iraq as a focus of the realigning power relationships within the Arab world between the Shia and the Sunnis. Each has its foreign sponsor pursuing its own interests. Standing firmly behind the Shia is Iran, with Syria nervously in attendance. Behind the Sunnis are the United States, the Europeans, and Saudi Arabia, the reluctant new power broker in pan-Arab politics as defined by the Sunnis. On May 20, 2007, militant Islam in its Sunni form suddenly declared its presence in Lebanon. Riding on the back of the great and enduring constant of the Arab world—the Palestinian question—a shadowy Islamic faction known as Fatah al Islam declared war on the Lebanese government, the Lebanese Shia, Israel, the United States, and Western culture from inside the walls of Nahr al-Bared, the seaside camp that is home to forty thousand Palestinians. Wielding the ideology of al Qaeda, the group was estimated to number 150 to 200 armed men. Some were Palestinians from Lebanon. Others were foreign jihadists who were veterans of Iraq now pursuing their agenda within the political instability of Lebanon.

Despite the paralysis that had gripped the Lebanese government since the assassination of Rafik Hariri, the Western-backed government headed by the Sunni Fouad Siniora; Hezbollah, populated by the Shia; the Christians, including Michel Aoun; most of the Lebanese people; and a significant percentage of Palestinians within Lebanon united behind the Lebanese army in this new assault on the Lebanese state. Sent north to crush the rebels, the force and symbol of the debilitated Lebanese government lay siege to the camp. In an ongoing barrage of indiscriminate shelling, it inflicted a high toll of civilian casualties that enflamed antigovernment feeling, as opposed to pro-Islamist feeling, among the Palestinians. The brief show of unity behind the events of Nahr al-Bared failed to break the logjam in the river of Lebanese politics. In the fall of 2007, partisans continued their ten-month-long encampment in Martyr's Square in support of Hezbollah's boycott of the government; the Shia speaker refused to call Parliament in session without Hezbollah participation; the Sunni prime minister struggled to hold the skeleton of the state together; the string of political assassinations continued; and the term of the pro-Syrian Christian president was running out. In a chilling reminder of 1958, 1974, 1982, and 1988, Lebanon once more faced the perilous task of electing a new president by the end of the year. As always, events in Lebanon fed on, and in turn fed, events in the Arab world.

In exposing the vulnerabilities of Israel, Hezbollah's stand in the summer war of 2006 emboldened Palestinians within the territories of the Palestinian Authority, particularly in Gaza. Ever since the Islamists of Hamas won the parliamentary election of January 2006, Israel had withheld taxes and duties belonging to the Palestinian Authority, under the terms of the Oslo Accords of 1993, while the United States and Europe shut off economic aid on the grounds that Hamas is a terrorist organization. With rival Fatah in its West Bank stronghold continuing to benefit from American aid pumped into its own militia, Gazans, sealed in the borders of their poor, overcrowded territory, bore the brunt of what became a humanitarian crisis. In June 2007, Hamas and Fatah went to war with each other over control of Gaza. Hamas won. With that victory, the future of the Palestinians became even more uncertain and the strength of Islamic political groups increased.

In Iraq, Shia and Sunnis continued their march to civil war while the United States and Iran faced off against each other to determine the future of the Fertile Crescent. Israel pondered defense against Arab anger that could no longer be contained by military force alone. The secular government of Syria pushed to open once more the door of Lebanon while closely watching the Islamists within its own borders. Islam as politics boiled both on and under the surface of every country of the Fertile Crescent. At the crescent's western point, Lebanon, unique to the Arab world, also reflected that world.

From an airliner approaching the eastern Mediterranean, a passenger sees not only Lebanon but the long stretch of coastline that is the Levant. Banking to land, the plane also provides a glimpse of the roadway to Syria and the Arab hinterland. It is a starkly visual reminder that Lebanon is the gateway to the Arab world and the doorstep of a region undergoing enormous change. The same factors that are feeding instability in Lebanon affect other countries that identify themselves as Arab: tribalism defined by family, clan, and confessional; borders often drawn by others; young, fragile national entities frequently created by colonial powers; the bitter contest between the Israeli state and the Palestinians; traditional societies reluctant to change; rule by elites that ignore the common good; collusion and intrusion of foreign powers; and issues of politics, economics, and culture that ebb and flow alongside those of religious tradition and modernity, authoritarianism and democracy. Finally there is the long-festering contest between Sunni and Shia, which has thrown off its veil to reveal to the West fourteen hundred years of enmity. In Lebanon, the West sees not only the form and direction of militant Islam in the Arab world but also the variety of the paths that crisscross Western security.

There are other conditions and challenges in the Arab world that vary in intensity from one Arab country to another: populations in which as many as one in three is under the age of fourteen; inadequate or poorly designed educational systems; economies unable to create jobs; too little water; limited or nonexistent political rights; societies struggling to define the role of women; and the crisis of identity, the most fundamental measure of who and what a person or society is.

In this age of globalization, the Arabs are entangled in the simultaneous movements of contraction and expansion where people of all cultures grapple with the global economy and debate universal values. At the same time, their inner selves retreat into the primordial ties of ethnicity, language, and religion. Although escaping the burden of rigid traditionalism, the West is not immune to the same forces. Between the Arab world and the West, the much-debated "conflict of civilizations" is inching forward to the peril of both.

AFTERWORD

The profile of Lebanon described in the preceding pages has provided Westerners a look inside the Arab world. Its purpose is not to make the reader a voyeur in the tangled lives of Arabs. Rather it is intended as a journey of insight into another people and another culture at a time when the tide of history is washing away aged sea walls, forcing the West and the Arab East into a lifeboat together. The interests of both demand keeping that boat afloat. And keeping it afloat means reaching cultural accommodation.

"Understanding" is perhaps the most used and abused word in the realm of human relationships. Nevertheless, comprehending the experiences, values, psychological anchors, broken moorings, soaring pride, and debilitating fears of the "other" is where accommodation begins.

Sadly, perhaps tragically, the Arab world and the West have never been able or willing to step out from behind their blinds of culture and religion, lay down the prejudices and perceptions they have carried for centuries, or meet as different societies with competing interests but a shared stake in their collective future. If East and West are to survive and prosper in a world in which they can no longer remain separated geographically, economically, or even culturally, then understanding must come from both sides. This book has been an attempt to begin that process in the West.

The river of time flowing from the Lebanon of the 1960s to the Iraq of post-2003 is cutting a new course through the Arab world. It is no longer adequate to speak of a geographic region defined on the west by the Nile and the east by the Tigris-Euphrates valley. With the political empowerment of the Shia, the Arab world has become the new Middle East, still beginning in Lebanon but rather than ending in Iraq, extending through Persian Iran into Afghanistan. Even so, it is on the ground of the Arab world where two cultures are walking toward the abyss. For it is within the Arab world where Islam and the West are the most intensely entwined. This is where they meet geographically. This is where the religions of Abraham—Judaism, Christianity, and Islam—are cradled. This is where the assumptions, perceptions, resentments, and realities of an unequal historical relationship are stored. This is where Zionist Israel, located geographically in the Arab East and anchored culturally in the West, sits as the great symbol of Arab humiliation. And this is where the globe's largest reserves of petroleum pool beneath the sands. Yet neither the Arabs nor the West generally recognize how much each is responsible for the fears facing the other or how near both are to the chasm that could swallow them. The irony is that as tension builds toward an explosion point, both the Arabs and the West are entrapped by many of the same insecurities, constrained by the same levels of intolerance, and plagued with their own internal conflicts over the definition of who they are as a people.

In 1949, the distinguished American historian Arthur Schlesinger opened his book *The Vital Center* with these words: "Western man in the middle of the twentieth century is tense, uncertain, adrift. We look upon our epoch as a time of trouble, an age of anxiety. The grounds of our civilization, of our certitude, are breaking up under our feet, and familiar ideas . . . [are] like shadows in the falling dusk." In the early years of the twenty-first century, the Arabs are experiencing that same uncertainty.

Spasms of change grip every Arab society. Long-festering wounds on the inside and new influences invading from the outside are eating away at ageless certainties, time-honored traditions, and venerable relationships within families, clans, and tribes. In the simplest expression of cause and effect, these multiple and varied forces can be bundled under the trendy term "globalization." Rather than opening up to the possibilities presented by a shrinking globe, many Arabs, particularly those shut off from globalization's economic benefits, are aligning themselves with political movements claiming that all the answers to the woes of the Arab world are found in Islam. Others are drawn to charismatic figures weaving vicious stereotypes and preaching hatred of Christianity and Judaism. Still others engage in acts of terrorism in defense of an identity enfolded in Islam.

Not since the Crusades have the Arabs and the West faced off so blatantly and simplistically under the flags of culture and religion. They do so because Islam is no longer just a religion. It is also politics. So is Christianity, particularly in the United States. In secular Europe, identity drawn from cultural aggrandizement performs the same function as religion in pitting Europeans against Muslims. It is as if two trains, one coming from Islam, the other from the West, are racing toward each other on the same track.

The highly controversial idea expounded by Samuel Huntington that the wars of the twenty-first century will be fought between civilizations rather than nation-states is neither entirely right nor totally wrong. Throughout history, wars have never resulted from dueling cultures alone. Underneath claims of cultural superiority hide motivations generated by competition for resources and advantages that secure interests. Such were the so-called wars of civilization between the Greeks and the Persians; the Greeks and the Romans; the Muslims and the Byzantines; the Christian Crusaders and Islam's defenders. At the same time, identity, tradition, theology, ideology, values, and perceptions provide the emotional energy to put armies in the field. And these same factors keep them there.

Through most of history, the West and the Arab East were separated from each other by mountains, oceans, and sheer distance. In the twenty-first century, stunning advances of technology in transportation and communication have shrunk the globe to the point where these two realms are constantly colliding. Not only are Westerners and Arabs bumping into each other, their encounters are reported by a mass media shaped by the particular culture in which it operates. Thus events are framed in terms of specific cultural attitudes. From these flow mutually hostile press reports and television coverage filled with conscious and unconscious bias. Further, fictional characters created through television and the movies exploit existing prejudices and perpetuate intolerance bred in mutual ignorance.

But the tensions are not only between cultures. Both Arabs and Westerners are tormented by conflicts within their own societies over the issue of who has the right to define religion and, by extension, society. Such conflicts are feeding extremism within cultures as much as between cultures. Inside the borders of a political state and religious faith, there are Muslims who abominate opposing interpretations of Islam and denounce those who seek reform of orthodoxy. There are Christians who claim to possess absolute truth and judge Christians outside their own strict theology as damned.

Nearly a thousand years ago, at the time of the Crusades, the Syrian Arab poet Osama bin al Munqidh wrote that most people divided the Arab Middle East into three unequal parts: Muslim, Christian, and Jew. To him, the truth was very different. In his eyes, that region was divided into only two parts: those who believe and those who think. Today it is the believers who are consuming the thinkers.

During the 1950s and 1960s, the future of the Arab world was in the hands of intellectuals and the educated political class. They saw in

Arab nationalism the renaissance of Arab culture and gave voice to the expectation that contact with the West would deliver modernization by breaking Islam's exclusive hold on the culture. The Palestinian intellectual Hazem Nusseibah has written of that time, "They believed in the blending of what was best in . . . Arab heritage and in contemporary Western civilization and culture, and they foresaw no serious problem which might impair the process of amalgamation."* As secularists, they called for the separation of religion from the state, the abolition of barriers between different sects and denominations, and banishment of clerical interference in political and judicial affairs.

By the mid-1980s, the elders of Arab politics had been pushed aside by cadres of the young who rejected intellectualism and engagement with the West in favor of theocratic politics and isolation. Coming of age in an atmosphere created by massive population increases, regional instability, and the ossification of their own political systems, this generation blamed the modernizers operating on Western models for the economic and political disappointments of Arab governance. They also accused them of neglecting to shield those they governed from cultural infringement or to confirm the authenticity of their identity. Seeking a redefinition of the role of religion in their lives, many have signed on with the politicized militants of Islam who reject any division between the city of man and the city of God. Believing that Islam encompasses both, they accuse secularism of suppressing religion, advancing Western ambitions to subjugate the Muslims, and bringing disorder into Arab society.

The furious and malignant anti-Westernism of conservative Islam is, in part, an expression of the Arab world's rage at itself. Judging themselves inferior to the West in terms of power and accomplishment, Islamic militants of the Arab world are attempting to prove that Arab

* Quoted in Fouad Ajami, *Dream Palace of the Arabs: A Generation's Odyssey* (New York: Vintage Books, 1999), p. 7.

institutions, the Arab way of life, and, in essence, the whole culture of the Arabs are superior to those of the West. In this mindset, Islam must be the pure Islam enunciated and lived by the Prophet. It must be free of contamination by reinterpretation or encroachment. And it must not be "reformed" because ultimate truth was articulated in the seventh century. This is the Islam of the Wahhabis. With hatred toward the West added, it is the Islam of al Qaeda and its fellow travelers. Those associated with al Qaeda in Mesopotamia are typical of those who sound the call to *jihad*: "Young men of Islam; gather together in fighting the Crusaders and the Jews, and remember Allah at all times . . . It is either victory or martyrdom . . . He whoever turns out to be a martyr, his soul will freely be flying around paradise . . . close to the throne of Allah."*

Although they see salvation in the past, these true believers employ current technology to disseminate their poison propaganda. In the souks of most Arab countries, stacks of DVDs, produced and distributed by militant Muslims, juxtapose images from the Crusades with images of the Iraq war. In others, a cross drips blood on the Kaaba. On the Internet, the voices of the jihadists exhort their followers and the undecided to become part of Islam's new century. Al Jihad al Islami, an organization implicated in the 1984 assassination of the president of American University of Beirut, Malcolm Kerr, issues its call to *jihad* on its Web site: "Islam . . . is a religion that sees its duty and commitment to form an Islamic state . . . Its mandate is to reform the whole world."† The target of the rhetoric of all is the West but it is also the Shia, the dissenters within Islam, and those Muslims who speak of the need for reform within their own faith.

Although the seeds of Arab discontent are within the Arab world itself, those seeds are fertilized and nourished by the West. As much

* Jihad Media Brigade, April 26, 2006, http://www.w-n-n.net, accessed April 17, 2007.

† http://www.al-islam.org/short/jihad/, accessed June 17, 2007.

as the Arabs feel victims of the West, Westerners possess and revel in a grand sense of superiority that developed first in Europe.

It was the pope of the Catholic Church of Rome who sent the Crusaders on the road to the Holy Sepulcher to wrest it from the "wicked race." At the end of World War I, European colonialism arrived in the Arabs' expropriated territories convinced of the moral correctness of their civilizing mission to the "backward" Arabs. Then during the 1960s, those same European masters began to allow their former Arab subjects to immigrate in the interest of adding cheap labor to their home economies. And then they stood by idly as these immigrant families packed into poor housing, sent their children to inferior schools, watched their young men be discriminated against in the job market, and lived as segregated communities on the fringes of society.

By the turn of this century, disillusioned immigrants of the first generation had been superseded by the angry second generation, who began to lash out against the culture and political system in which they were trapped. Before this century's first decade ended, Paris suburbs burned, the London underground became a bomb site, and Madrid's commuter system turned into a killing field. Total blame fell on the Muslims, with little or no consideration of the conditions at the root of the violence. Instead Europeans from Germany to Scandinavia have come to see the differing degrees of hostility within their societies between those whose native status is claimed by ethnicity and membership in the dominant culture, and recent arrivals, principally Muslims, who are not "European enough."

This animosity toward Muslims is spreading ever more rapidly among European populations who resent, with a certain justification, the burden of providing the generous benefits of welfare states to the "outsider." Yet the rising resentment is also fed by the human propensity to shut out those who are not part of the "national tribe" created by common language, customs, and history. But there is also a strong cultural bias. Most Europeans, like the Arabs of the Middle East, regard those of a different culture as inherently inferior. Once this attitude politely stayed in the communal cupboard. Now expanding right-wing, nationalist political movements in a number of European countries are openly demanding imposition on the minority the cultural norms of the majority, thereby throwing everything from language to head scarves into the political arena.

Across the so-called pond that separates Europe from America, Americans have assimilated their Muslim immigrants better than the Europeans have. They fit more comfortably in America's immigrant society and confirm what some Americans regard as the United States' unique mission. From the founding of the republic, a varying percentage of Americans have envisioned the United States as the city on the hill, the new Jerusalem, a beacon to all nations and all people.

With the start of the Spanish-American War at the end of the nineteenth century, the idea of the "Imperialism of Righteousness" reached full flower. Wilting after World War I, it bloomed again in World War II when Americans saw themselves marching into war as a chosen people destined to transform the world. Through the rest of the twentieth century, Americans measured every political/economic system and every culture by the standard of the American ideal. Yet what amounted to an attitude of cultural superiority was affable and absent of real animus. Then came September 11, 2001, and the explosion of American wrath against Islam.

On any given day, the kings of talk radio spew their venom on all things Muslim. Neal Boortz, broadcasting from Atlanta, pontificates on Islamic law of which he is woefully ignorant, and Rush Limbaugh, leaning into his microphone, warns against dark Muslim conspiracies against "freedom and the American way of life." Glen Beck on CNN insinuates that the first Muslim elected to the U.S. Congress is a terrorist. They are joined by the denizens of local television news who gravely report the danger to millions of American lives posed by nuclear weapons in the hands of "terrorists." Behind them are national news organizations that often pump out dire warnings of Armageddon. While pursing its high-profile "war on terrorism," Washington sounds the alarm about brewing plots without addressing terrorism's underlying causes or grasping the reality that terrorism in the hands of nonstate players is immune to military might alone. Feeding on it all are the large numbers of highly organized Christian conservatives.

The latter half of the twentieth century saw an explosion of television evangelists preaching to audiences hungry for validation of conservative Christianity. The message was "God not only loves you but he wants you to be prosperous and happy." It was not long before megachurches with thousands of members and a charismatic presence in the pulpit spread over the decorous landscape of suburban neighborhoods that constitute the heartland of a new religious/political conservatism. In them, politics moved from debating social policy and national security to a nasty confrontation between good and evil, right and wrong.

A host of conservative evangelists ranging from Franklin Graham, the son of Billy Graham, to Pat Robertson, the father of Christian Broadcasting, are now at war with Islam, which they judge as ultimate evil. All convey the same message as Rod Parsley, senior pastor of the twelve-thousand-member World Harvest Church of Columbus, Ohio, and star of *Breakthrough*, daily and weekly television broadcasts watched by millions. According to the Reverend Parsley, the United States cannot "fulfill its divine purpose until we understand our historical conflict with Islam. . . . The fact is that America was founded, in part, with the intention of seeing this false religion destroyed."* According to his version of the basics of Islam, "The God of Christianity and the god of Islam are two separate beings; Muhammad received revelations from demons and not from the true God; Islam is an anti-Christ religion that intends, through violence, to conquer the world."†

As they wage war on Islam, Christian fundamentalists ignore the centuries in which Christianity inflicted suffering on Jews they accused

---

* Rod Parsely, *Silent No More*, (Lake Mary, Fla.: Charisma House, 2005), p. 90.
† *Ibid.*, p. 96.

of "killing Christ" to embrace the state of Israel. Closing their eyes to the role Israel plays in the Arab world's endemic instability and growing radicalism, the apocalyptics within the Christian right seem willing to subject the Middle East to nuclear war in defense of Jerusalem, where Jesus Christ must return to preside over the "end times." They are joined by some within Judaism who have forged an unlikely alliance with Christian fundamentalists in the interest of retaining generous American support for the state of Israel.

Because Israel is geographically part of the Arab world and culturally entwined with the West, Israel plays a central role in the tensions between the Arabs and the West. Yet in the central dilemma of the Arab world—the Israeli-Palestinian issue—Jews within Israel and Jews in the Western world are bitterly divided over the future of the Israeli state at the edge of the Arab heartland. Within a community defined by Jewish nationalism, many regard their own religious radicals as the greatest threat to the early Zionist dream of a secular Jewish homeland.

Even before Zionism wrested Palestine from its majority Arab population, the Jewish pioneers were divided into competing definitions of the coveted Jewish homeland. David Ben-Gurion, regarded by most as the father of modern Israel, personified the idea that Palestine was to provide the Jews a homeland where they could free themselves of the pogroms of eastern Europe and set down thousands of years of Jewish culture. Vladimir Jabotinsky, the leader of the Revisionist wing of Zionism, wove the image of a Jewish state won by force of Jewish arms that would span from the Mediterranean coast of Palestine to the eastern border of Jordan. Ben-Gurion championed Israel as a secular state. Jabotinsky claimed the future Israel was about the restoration and redemption of Jews in the reconstructed kingdom of David. Those two dueling views still constitute the essential debate on Israeli identity and mission.

The settler movement is the crown jewel of what has become ultranationalism tinted with religious orthodoxy. Those filling its ranks are Jewish extremists who dehumanize Palestinians and repudiate the legitimacy of Islam. Some played a role in the assassination of Labor prime minister Yitzhak Rabin in 1995, and others are guilty of acts against Palestinians that fit easily into the definition of terrorism. A force in contemporary Israeli politics, they defy those who oppose them with a verse from the eighth chapter of Isaiah: "Hatch a plot, it shall be foiled; agree on action, it shall not proceed; for God is with us!"

But the profound debate in which the Israelis are engaged goes much deeper than the issue of settlements in the occupied territories, where Jews and Palestinians contest streets and neighborhoods measured by inches and feet. Rather it is about identity and the definition of Jewish society. As with Arab societies, the Israelis are waging an internal contest to determine who possesses their people's collective history and who holds the right to define the future. Conservative Christians of the United States are caught up in the same contest with liberal Christians and non-Christians. Europeans, fearing cultural nullification, gather against their immigrant populations to determine the answer to the same question.

The theologies, identities, and passions of militant Muslims, Christians, and Jews either are rooted in or arise out of territory within the Arab world. In defense of their own definition of "civilization," charges and countercharges fly between governments. Religious figures of competing faiths and sects, along with segments of political analysts, academics, journalists, and ordinary people, engage in strident one-sided diatribes. In the noise, reasoned dialogue has gone still. What is left is a sorry and ill-defined contest of cultures.

But in the final analysis, this war is not a clash of civilizations. Rather it is a struggle between believers and thinkers across cultures and within cultures over the very concept of "civilization" in the age of globalization. With the believers, armed with certitude, ignorance, and fear shaping how they themselves define and defend their universe, the lethal brew boiling within the Arab Middle East will likely spill over. This is the danger. Most Arabs, Westerners, and Israelis—Muslims, Christians, and Jews—are ignoring the warning signs that three faiths and three cultures, each pursuing its own political and economic interests, are on a collision course that could be catastrophic for all. That collision may well occur in Lebanon.

ACKNOWLEDGMENTS

Every book represents a collaborative effort, no matter how much time the writer spends in isolation stringing words and thoughts together. It is impossible to list everyone who contributed to this book, from friends who were solicitous of my time; to my traveling companions in Turkey who gave me space to edit in the most unlikely places; to my family, who soothed my stress and took care of my needs. But special mention belongs first to the Lebanese people who in all their diversity took me into their confidence and their homes. My thanks also go to R. K. Ramazani, who patiently listened to my ideas and offered help and assurance in conceptualizing this book; to the staff of the American University of Beirut and the Lebanese American University who gave me access to their student body; to students at the Lebanese University who talked to me about their hopes and fears; to Mary Mikhael of the Near East School of Theology, who opened the door to an unknown slice of Ras Beirut; to Samir Nasser and his family for their hospitality; to Rola el-Husseini for her advice and scholarship; to the many veterans in the field who come out of both academia and journalism who were willing to share their experience, observations, and opinions; to John Turner, assistant professor of history, Colby College, who so carefully read the manuscript and added so many welcomed suggestions; to my agent, Gail Ross, who is always there for me; and to my editors, Morgen Van Vorst and Elisabeth Kerr, who were so supportive in the conceptualization and execution of this book, and Starling Lawrence, editor in chief of W. W. Norton, who has so wisely recognized the value of books on the Middle East for the nonspecialist reader.

There is a very special friend who proved invaluable in helping me with my research on the ground in Lebanon. Although I have declined to name him because of the unstable political situation in Lebanon, he has my eternal gratitude. And as always, I thank my husband, Dan, who has now suffered through the process of writing six books.

Finally I want to pay tribute to my dear friend Barbara Bowen Moore, who died on October 14, 2006. Over the many years of our friendship, Barbara not only shared my fascination with the Arab world but also functioned as an enthusiastic cheerleader of my work. An extremely talented photographer, she took the photos of me that appeared on the jacket of several of my books, including this one. Her death has left a hole in my life.

SELECTED BIBLIOGRAPHY

Ajami, Fouad. *The Dream Palace of the Arabs: A Generation's Odyssey.* New York: Vintage Books, 1999.

Ajami, Fouad. *The Vanished Imam: Musa al Sadr and the Shia of Lebanon.* Ithaca, N.Y.: Cornell University Press, 1986.

Awal, Habib J. "Threat to Lebanon," *Commonweal*, August 8, 1947, pp. 394–398.

Betts, Robert Brenton. *Christians in the Arab East.* Atlanta: John Knox Press, 1978.

Blanford, Nicholas. "A Testing Time." *Middle East* (London), December 1997, pp. 9–12.

Blanford, Nicholas. *Killing Mr. Lebanon: The Assassination of Rafik Hariri and Its Impact on the Middle East.* London: I.B. Tauris, 2006.

Churchill, Charles H. S. *The Druzes and the Maronites under Turkish Rule from 1840 to 1860.* London: Bernard Qaritch, 1862.

Cole, Juan R. I., and Nikki R. Keddie. *Shiism and Social Protest.* New Haven, Conn.: Yale University Press, 1986.

Dib, Kamal. *Warlords and Merchants: The Lebanese Business and Political Establishment.* Ithaca, N.Y.: Ithaca Press, 2004.

Dorraj, Manocher. *From Zarathustra to Khomeini: Populism and Dissent in Iran.* Boulder, Colo.: Lynne Rienner, 1990.

Durant, Will. *The Age of Faith.* New York: Simon and Schuster, 1950.

Fromkin, David. *A Peace to End All Peace: The Fall of the Ottoman Empire and the Creation of the Modern Middle East.* New York: Henry Holt, 1989.

Hameed, Mazher A. *Arabia Imperiled: The Security Imperatives of the Arab Gulf States.* Washington, D.C.: Middle East Assessment Group, 1986.

Hamzeh, Ahmad Nizar. *In the Path of Hizbullah.* Syracuse, N.Y.: Syracuse University Press, 2004.

Hanf, Theodor. *Coexistence in Wartime Lebanon: Decline of a State and Rise of a Nation.* London: The Center for Lebanese Studies in association with I. B. Tauris, 1993.

Hitti, Philip. *The Arabs: A Short History.* Princeton: Princeton University Press, 1949.

Holden, David, and Richard Johns. *The House of Saud.* London: Holt, Rinehart and Winston, 1981.

Hourani, Albert. *Europe and the Middle East.* Berkeley: University of California Press, 1980.

Johnson, Michael. "Fractional Politics in Lebanon: The Case of the 'Islamic Society of Benevolent Intentions in Beirut,'" *Middle Eastern Studies*, January 1978, pp. 56–75.

Khalaf, Samir. *Civil and Uncivil Violence in Lebanon: A History of Internationalization of Communal Conflict.* New York: Columbia University Press, 2002.

Khashan, Hilal. *Inside the Lebanese Confessional Mind.* New York: University Press of America, 1992.

Maila, Joseph. "The Taif Accord: An Evaluation," in *Peace for Lebanon? From War to Reconstruction*, Deirdre Collings, editor. Boulder, Colo.: Lynne Rienner, 1994.

McDowall, David. *Lebanon: A Conflict of Minorities.* London: Minority Rights Group, 1983.

Nasr, Vali. *The Shia Revival: How Conflicts within Islam Will Shape the Future.* New York: W. W. Norton, 2006.

Norton, Augustus Richard. *Amal and the Shi'a: Struggle for the Soul of Lebanon.* Austin: University of Texas Press, 1987.

Parsely, Rod. *Silent No More.* Lake Mary, Fla: Charisma House, 2005.

Pryce-Jones, David. *The Closed Circle: An Interpretation of the Arabs.* New York: Harper Perennial, 1991.

Rabinovich, Itamar. *The War for Lebanon, 1970–1985.* Ithaca, N.Y.: Cornell University Press, 1985.

Randal, Jonathan C. *Going All the Way: Christian Warlords, Israeli Adventurers, and the War in Lebanon.* New York: Viking Press, 1983.

Theisger, Wilfred. *The Marsh Arabs.* London: Longmans Press. 1964.

Vatikiotis, P. J. *Nasser and His Generation.* New York: St. Martin's Press, 1978.

Wright, Robin. *Sacred Rage: The Wrath of Militant Islam.* New York: Simon and Schuster, 1985.

INDEX

president of, 53, 59, 61–63, 100–101,
    109, 113–18, 123, 131–33,
    140–42, 146, 195–96, 202, 203,
    207–10, 226, 231, 243, 252
prime minister of, 53–54, 63, 123,
    133–37, 139, 152, 176, 203,
    207–10, 229, 230–33, 238–42,
    252
reform movement in, 101, 105, 108,
    138–40, 145–46, 161, 238–40
refugee situation in, 71–74, 80–84,
    87, 89–96, 104, 117–18,
    148–50, 163, 169, 175, 176,
    177, 195, 244, 251–52
as republic, 52–55, 60, 65, 145–46,
    153, 160–61, 203, 232
reunification of, 150, 152–55, 203,
    232
revolt of 1840 in, 35–36
Saudi Arabia's relations with, 99,
    138–39, 207, 251
Second Republic of, 153, 203, 232
sectarian conflict in, 34–39, 41,
    48–58, 59, 60–65, 68–69, 83,
    84, 96, 98–123, 130–43, 145,
    146–47, 149, 153–55, 187,
    190, 197n, 206, 207, 225–27,
    229, 238–40, 242, 246–47,
    253–54
Shia Muslims in, see Shia Muslims
social conditions of, 3–4, 14, 29,
    36, 49, 66–67, 68, 90, 91, 96,
    98–100, 101, 105, 107, 109–10,
    112, 119–23, 144–45, 161–62,
    168, 230–31
southern region of, 49, 91, 108,
    115–19, 131, 136, 148–50, 160,
    161–65, 166, 169–81, 191,
    199–200, 201, 205, 210–11,
    227, 229, 237, 246–50

sovereignty of, 55, 60, 65, 140, 153,
    154–55, 160–61, 203, 206–11
Sunni Muslims in, see Sunni Muslims
Syria's relations with, 7, 13, 99,
    108–9, 151, 153, 155, 160, 176,
    181, 191–92, 199, 200, 201–10,
    211, 230, 232, 239–44, 245,
    246, 247, 250, 251, 252, 253
Syria's withdrawal from, 209–10, 230,
    240–44, 245, 246, 247
Taif Accord for (1989), 138–40, 147,
    150, 152, 153, 154, 173–74,
    176, 200, 201, 203, 229, 230,
    242
taifiyya (power sharing) in, 242
taxation in, 67, 113, 120–21, 134, 151
tourism in, 10–11, 21–22, 54, 109,
    246, 251
tribalism in, 54, 55–56, 68, 104,
    142–43, 146, 225, 253
unemployment in, 152
UN involvement in, 82, 116, 169,
    179, 208, 209, 210, 245–46, 250
upper class of, 67
U.S. Marines operation in (1958),
    62–63, 85, 108
U.S. relations with, 62–63, 85, 108,
    109, 113, 116, 117, 118, 172,
    173, 190, 193–98, 201, 202n,
    205, 206, 207, 208, 211, 218,
    250–51
warlords in, 35, 36, 49, 64–65, 101,
    110n, 111–12, 120–23, 141,
    142–43, 145–46, 147, 228, 231,
    236
Western influence in, 48–49, 50, 51,
    53, 102, 103, 105, 109, 130–31,
    153, 170, 171–73, 181, 225–26,
    245–46, 251, 252
women in, 107, 152, 163, 170